The
Princeton
Review

Cracking the
AP English Language
and Composition Exam

RICHARD HARTZELL

2006–2007 EDITION

RANDOM HOUSE, INC.
NEW YORK

www.PrincetonReview.com

The Independent Education Consultants Association recognizes The Princeton Review as a valuable resource for high school and college students applying to college and graduate school.

The Princeton Review, Inc.
2315 Broadway
New York, NY 10024
E-mail: booksupport@review.com

ISBN-10: 0-375-76536-0
ISBN-13: 978-0-375-76536-0

Editor: Rachel Warren
Production Editor: Patricia Dublin
Production Coordinator: Jennifer Arias

Manufactured in the United States of America.

10 9 8 7 6 5 4 3 2 1

2006–2007 Edition

ACKNOWLEDGMENTS

Even though there is only one author, a team of people contributed to the creation of this book.

First of all, I want to thank Paul Tipton for his sage counsel and Kamilla Khaydarov and Rachel Newman, who wrote the student essays. Also, thanks go to my assistant, Kathryn Lee. Her cheerful manner and professional support proved invaluable; I could not have completed the text without her help.

Next, I want to express my sincere appreciation to my editors, Ellen Mendlow and Rachel Warren. Ellen expressed confidence in my ability to put together the text and got the book started. Rachel's work entailed not only editing every chapter (more than once!), but also tapping into her reserves of patience and sense of humor. Her job was perhaps more difficult than mine.

I cannot fail to mention both my wife Susana and Laura, who, for months on end, allowed me to replace them with my computer screen and tolerated the very, very occasional bouts of bad humor that resulted from my sequestration.

And finally I'd like to thank my colleague and friend Robb Cutler for suggesting that I take on this project; I have forgiven him.

CONTENTS

PART I

Welcome to the Exam

1

A Brief Introduction to the AP English Language and Composition Exam

WHY DO YOU NEED THIS BOOK?

This book was written for the student whose goal is to achieve the best possible score on the AP English Language and Composition exam. We at The Princeton Review believe that the best way to achieve this goal is to understand the test—and especially how the test is written. If you understand the limitations that test writers face, you will approach the test in a way that enables you to earn your maximum score—and that's probably what matters most to you right now. Even if your English Language teacher spends most of the class time discussing her favorite books instead of teaching you about rhetoric, you can still ace the exam with the help of this book. However, if you had excellent English instruction in a course specifically centering on the nuts and bolts of AP English Language, then this book will help you review what you learned and give you valuable test-taking strategies that will ensure your success.

You may not be surprised to learn that there is no standard AP English Language and Composition course curriculum. The course that you took is undoubtedly different from the one given at a high school in a neighboring town, and both are different from one given ten states away. Despite this diversity, however, the courses share a common task: to teach you to read and write English at a college level. Likewise, the AP English Language and Composition exam shares the goal—it attempts to test you on whether you read and write English at a college level.

How Is This Book Organized?

In this book, we start by giving you a brief overview of the test—we tell you about the history of the test, what it looks like, how to sign up for it, and what your score means. Then, in Parts II and III, we go through some strategies and techniques for approaching the two parts of the exam: the Multiple-Choice section and the Essay section. The content review portion of the book, Parts IV and V, prompts you to use the techniques you learned in Parts II and III to answer the sample questions and drills you see there. You need to get as much practice using these techniques as you can, and that means using them whenever you have an opportunity.

Got it? Now let's find out more about the exam itself.

Know the Exam, and Practice, Practice, Practice

There's more to doing well on a standardized test like the AP English Language and Composition exam than simply knowing all about English. After all, how often have you answered questions incorrectly on a test even though you really knew the material? To do well on the AP English Language and Composition exam, you need to know not only *what* will be tested, but also *how* it will be tested. How many multiple-choice questions are there, and what are they like? This is helpful knowledge to have, if only so you know how to budget your time on test day. What kinds of essays are on the exam, and what do the essay readers expect? If you know what they expect, you can practice giving it to them on practice tests—well before test day.

This knowledge brings us to our next point: It is absolutely essential that you *practice* before going into "the big game." Doing some trial runs—answering AP-type multiple-choice questions and writing AP-style essays—is one of the best ways for you to get ready for the AP English Language and Composition exam. Think about it. If you are a tennis player, you probably practice every day. You practice serving, you practice your backhand, and you play matches against your teammates. This type of practice helps you become as prepared as you possibly can for real matches. In the same way, going through drills and taking some full-length practice tests will help you be as prepared as you can be for the AP English Language and Composition exam.

So what can you do besides faithfully complete the drills and practice tests in this book? Well, there are practice questions and free essay questions from past tests on The College Board website, so go through those if you feel like you want more practice after you've finished with this book. Their website is: www.collegeboard.com/student/testing/ap/about.html.

You can also get more information by contacting The College Board directly at the following address:

The AP Program
PO Box 6671
Princeton, NJ 08541-6671
Phone: 609-771-7300 or 888-225-5427 toll-free in the United States and Canada
TTY: 609-882-4118
E-mail: apexams@info.collegeboard.org

A BIT OF HISTORY YOU MAY WANT TO KNOW

Once upon a time, in Ancient Greece, there were scholars who decided that rules for written and oral expression needed to be formalized; among these were Plato and Aristotle. This marked the birth of rhetoric. The Roman rhetoricians continued to develop this important art because they understood the importance of speech in ruling a vast empire.

In Europe, during the Middle Ages, the rules of rhetoric became even stricter. It was determined that to give "proper" form to thought, one had to follow certain rules of expression. By the time the Renaissance rolled around, the goal of expression was to match the models of Antiquity. Everyone was striving to live up to the brilliance of the past.

The rest of the story, as it pertains to your AP exam and you, can be summed up in this way: For centuries, writers struggled to liberate themselves from the yoke of formal rhetoric, to invent new forms, and finally to use no forms at all. By the second half of the twentieth century, they had succeeded. Freedom at last! Unfortunately, there was an unanticipated side effect: Reasoned discourse all but disappeared. Horrified professors began to complain that university students were handing in disorganized, illogical drivel. The pendulum began to swing the other way; freshman composition became a mandatory college course; the formal study of grammar, usage, and rhetoric returned. And high school students, hoping to place out of the freshman composition course in college, began to flock to AP English Language and Composition courses.

AP ENGLISH—DON'T CONFUSE THIS EXAM WITH ITS SISTER

When you sit down to take the AP English Language and Composition test in May, about 199,999 other students will also be sitting down in testing centers around the world to take the same exam. The sister exam to this one (which is often confused with this test) is entitled the AP English Literature and Composition exam. It is also given in May, and is taken by about 240,000 students each year. The reason for the existence of these two similar tests is that different freshman college English courses emphasize different things. The Language test assesses knowledge and skills in expository writing or rhetoric, while the Literature test assesses knowledge and skills in dealing with literature, including poetry, which is not tested on the Language test.

The number of students who take the Language exam has grown dramatically over the last five years, while the number of students who take the Literature exam has increased only slightly. If the trend holds, the Language exam will become the more popular one before the end of the decade.

The tests are similar in format and are scheduled on different days during the AP weeks, so it is possible to take both exams in the same year. If you are a strong student of literature, it may be a good idea to take both exams—many students do.

Interestingly enough, almost all of the students who take the Literature and Composition exam take a course that's specifically designed to prepare them for the test. However, many schools do not have a course that specifically covers AP English Language and Composition. In fact, more students take the AP English Language and Composition exam without a specific preparatory class than any other AP subject exam. Like the other AP exams, there is no prerequisite for either AP exam in English; anyone who wants to take the tests may do so.

AND DON'T BE SHY...

As you know, AP English courses, like other AP courses, are essentially first-year college courses. Actually, AP English courses are often better than their corresponding courses at college. This is partly because nearly everyone in an AP course is a strong student who wants to be in class; as a general rule, the more excited the class, the more inspired (and interesting) the teacher will be. So, if AP English is available at your school, and if you're motivated and interested, take it if you have not done so already.

Even if you cannot take the course, if you're a strong student and you're just thinking about taking the test—you should do it. Sign up for the AP English Language and Composition exam, study the material in this book, and go for it! AP English credit enables you to skip ahead of the pack, saves money, looks great on your transcript, and opens up your college schedule so you can get to the really interesting courses faster. Even if you place out of only freshmen English (but don't get any credit for that course), it will have been worth it.

SO WHO WRITES THE AP ENGLISH EXAM—AND WHAT DOES IT LOOK LIKE?

The AP English Development Committee writes the test, but ETS (Educational Testing Service) is involved in crafting it too. The AP people (English instructors from high schools and universities) pick the passages and write first drafts of the test questions, but then the ETS people step in and fine-tune the test. ETS's primary concern is to ensure that the test, especially the Multiple-Choice section, is similar to previous versions and tests a broad spectrum of student ability.

Luckily for you, ETS has predictable ways of shaping questions and creating the wrong answers. On multiple-choice tests, knowing how the wrong answers are written and how to eliminate them is very important. We'll discuss this topic in detail in the next chapter, entitled Cracking the System: The Multiple-Choice Section. So let's answer the second question in the heading of this section...what will the test look like?

The Format of the AP English Language and Composition Exam

Below is a helpful outline that describes the basic format for the exam. The total time allotted for the completion of this exam is 3 hours, or 180 minutes.

Section I: Multiple Choice (60 minutes)—counts for 45 percent of your grade
Total number of questions: 50–55

Section II: Free Response (120 minutes)—counts for 55 percent of your grade
Composed of three essays, which The College Board describes in the following way:

1. Analysis of a passage and exposition/presentation of the analysis (40-minute essay on a passage that ETS provides)

2. Argumentative essay (40-minute essay that supports, refutes, or qualifies a statement provided by ETS)

3. In 2006—another analysis and exposition essay (40-minute essay on a passage that ETS provides)

or

In 2007—a synthesis essay (55-minute essay that integrates information from a variety of sources that ETS provides)

WHAT YOUR FINAL SCORE WILL MEAN

After taking the test in early May, you will receive your scores sometime around the first week of July, which is probably right about when you'll have just started to forget about the entire harrowing experience. Your score will be, simply enough, a single number that will either be a 1, 2, 3, 4, or 5. Here is what those numbers mean.

Score Meaning	Approximate percentage of all test takers receiving this score	Roughly equivalent first-year college course grade	Will a student with this score receive credit?
5—Extremely qualified	8.7%	90–100	Yes
4—Well qualified	17.8%	80–89	Yes
3—Qualified	31.7%	70–79	Maybe
2—Possibly qualified	33.0%	60–69	Very Rarely
1—Not qualified	8.8%	F	No

Your Multiple-Choice Score

In the Multiple-Choice section of the test, you are awarded one point for each question that you answer correctly, you receive no points for each question that you leave blank, and lose a quarter of a point for each question that you answer incorrectly. This quarter point deduction is the infamous "guessing penalty." While you should never make random guesses, you should use process of elimination (POE, as discussed in Part II) to narrow down the choices whenever possible, and make educated guesses.

Your Free-Response Score

Each AP essay is scored on a scale from 0 to 9, with 9 being the best score. Essay readers (who are high school or university English instructors) will grade your three essays, and the scores for your three essays will be added together. The resulting total (which ranges from 0 to 27) constitutes your free-response score.

We will go into the details of essay scoring in Part III, but in general an essay that receives a "9" answers all facets of the question completely, making good use of specific examples to support its points, and is "well-written," which is a catch-all phrase that means its sentences are complete, properly punctuated, clear in meaning, and varied (they exhibit a variety of structure and use a large academic vocabulary). Lower-scoring essays are considered to be deficient in these qualities to a greater or lesser degree, and students who receive a "0" have basically written gibberish. If you write something nasty about your teacher or craft something else that is not on the topic, you will receive a blank ("—"). This is equivalent to a zero.

The essay readers do not award points according to a standardized, predetermined checklist. The essays are scored individually by individual readers, each of whom scores essays for only one prompt. Thus, you will have three different readers, and each reader will be able to see only the single essay that he or she reads. The readers do not know how you did on the other essays or what score you received on the multiple-choice section.

Your Final Score

Your final score of 1 to 5 is a combination of your scores from the two sections. Remember that the Multiple-Choice section counts for 45 percent of the total and the Essay section counts for 55 percent. This makes them almost equal, and you must concentrate on doing your best on both parts. ETS uses a formula to calculate your final score that would take almost a full page to diagram, but it isn't worth showing here. Given that neither you nor anyone else (including the colleges) will ever know what your individual section scores are, there is no reason to get too wrapped up with the specifics.

If you like statistics, however, here is some useful information: If you can get a score of 36 (number correct minus $\frac{1}{4}$ the number wrong) on a Multiple-Choice section with 54 questions, you have exactly a 99 percent chance of getting *at least* a score of 3 on the exam.

Getting Credit

So how do you get credit from colleges for taking this exam? First, you must attend a college that recognizes the AP Program (most colleges do); second, you need to get a good score on one of the two AP English exams (Language and Composition or Literature and Composition).

Your guidance counselor or AP teacher should be able to provide you with information on whether the schools to which you're applying award AP credit. They can probably also tell you how much credit you can get and what scores you need to get the credit. You can also sometimes get the information you need from the college's website. By far the most reliable way to find out what you need to know is to write or e-mail (do not call) the admission office of the schools that interest you and ask about their AP policy. When someone from admission responds, take the e-mail or letter (that's why you didn't call!) with you when you register for courses. College registration does not always go smoothly, and you don't want to have to argue with an admission clerk over things like credit (or placement).

In general, the AP exams are widely accepted, but minimum scores and credits awarded vary from school to school. A 4 or a 5 will always get you credit when it is available. A 3 works at many schools, especially larger universities, but unfortunately, a score of 1 or 2 will get you neither credit nor placement.

As you saw from the table, only about 25 percent of the students who take the AP English Language and Composition exam earn a 4 or a 5, and about 42 percent receive a 1 or a 2. The rest—33 percent to be exact, receive a 3. This isn't an easy test, but it's well worth the effort that it takes to do well. And again there's good news: With so many poorly prepared students taking the test, you can use this book and walk into the testing center with an important advantage.

Just a couple more topics and we'll move on to strategies and techniques.

HOW TO REGISTER TO TAKE THE EXAM (AND OTHER USEFUL INFORMATION)

This test is administered once a year, in early May, and the fee is a whopping $82.00. Your high school guidance counselor should have all the information you need to sign up to take the AP English Language and Composition exam. You will have to fill out some forms and make sure the timing of this exam doesn't conflict with any other AP exams you may be taking. Since you'll be preparing so much for this exam, it would be a shame to encounter a scheduling conflict on test day.

On test day, be sure to wear comfortable clothes and shoes; consider dressing in layers if you don't know what the temperature in the testing room will be like. Bring a snack to eat during the break if you think you'll get hungry. Also, remember to bring at least two number-2 pencils and a few good blue or black pens (those are the only two colors allowed on the AP exam).

Finally, and most important, don't forget to get a good night's sleep before test day.

HOW TO USE THIS BOOK

While you may be tempted to skip right to the content review portion of this book—Parts IV and V—we strongly recommend that you read the chapters on test-taking techniques before you work through the content review. These chapters will give you a better idea of what you're doing and show you important techniques for approaching the sample questions, drills, and two full-length tests.

After you have taken the practice tests, we advise that you read all the explanations, even the explanations to the questions that you've answered correctly. Often, you will find that your understanding of a question or the passage will be broadened when you read the explanation. Other times, you'll realize that you got the question right, but for all the wrong reasons. Also, sometimes we learn the most from other students, and we strongly recommend that you read the sample essays, which several different well-prepared students wrote just days before they took the real exam.

MOVING ON...

At this point, we've described the basics of the AP English Language and Composition exam. You probably have a lot of unanswered questions, such as *What are the passages like? What kinds of questions are on the Multiple-Choice section? How should I approach the essays to ace them? Does good handwriting count? When should I guess?*

We'll answer all these questions and many more in the chapters that follow.

PART ◆ II

Cracking the System: The Multiple-Choice Section

2

Cracking the Multiple-Choice Questions

RELAX!

The Multiple-Choice section of the AP English Language exam will test your ability to take multiple-choice tests more than it will test your knowledge of English. If you're already an accomplished test taker, then wonderful! Our techniques will probably not help you much—because you don't need much help. However, if you get high grades in class but consistently underachieve on standardized tests, you can relax—using our techniques on these multiple-choice questions will make a huge difference on test day. Finally, if you fall somewhere in-between (most students do), using our techniques for the Multiple-Choice section will probably earn you half a dozen more points than you would have gotten if you hadn't used them.

WILL THE PASSAGES ON THE EXAM LOOK FAMILIAR?

Probably not. The Multiple-Choice section is made up of 5 to 7 passages, which are followed by 5 to 12 multiple-choice questions about each passage. Although most of the passages will come from works of the nineteenth and twentieth centuries, you should count on seeing at least one that was written before 1800. Typically, students have the greatest difficulty with the older passages since the style is so different from what they're used to seeing in their everyday lives. Again, don't worry. Our practice tests include passages from earlier works just like the real exam does.

Think about it—almost any prose written in English or translated into English is a candidate for inclusion on this test. Variety is the byword! Imagine all the different *types* of writing that could be included: works of fiction, essays, biography (or autobiography or diary entries), speeches, letters, pieces of journalism, literary (or any aspect of cultural) criticism, science and nature writing, and writings about politics or history. Contemporary and classic, controversial and commonplace, and male and female perspectives are just some of the contrasts you should anticipate among the passages.

The passages will also run the gamut as far as types of diction, syntax, imagery, tone, style, and points of view. The teachers and professors who write the exam want to include as many rarely seen passages as they can. The idea is to get you to focus on rhetorical devices, figures of speech, and intended purposes of writings that you have not already articulated. Drawing inferences about a passage you've studied in class is less of a challenge than seeing how you deal with new material; this is a much more valid test of your ability to see how writers' language works.

QUESTIONS OF ANONYMITY

In addition to being totally new to you, the actual passages you'll see on the AP exam will be missing some context clues that you're probably used to having—for example, introductory material such as historical context, a title, explanatory notes, and even the names of the authors. Some passages *will* have titles, but most of them will be identified only by their date of publication.

These omissions may be some of the most obvious differences between the reading you've done before the exam and the reading you will do during the exam. And you probably won't realize how helpful these little contextual clues are in understanding the passage until you encounter one of these anonymous passages—it would mean something very different to you if you saw that a piece was written by Abraham Lincoln, than if it were written by Homer.

Okay, let's start talking in more detail about how to approach the questions.

THE BIG PICTURE

Some people may advise you to read the questions that pertain to the passage before you read the passage. Do NOT take that advice! If you do this, you run the risk of automatically filtering your reading through the lens of a particular question or questions. You might ignore certain important aspects of the paragraph in your search for the answer to the questions you read. Get the real sense of the passage before you dive into specific questions. Imagine that the first question will be, "What's the gist of the passage?" In other words, the forest will have a quality of its own, and you need to be comfortable within that forest before you can analyze its trees; *read for the big picture*. Some of the multiple-choice questions will ask you to summarize the author's dominant tone, style, and point of view. To do this, you'll need to have a sense of the big picture. In fact, several of the questions will probably try to trick you into identifying the wrong answer because you're focusing too narrowly on the sentence (or section) to which the question refers.

In a minute, we'll introduce you to a typical passage on the AP English Language exam. However, first we'll talk more about two other important techniques you should use when tackling these questions—the Two-Pass system and POE.

PACE YOURSELF! THE TWO-PASS SYSTEM

There are 54 questions on the Multiple-Choice section of this exam, and you have a total of 60 minutes to complete it. This means that you have about one minute to answer each question. To most efficiently use your time, you should employ what we call the Two-Pass system. Basically, this means that you make a first pass at the Multiple-Choice section, answering the questions you easily can and circling the harder ones so that you can go back later. This system works well since, in this section, all the questions are worth the same number of points—regardless of whether you think they're easy or hard!

As you know, on the AP English Language exam, the Multiple-Choice questions are based on passages. We've also told you that there will be a total of 5 to 7 passages on your test. Since you have 60 minutes total, this means you should be spending about 8 to 12 minutes on each passage and its questions. Glance through your test when you get it to see how many passages there are. If you spend 15 minutes on the first 3 passages, you won't have time to even read the last passage!

Here are the steps to take when using the Two-Pass system.

1. Answer all the easy questions first.

2. Circle the hard questions.

3. Look at your watch to see how much time you have left out of whatever number of minutes you allotted for this passage (between 8 to 12). If you have 5 minutes left, tackle questions you circled: If you have no time left, then come back to the circled questions after you've safely finished the rest of the passages in the section (if there's time).

POE AND GUESSING

You've probably heard about the techniques called "process of elimination" and "educated guessing." Whatever you know about these techniques, you should know that on this exam, your chances of guessing correctly on a question will go up if you can eliminate one or more answer choices. This means that if there are questions on this exam that you don't know the answer to, and there will be, apply POE and guess.

But, does guessing really help? Some people believe that it can actually hurt your score. Here's why that isn't true. On the AP English Language and Composition exam, each question has five answer choices. Now, say you need to guess on five questions. If you guess blindly on every question, then according to the basic laws of statistics, you will get 1 in 5 questions right and lose $4 \times \frac{1}{4} = 1$ point for guessing wrong, so the net gain will be zero. (Remember that you get one point for guessing the answer to that one question correctly.) However, if you use POE in conjunction with guessing, your chances of guessing the correct answer go up, and the net gain of points increases as well. In other words, if you can eliminate at least one answer choice on a question, you should feel safe—no, confident—to guess.

Let's recap:

- Read the passage for the big picture.
- Pace yourself (use the Two-Pass system).
- Use POE on *every question*!

Now you're ready to try your first sample passage.

SAMPLE PASSAGE #1—HERE'S HOW IT'S DONE

This paragraph was taken from Henry David Thoreau's *Walden*.

One day when I went out to my wood-pile, or rather
my pile of stumps, I observed two large ants, the one
red, the other much larger, nearly half an inch long, and
Line black, fiercely contending with one another. Having once
5 got hold they never let go, but struggled and wrestled
and rolled on the chips incessantly. Looking farther, I
was surprised to find that the chips were covered with
such combatants, that it was not a *duellum*, but a *bellum*,
a war between two races of ants, the red always pitted
10 against the black, and frequently two red ones to one
black. The legions of the Myrmidons covered all the hills
and vales in my wood-yard, and the ground was already
strewn with the dead and dying, both red and black.
It was the only battle which I have ever witnessed, the
15 only battle-field I ever trod while the battle was raging;
internecine war; the red republicans on the one hand,
and the black imperialists on the other. On every side
they were engaged in deadly combat, yet without any
noise that I could hear, and human soldiers never fought
20 so resolutely. I watched a couple that were fast locked
in each other's embraces, in a little sunny valley amid
the chips, now at noonday prepared to fight till the sun
went down, or life went out. The smaller red cham-
pion had fastened himself like a vice to his adversary's
25 front, and through all the tumblings on that field never
for an instant ceased to gnaw at one of his feelers near
the root, having already caused the other to go by the
board; while the stronger black one dashed him from

side to side, and, as I saw on looking nearer, had already
30 divested him of several of his members. They fought
with more pertinacity than bulldogs. Neither manifested
the least disposition to retreat. It was evident that their
battle-cry was "Conquer or die." In the meanwhile there
came along a single red ant on the hillside of the valley,
35 evidently full of excitement, who either had dispatched
his foe, or had not yet taken part in the battle; probably the latter, for he had lost none of his limbs; whose
mother had charged him to return with his shield or
upon it. Or perchance he was some Achilles, who had
40 nourished his wrath apart, and had now come to avenge
or rescue his Patroclus. He saw this unequal combat from
afar—for the blacks were nearly twice the size of the
red—he drew near with rapid pace till be stood on his
guard within half an inch of the combatants; then, watch-
45 ing his opportunity, he sprang upon the black warrior,
and commenced his operations near the root of his right
fore leg, leaving the foe to select among his own members; and so there were three united for life, as if a new
kind of attraction had been invented which put all other
50 locks and cements to shame. I should not have wondered
by this time to find that they had their respective musical
bands stationed on some eminent chip, and playing their
national airs the while, to excite the slow and cheer the
dying combatants. I was myself excited somewhat even
55 as if they had been men. The more you think of it, the
less the difference.

THE ANALYSIS

Having read the passage, what would you say the big picture is? The dominant rhetorical strategy
Thoreau employs in this passage is the analogy that compares the behavior of the ants with that of
human beings. Is he writing to shed some scientific light on the behavior of ants? No. He's dwelling
on details about the insects to lead us to a revelation about human beings. He's asking us to see that
people are like ants and is commenting on the inappropriateness of associating warfare with gran-
diloquence and romance. Thoreau is basically asking, *What difference do the struggles of the ants make,
when we examine them from far above? Likewise, what difference does human warfare make, when seen from
far above or even from a divine perspective?*

This is the big picture. As you read the passage, you need to keep in mind his reason for taking
this strong interest in ants and not get waylaid by the particular events taking place in the narrative.
The last line of the passage should help you make the important conceptual leap. Thoreau outright
says, "I was myself excited somewhat even as if they had been men. The more you think of it, the
less the difference."

Okay, let's move on. As we mentioned earlier, some types of big-picture questions you'll see on
this exam will ask you to characterize the speaker's tone, style, or attitude in the passage. Another
type of big-picture question that you'll see will ask you to describe how a particular detail fits into
the big picture—what a particular word means in context or how the reader is meant to interpret a
word based on the tone, style, or attitude of the passage as a whole. Let's look at a typical big-picture
question.

1. The author's tone in this passage can best be described as one of

   (A) suspicion and confusion
   (B) horror and shock
   (C) detachment and criticism
   (D) condescension and bemusement
   (E) admiration and empathy

The correct answer is (D). While it may be tempting to take the words at face value and interpret the ants as heroic, remember that this is a big-picture question, so you need to consider the overall meaning or intent of the passage. Remember that Thoreau's intention is to make the point that the observer is to the ants as some higher being would be to humans. This is why *condescension* is a valid answer.

By the way, you'll see this type of question—with answer choices that contain two elements joined by the conjunction *and*—quite a lot on the exam. It's one of The College Board's favorite types of questions. When you're looking for the correct answer, remember that both elements of the answer choice must be correct, so the easiest way to approach this type of question is to try to eliminate just one of the elements; if one of them is wrong, then the whole answer choice can be eliminated. For example, *detachment* (C) is a plausible answer, but *criticism* is not; so (C) can be eliminated.

In case you didn't notice, Thoreau makes three references to Greek history, literature, and art in this one paragraph. Do you know who the Myrmidons were? Do you know the story about the Spartan mother who says to her son, "With it or on it"? Do you understand the relationship between Patroclus and Achilles? Don't worry. This kind of specialized knowledge will never be tested explicitly. If you miss certain pieces of the big picture, don't be disheartened! Just like when you put together a jigsaw puzzle, if you have the general outline and can fill in major portions of the content, then you can imagine the entire picture even if a few pieces are missing.

Here is another typical big-picture question that gets at pretty much the same issues as the previous one.

2. In this passage, the author exaggerates the greatness of the ants' struggle to

   (A) exaggerate the greatness of nature
   (B) show the true greatness of nature
   (C) demonstrate the importance of war
   (D) illustrate the fierceness of ants
   (E) suggest the exaggerated greatness of humans

The answer is (E). The other answers—particularly (C) and (D) may have also looked good to you—they were deliberately put in there to trap readers who didn't pay attention to the big picture.

Got it? Okay, now, let's take a look at what types of details will be tested—and how.

DETAILS AND THE BIG PICTURE

You now know that for each passage you come to in this section, without dwelling too much on the details, you'll read the passage to get the big picture. Big-picture questions often come either at the beginning of the question set or at the end, and the detail questions are sandwiched in between.

Let's assume that the passage by Thoreau was the first one on the test and that the two questions that we already looked at were the first two questions about the passage. The next two are as follows.

3. In lines 1–2, Thoreau changes "wood-pile" to "pile of stumps" because he wants to

    (A) enhance the sense of realism in the passage
    (B) trivialize the setting of the action
    (C) be thoroughly truthful in his depiction
    (D) create a sense of drama
    (E) make the setting more natural

You can immediately eliminate choices (A), (C), and (E); you know from getting the big picture that Thoreau probably wouldn't be trying to "enhance the sense of realism," or "be thoroughly truthful." Nor is he trying to "make the setting more natural;" the setting is just about as natural as it can get. Even if you thought that (D) reinforced your view that the battle of the ants was a serious epic drama and chose that answer, you may have been saved at the last minute if you noticed that (B) lined up nicely with the answer choices from the first two questions. If you got those two questions right, then (B) would have been a choice that reinforced your confidence.

Take a look at the next question on this passage.

4. All of the following humorously aggrandize the battle EXCEPT

    (A) it was not a *duellum*, but a *bellum* (line 8)
    (B) the hills and vales of my wood-yard (lines 11–12)
    (C) human soldiers never fought so resolutely (line 20)
    (D) whose mother had charged him to return with his shield or upon it (lines 37–39)
    (E) Or perchance he was some Achilles (line 40)

Again, in case you missed the big picture, the exam writer goes so far as to *say* that the battle is humorously aggrandized. If there was ever any doubt about the seriousness of the author's point of view toward the ant war, that doubt should immediately disappear.

Let's look through the answer choices, starting with (A). Even if your Latin is weak or nonexistent, you can probably see the word "duel" in *duellum*, and *bellum* (war) is defined in the context; if you catch the pun (knowing that *duellum* is the ancient Latin word for war and the etymological root of *bellum*), then the humor is even more obvious. The "hills and vales" (B) are, of course, only minuscule piles of wood chips or sawdust. Hopefully the humor in the personifications in (D) and (E) was also apparent. The correct answer is (C); in fact, it is almost the only line in the passage that could be considered not tinged with humor.

The Details

After you have read the passage to get the big picture—don't read it again to try to get all the details. Instead, as you come to detail questions that refer you back to specific lines in the passage, go back to those places and read more closely. You should *always* reread those lines; do not rely on your memory, and do not reread the entire text. When a question refers you to words or lines in the same part of the passage, make sure you "read around the lines"; that is, you should read the sentence before the sentence in question, read the sentence itself, and finally read the sentence that follows the one in question. You want to read as little as possible, but as much as is necessary, and this is an art that you must develop over time. Our practice tests at the end of the book will afford you ample practice for you to hone your skills.

Let's move on. Most of the non–big picture questions on the passage will focus on detailed information from very specific parts of the passage. Remember, do NOT go back and read large portions of the text; if you cannot answer a question without extensive reading, then you should leave the answer blank and return to it, in your second pass through the questions in the section. Here are a couple of examples of this type of question.

5. In context, "pertinacity" (line 31) most nearly means

    (A) pertinence
    (B) loyalty
    (C) perspicacity
    (D) obstinacy
    (E) attentiveness

On this type of question, oftentimes just knowing the definition of the word will not be enough to enable you to answer the question correctly, and the indication that you are to find the meaning "in context" almost guarantees that the answer won't be the first meaning that pops into your head. "Pertinent" wouldn't be right, and "pertinence" (being pertinent) is also incorrect. If you go back and look at the context—especially the word "bulldogs"—you should be able to eliminate all the answers except (D). Another clue is the adverb "resolutely" that appears slightly earlier in the passage. The ants are fighting resolutely and obstinately—like bulldogs.

Let's go through a couple more.

6. The phrase "who had nourished his wrath apart" (lines 39–40) most nearly means

    (A) who was hungry for battle
    (B) who worked up great anger in private
    (C) who was only partly angry
    (D) who fought alone
    (E) who feasted alone

7. The phrase "who had nourished his wrath apart" (lines 39–40) serves mainly to

    (A) create the impression of an epic tone
    (B) sustain the seriousness of the author's point of view
    (C) highlight the extent of the hatred between the enemies
    (D) underscore the loneliness of the combatants
    (E) emphasize the cannibalistic nature of the combatants

Question 6 is a translation question. What does "who nourished his wrath apart" mean in simple English? The answer is (B).

Question 7 is more of a big-picture question—remember that these generally occur at the beginning and ending of the group of questions that pertain to one passage. On a real test, you would not see two questions on the same quotation, but we want you to see how the exam writers can approach material from different perspectives. We have already determined that there is a playful humor in the humanization (*anthropomorphism*) of the combat of the insects, and this allows us to eliminate answer (B), which is there just to trick students who missed the big picture. The correct answer is (A). There is "the impression" of an epic tone (rather than a true epic tone) because, once again, Thoreau's aim is to have us understand the futility and insignificance of events in the grand scheme of things.

One final note about detail questions: Do not forget the big picture when answering the detail questions. Often, the test writer will inadvertently give away important information about the big picture in the phrasing of the detail questions and answers, as they did in the sample questions on page 20. Sometimes the detail questions will cause you to reevaluate your big-picture view of a passage; if your view is correct, the detail questions will probably confirm that view.

TO SUM UP

- Begin each passage by reading for the big picture.

- Concentrate on the author's goal, tone, and point of view.

- Do not read stubbornly; you do not need to understand or follow everything; some (even many) details can escape you—focus on the big picture!

- Always return to the passage when multiple-choice questions refer you to specific lines.

- Always read around the lines; the context of the lines is almost always critical in determining the correct answer.

- Pace yourself! Remember our Two-Pass system. Dividing the section into chunks for each passage should help you out.

- Don't forget about POE and educated guessing! If you can eliminate two answer choices, your chances of guessing correctly increase a lot.

A FINAL NOTE

Do NOT expect to be entertained by the passages! Every now and again, you will encounter a passage as clever and entertaining as Thoreau's, but that will be the exception. The test writers often (purposely?) choose passages that are dry, humorless, and downright boring. This exam is about toughness—mental toughness. Your ability to concentrate and think methodically and critically even *when you're not interested* is as important as anything when it comes to scoring high. You are in luck because the vast majority of the passages in the sample tests in this book are every bit as dry, humorless, and boring as the ones that you'll encounter on the real exam! If you read the passages and answer the questions under actual testing conditions, you will be ready for the rigors that await.

PART ◆ III

Cracking the System:
The Essays

3

Basic Principles of the Essay Section

THE FORMAT AND CONTENT OF THE ESSAY SECTION

The format of the AP English Language Essay section will undergo a significant change in May, 2007, so we're including all of the information you'll need for both the 2006 and the 2007 tests—pay attention to whichever one applies.

In May, 2006, the Essay section of the exam will be made up of the following:

- One analytical/expository essay
- One argumentative essay
- One additional essay—EITHER analytical/expository OR argumentative

In May, 2007, the Essay section of the exam will be made up of the following:

- One analytical/expository essay
- One argumentative essay
- One document-based (DBQ) essay

In Chapters 4 through 6, you will learn more about each kind of essay and how to go about writing the best possible essays in the time that's allotted—a total of 2 hours, or 120 minutes. At the test site, you will receive all the paper you need (including scratch paper), and you will be instructed to write in pen. Remember to bring two or three blue or black ink pens with you.

As we mentioned, you'll have two hours to complete the Essay section. While the test administrator will give you some approximate guidelines for time management, you will not be told how much time to spend on each essay or when to move on to the next essay. Time management is important! Before you set foot in the test center, you must practice writing 40-minute essays. Of course, if your school has not provided you with practice, the tests at the end of this book will give you an opportunity to hone your skills. Do not fool yourself into believing, as so many other students (and teachers), that any type of writing will prepare you to write the AP English Language and Composition exam. Writing a cogent, organized essay under rigid time constrictions is a special art; writing three consecutive essays under such conditions requires special training and lots of practice. Fortunately for you, this book provides you with both.

THE IMPORTANCE OF THE ESSAY SECTION TO YOUR SCORE

The Essay section of the AP English Language and Composition exam counts for 55 percent of your total score, so this means that it's only slightly more important to your overall score than the Multiple-Choice section of the test. However, the Essay section will *feel* like it's more important because two-thirds of your time will go into producing the essays. Students tend to look at the Essay section with a combination of awe, fear, and excitement. It's one thing to send off some pencil marks on an answer sheet for mechanized correction; but it's quite another to submit your writing to an anonymous person for personal judgment. The Essay section is the only place in this exam where your personality—at least to a limited degree—will shine through to test graders.

Keep this in mind: Although the Multiple-Choice and Essay sections are roughly equal in the ETS scoring process, there is a big difference between the way that you'll approach each of these sections. Preparing for the Essay section of the exam is more than just memorizing and applying techniques.

READY, SET, WRITE!

As we've discussed, you will write your AP essays under intense time pressure and without a preparatory lesson. That is not what you're used to. In the past, editing and rewriting may have been an important part of your in-school essay writing. Perhaps your teachers have insisted that you turn in drafts of essays and required you to revise the drafts. If so, then you know that good writing takes patience and care; the "ready, set, write" attitude that test writers expect you to adopt when writing the AP essays runs opposite to the right way to approach most writing and is, hopefully, diametrically opposed to the way your teachers have trained you to write. Unfortunately, just because you have the ability to write a superlative essay when time is not a factor does not guarantee that you'll be able to write a good one in 40-minutes. That's why you're reading this chapter.

The closest thing you may have experienced to writing the essays for the AP test is probably an in-class essay test, but even in that case there are significant differences. For example, in-class essays usually come after you've spent several classes on the subject at hand and know what your teacher expects you to have learned. Also, on in-class essay tests, the teacher wants to see what you know, not just how well you write. On the AP exam, you will be writing cold on a passage you read just two minutes prior for the first time. You'll have no time to revise—only proofread—your work, and you'll be graded at least as much on the form and writing as on the content. The AP essays call for a kind of speed writing; you have to come up with good ideas and get them down efficiently—on the very first try.

This isn't the best way to write, but remember that everyone else is working under the same conditions. If you know how to make the most of the conditions, you will have a leg up on most other writers and your essays will stand out as being stronger than average. It's a little late in the game to learn how to write well; but it isn't too late to learn how to write a high-scoring AP essay.

YOUR TEACHER KNOWS YOU

In school, you write essays for teachers who know you and who are probably influenced by that knowledge. They know what your writing looked like at the beginning of the year, they know that it has or has not improved, they know whether you do your homework assiduously; they know whether you contribute keen insights to class discussion; they know that your real passion is for football, field hockey, dance, painting, physics, or reading. They may even know about special circumstances in your life that are affecting your work.

When you write your name on the first page of an essay, your teacher already knows a thousand things about your essay, and these are part of your teacher's reading. Inevitably, that familiarity has some effect on the grades that you receive.

The AP reader doesn't know you at all.

YOU KNOW YOUR TEACHER

Also, remember that you do not know anything about the reader of your AP essays. Who is he or she? In school, you know your teacher. You are accustomed to his or her demands; you know what that teacher wants to hear. You may know that he or she detests misspellings, loves it when you use humor, or gives extra credit for originality. Or, you may know that he or she is old and cantankerous and takes off more points for a misplaced book than for a misplaced modifier. Your AP essays will be written to a featureless face: Is it a kind face? Mean? Crazy? You will never know.

ALL ABOUT AP ESSAY SCORING

THE ZERO-TO-NINE SCALE

As we mentioned in Part I, each of your essays will be given a score between 0 and 9, with 0 being the worst score you can get, and 9 being the best. However, the scores are *not* spread out evenly over that range; the majority of essays receive a grade of 4 or 5. Here is how the scores break down.

Score	Approximate percentage of students receiving score
9	1%
8	5%
7	10%
6	20%
5	23%
4	22%
3	15%
2	3%
1	1%
0	less than 1%
–	less than 1%

As you can see, about 65 percent of the essays receive a score in the middle range: 4, 5, and 6. The high and low scores taper away pretty quickly. ETS does not *tell* its essay readers to bunch up the scores this way (in fact ETS often chastises the readers for this bulge in the middle), and they don't manipulate the results to make them produce this bell curve. It works out this way because most of the essays are, indeed, average. In fact, reading essays often becomes drudgery because there are so many middle-of-the-road essays. With this in mind, your goal is to have your essays stand out from the rest. Your goal should be to *at least* get a 6 or 7, and it's even realistic to expect at least one score of 8 if you practice enough before test day.

HOLISTIC SCORING

The essays are scored holistically. What this means is that the reader goes through your essay and gets an overall impression, which is translated into a single number (your essay's score). There is no checklist of points; you won't receive 2 points for style, 2 points for grammar, 1 point for vocabulary, and 1 point for a clear thesis statement.

About a week before the actual grading sessions, ETS goes through several essays to get a sense of how students did—this is the beginning of the calibration process. Next, the ETS table leaders comb through the student writing looking for representative essays: the perfect 9 essay, the perfect 5 essay, and so on. The table leaders use these sample essays to train (calibrate) the readers. For nearly an entire day, the table leader and readers—working on a single essay prompt—read essays together and discuss the grades that they would assign. Once the readers can grade sample essays the way the table leader can, the group is ready to embark on the grading process. ETS scrupulously applies certain control processes; for example, over time, a reader will end up rereading and correcting certain essays chosen at random, and the two sets of scores will be compared for consistency. To check consistency from one reader to another, every reader (without knowing it) grades essays that another reader has already graded. However, despite all this checking and rechecking, there is no way around one key fact: The readers are individuals who will make subjective judgments.

THE READER WANTS AN ESSAY THAT IS EASY TO SCORE

Readers are dedicated high school, college, and university instructors who take a week out of their year to come to one site to grade essays. It's your job not to contribute to the monotony and to make sure your essay stands out from the hundreds of ho-hum essays that each reader will score.

You need to strive to write an essay that's obviously better than average. The person who reads your test should feel confident about giving you at least a 6. Remember that three-quarters of the essays are average or worse, and readers are always hoping to come across something outstanding. Usually, the essays are generic and have no distinctive style to them, and often the essays barely address the prompt. If an essay starts out dull and poorly written, the reader may tune out and miss an excellent and well-written point later in the essay; likewise if an essay ends with a long, boring paragraph, the reader may forget some of the great points that were made earlier in the essay. But before we examine some basic tips for making it easy for the reader to give you a high score, let's look at the kind of scoring guide that the readers use.

A TYPICAL SCORING GUIDE

As we discussed briefly, the readers receive a scoring guide for the essays that they will grade. The scoring guides for all of the AP essays are very similar. What follows is a combination of the various guides, without the details that are particular to any specific passage or prompt. As you look over the scoring guide, notice how little specific guidance ETS actually provides. The readers are actually given considerable leeway.

Scores 8–9

These are well-organized and well-written essays that clearly address the prompt. These essays include apt, specific examples to explain or argue a point. When appropriate, these essays clearly explain elements such as rhetorical strategies, diction, imagery, and point of view. While not flawless, these works demonstrate an understanding of the passage or concept and of the techniques of composition. The writers of these essays express their ideas skillfully and clearly.

Scores 6–7

The content of these papers resembles that of the higher-scoring essays, but it is less precise and less aptly supported. These essays deal with elements such as rhetorical strategies, diction, imagery, and point of view, but they are less effective than the essays in the upper range. Essays that receive a score of 7 generally exhibit fewer mechanical errors and use slightly better specific examples than those that receive a score a 6.

Score 5

These essays are superficial. Although not seriously off topic or completely lacking in merit, they miss the complexity of the prompt or of the passage and offer only a perfunctory analysis. The treatment of elements such as rhetorical strategies, diction, imagery, and point of view is overly generalized. The writing adequately conveys the writer's thoughts, but the essays are mechanical, poorly organized, or simplistic.

Scores 3–4

These essays attempt to address the prompt, but they reflect an incomplete understanding of the prompt or of the passage (or both); they do not address the prompt adequately. The discussion is unclear or simply misses the mark. The treatment of rhetorical elements is scanty or unconvincing, and there is little support for the writer's statements. Typically, these essays reveal marked weaknesses in the writer's ability to handle the mechanics of written English.

Scores 1–2

These essays contain the shortcomings found in the essays that are given a score of 3 and 4, but to a more pronounced degree. These essays either completely misunderstand the prompt or the passage (or both) or fail completely to address the prompt. Typically, these essays are incoherent, inchoate, or both. The writing evinces no control of written English, and the organization is poor.

Score 0

This is a response that fails to address the question. There may be a reference only to the task at hand.

Score " — "

This indicates that the response is completely off topic or that a response has not been made. The essay, of course, receives no points.

ANALYSIS OF THE SCORING GUIDE

The scoring guide should tell you two important things:

- First, that the high-scoring essays are *clear*. They are not perfect. They aren't moving and profound. They're simply clear. Practically every point made in the 8 to 9 score description is just another way of saying *clear*. "Well-organized" means clearly organized. "Apt, specific examples" is another way of saying that the writer has used clear examples. Clarity is your goal.

- Second, notice the jump that happens at the 5 score. Notice how the whole tone of the guide changes. Suddenly the guide is not talking about the fine points of addressing the prompt; it is talking about the life-choking drabness of it all. You can almost hear the guide's author muttering under his or her breath, "I wish we could give these essays an even lower score; they are so boring!" The 5 essay is just a trap; many 5 essays are written by good students, and most of these students probably think they wrote a pretty good essay. But in actuality they wrote only an adequate essay, a mechanical essay, a commonplace essay—a boring essay. After grading the fifty-fifth essay of the day, a reader writes down a 5 and picks up another essay from the pile, praying: "Please, not another drab, boring 5 essay!"

If you understand what you read and can write reasonably well, your goal should not be a 5. It should be at least a 6 or 7. You will almost certainly do better than even a 6 or 7 by following a few basic tips and familiarizing yourself with the types of essays you will be required to write.

HOW TO MAKE IT EASY FOR THE READER TO GIVE YOU A HIGH SCORE

Just a little more than half the points you're given for your essay will come from an assessment of its content, but the reader has to be able to get to that content. There are a few vital things that you must do to let your excellence shine through with full impact. Ignore these basic tips at your own peril. They pertain to the superficial aspects of your writing, but a clear surface is the first step toward getting a high score.

NEATNESS COUNTS

Do everything that's reasonably possible to make your essays readable. Your writing does not have to be pretty, but it needs to be legible. Think before you write! If your thoughts are clear before you write, you will express yourself more clearly in the essay; if your thoughts are a mess, your essay will be a mess too.

Some test advisers will urge you to print, rather than use cursive. This is bad advice, unless you ordinarily print instead of using cursive when you write. Do not waste time by slowing down your writing or, worse, learning how to print on the day of the test. Your handwriting can be almost indecipherable for the common reader. In the past, students with absolutely horrific cursive handwriting have scored decently on the AP English Language and Composition exam.

The general appearance of the essay is what's most important. An occasional scratch-out is perfectly fine; a scratch-out every third word is a sign that you don't know what you're doing. Messy essay writing is like a guy showing up for a job interview with his shoes untied, his fly unzipped, his belt skipping a few loops, ketchup all over his shirt, and his hair unwashed. First impressions count, and it is easy to dismiss a mess. Think, organize, and let your writing flow.

These days, using a word processor makes perfect sense for most writing that you do. Students like the auto-correct, spell-check, and auto-almost-everything functions that are part of word-processing programs; teachers like having fewer mistakes to correct—and the increased legibility. However, if your teacher truly cares about how prepared you are, most of your essays in your AP class will be in class and written by hand. Do *not* use your computer when you're writing the practice essays in this book. A significant part of your preparation for the exam should be to practice writing your essays by hand. Far too many students produce their only handwritten essays of the entire year on the day of the exam, and that's a huge handicap.

INDENT

Your reader's first impressions are, indeed, crucial. The messy-looking character at the job interview has an uphill battle on his hands, if he hasn't lost his chance already. The overall look of your essay is a first impression. It is the smile on your face as you walk in the door. Your essay should look neat, organized, and clear. Make your paragraphs obvious. Indent twice as far as you normally would.

When in doubt, make a new paragraph. Have you ever opened a book and seen nothing but very long paragraphs? Your next thought is probably, "Do I really want to read this?" That's exactly what readers think when they see an essay without paragraphs. Make sure readers can see the paragraphs at first glance. Also, get in the habit of checking your essays for balance. All of the paragraphs should be approximately the same length, if possible.

Neat presentation, regular handwriting, and balanced paragraphs will put readers on your side before they even read a line.

WRITE PERFECTLY...FOR THE FIRST TWO SENTENCES

If your essay looks neat, the reader will start feeling relaxed and optimistic. It's up to you to write a brilliant beginning that will set the tone for the entire essay and sustain the reader's positive attitude. Put a lot of care into writing the first two sentences, and don't make any mistakes. If you're unsure about the spelling of a word, don't use it! Don't worry so much about the rest of the essay; the readers expect little mistakes. If you try to write the whole essay perfectly, you may write too slowly and run out of time, or worry too much and write dull, overwrought, and perhaps recondite paragraphs. All it takes is two good first sentences to convince the reader that you can write a good sentence when you have time to do so. As long as the rest of your essay is clear and well organized, the glow of a good beginning can carry over the entire essay.

WRITE WITH PIZZAZZ

Take some risks when you write your essays; you may fall flat every once in a while, but the reader will appreciate your effort and reward it. Bored students write boring essays. Be decisive and let yourself go. For example, you may write, "The candidate's appearance was neat, and the boss gave him the job right away." That may be true, but the sentence is mundane at best. A better sentence would be something like, "The candidate's Armani suit and sleek silk tie captivated the boss, who slipped a contract across the table without comment or hesitation." Or, "The creases on the candidate's suit were as sharp as the pencil that the boss had tucked behind his ear, and, faster than a New York second, the wizened old man produced a contract and a pen." Over the top? Who cares! Nobody expects you to write like Toni Morrison or Neil Postman. In fact, the reader expects you to write like someone who is suffering through a tedious, nerve-racking exercise—because that's exactly how most of the other essays come across. If you write like someone who enjoys writing, the reader will enjoy reading your essay and reward you.

This does not mean that you should write tangled, complex sentences; in fact, you should try to avoid them. All you need to do is pay attention to diction (word choice). When you find yourself using a generic verb such as *look*, *see*, *says*, *walk*, *go*, *take*, or *give*, or a generic noun such as *street*, *house*, *car*, or *man*, ask yourself if there isn't a more precise, more colorful word that you could use instead. Why write "house" when you're referring to a mansion, shack, or cabin? Why write "car," when you really mean jalopy, Porsche, or limousine? A little bit goes a long way: You could even make it appear that writing the essay was fun, which may very well be the case.

Obviously, there can be too much of a good thing, so don't go overboard. Just try to let your writing flow naturally; from time to time, however, think about alternative diction.

Do not use contractions or shorthand symbols such as "&" or "w/" or "tho." Get in the habit of using a relatively high level of discourse when you write essays for class. The AP reader will not necessarily take off points if you neglect this advice, but you will not impress anyone with e-mail or instant messenger–style writing.

ANSWER THE QUESTION

If you write a great essay that does not address the prompt well, you will get a lousy score. All three essays are directed essays, and, in the next chapter, you will study the types of prompts that you will encounter on the exam. It is extraordinarily easy to figure out how to address each prompt as long as you remain cool, read the prompt slowly, and follow the advice we give you. For now, every prompt has telltale signs that allow you to "answer the question"—even if you do not fully understand it.

Budget Your Time

As we mentioned, you can take as much or as little time as you like to write each of the three essays, as long as the total time does not exceed two hours. Each essay is worth the same number of points, however, so it's essential that you allot about 40 minutes for each essay. A slightly better score on one essay will not make up for a bad score on another, and if you spend an hour on your first essay, you will not have enough time to write the other essays well.

With this in mind, when you approach the essays, you should definitely have a plan for budgeting your time. As we mentioned above, you have 2 hours total or about 40 minutes for each essay. It is wise to use part of your 40 minutes for planning and jotting down an outline for the essay you're about to write; usually, 3 to 5 minutes is sufficient for this. In the next few chapters, you learn specific steps you can take to effectively plan your answers to all three types of essay prompts (analytical, argumentative, and [for 2007] synthesis). Basically, you should first examine the question and circle key words and phrases, jot down a few notes (more on this in a bit), and begin to write your essay. It may also be helpful to write your thesis statement (or at least a key phrase) at the top of the page to keep you on track. Also, try to save a few minutes at the end for proofreading. You'll be surprised at the improvements you can make to your essay in the last minute or two, simply by correcting little mistakes in wording or grammar.

Ordering the Section

Just as with the reading passages in the Multiple-Choice section of the exam, you may write the essays in any order you like. However, you should probably not do this unless the first prompt makes you feel extremely uncomfortable. After all, you still have to write all three essays, and leaving the most difficult essay for the end (a common technique for many students), when you are tired and restless, isn't a great idea. In any event, once you learn how to identify the various kinds of prompts, there will be no such thing as a difficult essay. For most students, it is better to save time and tackle the essays in the order in which they are presented.

FOR AND AGAINST THE FIVE-PARAGRAPH ESSAY

If you consider yourself a weak writer, the standard five-paragraph form of an essay may provide you with a safe and much-needed method for writing your essay. However, if you're a good writer, it will restrict you and prevent you from creating an essay that's as inspired as it may be otherwise.

Good and weak writers should take, the "five" in "five-paragraph essay" with a grain of salt. Your essay should have a brief introduction and a brief conclusion that isn't just a repetition of the introduction. Three body paragraphs often make sense, but you could also have only two, or four, depending on the prompt. Good writers should not restrict themselves to five paragraphs.

The Organization

The nice thing about the five-paragraph essay is that it provides you with a framework for organizing your ideas and achieving your goal—a high-scoring essay. Using this format, you will do the following:

1. State a thesis (often, the prompt does this for you).

2. Identify two to four—preferably three—ideas that will allow you to prove your thesis.

3. Wrap up your essay with some final thoughts.

For example, consider the following prompt, which is typical of some of the real essay prompts:

> The statement "patience is a virtue" has become proverbial, but is it true? Is patience a virtue? Drawing from your readings or from your own experience, support, refute, or qualify the validity of the statement.

So, what are you going to do? Will you support, refute, or qualify?

First, simply put down on scratch paper whatever crosses your mind, pro or con.

- Patience helps you avoid making rash decisions, which are almost always bad. There was that time when you forgot your house key and, instead of waiting for your parents to come home, you broke a window to get into the house. The neighbors called the cops and… Patience is a virtue!

- Patience is a touchstone for love and friendship. Wow, there are lots of examples!

- Too much patience may prevent you from seizing an opportunity. Bill Gates lost patience with his university work and dropped out. I'll bet he's happy that he wasn't patient. Patience is not a virtue!

At this point, you could forget about the third idea, but why? You are set up to qualify the adage, and your thesis practically writes itself: *Patience is not an absolute virtue; while most often one does well to heed its voice, inevitably there are times when it is better to turn a deaf ear.*

You have already written half of the introduction and much of the essay.

THE OUTLINE

Do NOT waste time writing a formal outline! You need time to write and to write well, and your time is extremely limited. Solid organization is important, but quantity is also relatively important. Don't let anyone fool you into thinking that a wonderfully organized one-page essay will do the trick; it won't. Depending on the size of your handwriting, you should plan to fill two to three of the lined pages in the essay booklet. The test is not designed for the kind of carefully thought-out work that results from multiple drafts; this is a sprint, and you'd better get out of the starting blocks fast.

You should write down the main idea and a few notes (in your own code or shorthand) for each planned body paragraph. Although for purposes of clarity we used a few too many words in the bullet points above, they contain the basics of the outline. A more realistic version might be worded as below.

- Rash decisions; house key/cops

- Love/friendship; waiting for Jim; looking for lost notebook with Stephanie; time when Angela waited for me

- Bill Gates

Even this is a bit wordy. Write down only enough to remember what you want to include—for example, Bill Gates's name is enough to remind you about dropping out of college and going on to found Microsoft.

THE INTRODUCTION

Perhaps surprisingly, the introduction is usually the weakest part of an AP essay. Long introductions take up time that should instead be devoted to the essay, and they tend to leave the reader confused, bored, or both. You should write around three sentences in your introduction. The first will be your thesis statement, and the second and third will contain the enumeration of the main points that will substantiate your thesis. Basically, you will announce what you intend to explain or prove and give a road map to the rest of the essay. Here's what you could do with the information that you just came up with.

> Patience is not an absolute virtue; while most often one does well
> to heed its voice, inevitably there are times when it is better to turn
> a deaf ear. Patience impedes rash decisions, which are almost always
> bad; furthermore, it is the true touchstone for love and friendship.
> However, patience can also be an impediment to decisiveness, which is
> often an ingredient for greatness.

Is this a great introduction? No, but it isn't bad either. The student has already proven that he or she is addressing the prompt and, specifically, chosen to qualify the adage. Also, the reader knows that the writer has a plan; in fact, all that's lacking now is good choice and presentation of examples drawn from his or her experience or readings.

A great writer could use the same material and write a more elegant introduction; a not-so-great writer could use the same material and lose it in a cloud of verbiage. If you are anything but an incredibly gifted writer, then less is more when it comes to introductions.

THE BODY PARAGRAPHS

Present the body paragraphs of your essay in the order in which you presented the topics in the introduction. Begin each of the three body paragraphs with a sentence that is roughly equivalent to the appropriate phrase in the introduction; this will be your topic sentence. If possible, do not use identical wording. For example, you may begin your first body paragraph with the following:

> More often than not, when it comes to making decisions, patience is
> definitely a virtue.

Then you may use the example of the lost house key, and maybe you'd add more examples as they come to you (perhaps you jotted these down in your outline before beginning the essay). It could be fun to write about the lost key, the " break-in," the arrival of the police on the scene, and the ensuing arrival of your terrified parents. Good narration can earn you big points. What's so hard about narrating a humorous anecdote? However, don't get too carried away with your anecdotes; remember to stay on the topic.

End each paragraph with either a "clincher," which is a sentence that drives home your point, or a transitional sentence, which is one that leads the reader naturally into the next paragraph.

> (Clincher) One thing is for sure: Patience is a virtue that my parents expect me to
> practice in the future!

> (Transition) Although the police were not thrilled with my rash decision, my parents
> bore the event with patience; surely they proved their love for me that day.

That transition sentence gets you ready to start the next paragraph (about how patience is a touchstone for love and friendship). You write two more body paragraphs, and you're practically done!

THE CONCLUSION

Sometimes an essay will end suddenly, and the reader will be left staring at the blank lines, wondering if the student ran out of time, ran out of ideas, or ran out of the room. Worse are the essays that end with a rambling, repetitive, boring rehashing of the introduction; this can erase some of the positive impressions earned in the body paragraphs.

Seldom will you have time to write a brilliant conclusion, so do the next best thing: Keep it short. If you can, invite the reader to reflect upon what you have written. As we mentioned in the planning stage, you may have a lot to say about what constitutes a virtue in the first place, so one possibility would be to end with something like the following:

> If patience is a virtue, like thrift, modesty, or generosity, it is not an absolute guide. Perhaps the only absolute virtue is the gift of knowing when to obey a virtue—like patience—absolutely.

That's a lot of information to digest, but as you go through the next chapters you can always revisit this one to refresh your memory. For now, let's go through the major points of this chapter one more time before you move on.

SUMMARY

GENERAL ESSAY INFORMATION

- There are three essays; work on them as equally as possible.
- You have 2 hours total, or 40 minutes for each essay.

ESSAY SCORING

- Each essay is scored by a reader who grades only that particular type of essay.
- Each essay is given a score from 0 to 9.
- The essays are scored "holistically." There is no checklist of available points.
- The reader wants to read good essays that are easy to score.
- When in doubt, the reader will grade your essay in the middle range of scores.
- Clear essays earn high scores, generic and boring essays earn mid-range scores, and bad essays earn low scores.

PRESENTATION

- Do everything in your power to make the essay appear neat.
- Write confidently in the manner in which you feel most comfortable; there should be a regular flow to your writing.
- Make your paragraph indentations easy to spot.

- Your first two sentences should be grammatically perfect. Your reader will quickly make a judgment about your ability to write. Once the reader has decided that you can write a clear sentence, he or she will cut you some slack later on.

- Vary your diction and sentence structure. A little extra effort when choosing verbs and nouns will pay great dividends.

- Do not use contractions or shorthand (e.g., "&" for "and").

- Address the prompt; write what they want to hear, not what you want to say.

- If you are perplexed by the first prompt, do the questions in whatever order you feel comfortable with; however, reordering the prompts takes time. If at all possible, do the essays in the order in which they are presented.

- If you do not have a good organizational track record, use "five-paragraph" form. It is always better to have too much organization than too little.

- Do not waste time crafting an outline; jot down just enough to capture the gist of a plan of attack for each body paragraph.

Now that you have a general idea of how the Essay section is structured and scored, let's move on to a few more specifics about the different types of essays you'll see. The next three chapters outline how you should go about answering the three different kinds of prompts: the analytical, argumentative, and (for 2007) synthesis questions.

4

The
Analytical/Expository
Essay

SAMPLE ESSAY #1 — HERE'S HOW IT'S DONE

You will be asked to write an analytical/expository essay for the AP English Language and Composition exam. You can count on that. But you should look at this as a good thing because you can practice and perfect the process of writing this type of essay before exam day. Let's start by taking a quick look at the instructions for our first sample essay.

THE DIRECTIONS

ENGLISH LANGUAGE AND COMPOSITION

SECTION II

Total Time—2 hours

Question 1

(Suggested time—40 minutes. This question counts as one-third of the total essay score.)

The passage below is extracted from Booker T. Washington's most famous speech, known as "The Atlanta Compromise Address." Washington presented the address to the Cotton States and International Exposition in 1895. Read the entire passage carefully. Then write an essay analyzing the rhetorical strategies that Washington uses to convey his point of view.

THE FIRST TIME YOU READ THE PROMPT

You should read this part twice pen in hand. The first time, you should read only to identify the type of essay they're asking you to write and what you're supposed to do. Also underline any directions that the essay gives you. Your instructions should now look as follows:

The passage below is extracted from Booker T. Washington's most famous speech, known as "The Atlanta Compromise Address." Washington presented the address to the Cotton States and International Exposition in 1895. Read the entire passage carefully. Then write an essay <u>analyzing</u> the <u>rhetorical strategies</u> that Washington uses to convey his <u>point of view</u>.

Prompts for analysis/expository essays, will always contain marker words, such as *analyze, analysis, analyzing*, and so on. For this question, you're expected to analyze Washington's rhetorical strategies. The prompts will not always have a marker to show that you are required to present your analysis in an *expository* essay, but it will be obvious that you are required to explain. Often, but not always, the prompt will contain the word *explain*. Basically, if the prompt doesn't instruct you to argue (or take a stand on an issue), then you'll be expected to explain something. Sometimes, the prompt will give you the point of view or position, but sometimes it won't. As you can see, this prompt does not give you the point of view. In this case, *What is his point of view?* amounts to *What is his position?*

Before reading the essay for the first time, you know that you have two main tasks. As you read the passage, you'll need to

1. figure out Booker T. Washington's point of view, and

2. identify the rhetorical strategies he uses.

By the way, almost all AP English Language and Composition exams require that you identify or analyze rhetorical strategies, so it is essential that you spend a lot of time studying the chapters 8 through 10, which are devoted to rhetorical strategies.

The Second Time You Read the Prompt

The second time you read the prompt, you should circle clues or key elements that you know or need to figure out. For example, for this question, you should circle Booker T. Washington's name. Hopefully you know that he was a famous African American leader and scholar of the nineteenth century; many public schools in the United States are named after him. If you do not know that, then you would have to glean the information from the text. "Most famous" is another clue; this implies that this person gave several famous speeches, and this tells you something important about Booker T. Washington if you do not know about his fame to begin with. You should also note the date of the speech, for it gives a clue about the speech's historical context, which will be important. Washington delivered the speech in the South (Atlanta, Georgia) just 30 years after the Civil War. Finally, the audience is important. It is easy to guess that the attendees of the Exposition were mostly white, and this is confirmed early in the reading passage—which you are ready to read.

The Passage

One-third of the population of the South is of the Negro race. No enterprise seeking the material, civil, or moral welfare of this section
Line can disregard this element of our population
5 and reach the highest success. I but convey to you, Mr. President and Directors, the sentiment of the masses of my race when I say that in no way have the value and manhood of the American Negro been more fittingly and
10 generously recognized than by the managers of this magnificent Exposition at every stage of its progress. It is a recognition that will do more to cement the friendship of the two races than any occurrence since the dawn of our freedom.
15 Not only this, but the opportunity here afforded will awaken among us a new era of industrial progress. Ignorant and inexperienced, it is not strange that in the first years of our new life we began at the top instead of at the bottom;
20 that a seat in Congress or the state legislature was more sought than real estate or industrial skill; that the political convention or stump speaking had more attractions than starting a dairy farm or truck garden.
25 A ship lost at sea for many days suddenly sighted a friendly vessel. From the mast of the unfortunate vessel was seen a signal, "Water, water; we die of thirst!" The answer from the friendly vessel at once came back, "Cast down
30 your bucket where you are." A second time the signal, "Water, water; send us water!" ran up from the distressed vessel, and was answered, "Cast down your bucket where you are." And a third and fourth signal for water was answered,
35 "Cast down your bucket where you are." The captain of the distressed vessel, at last heeding

the injunction, cast down his bucket, and it came up full of fresh, sparkling water from the mouth of the Amazon River. To those of my
40 race who depend on bettering their condition in a foreign land or who underestimate the importance of cultivating friendly relations with the Southern white man, who is their next-door neighbor, I would say: "Cast down your bucket
45 where you are"—cast it down in making friends in every manly way of the people of all races by whom we are surrounded.
Cast it down in agriculture, mechanics, in commerce, in domestic service, and in the
50 professions. And in this connection it is well to bear in mind that whatever other sins the South may be called to bear, when it comes to business, pure and simple, it is in the South that the Negro is given a man's chance in
55 the commercial world, and in nothing is this Exposition more eloquent than in emphasizing this chance. Our greatest danger is that in the great leap from slavery to freedom we may overlook the fact that the masses of us are
60 to live by the productions of our hands, and fail to keep in mind that we shall prosper in proportion as we learn to dignify and glorify common labor, and put brains and skill into the common occupations of life; shall prosper
65 in proportion as we learn to draw the line between the superficial and the substantial, the ornamental gewgaws of life and the useful. No race can prosper till it learns that there is as much dignity in tilling a field as in writing a
70 poem. It is at the bottom of life we must begin, and not at the top. Nor should we permit our grievances to overshadow our opportunities.

To those of the white race who look to the
incoming of those of foreign birth and strange
75 tongue and habits for the prosperity of the
South, were I permitted I would repeat what I
say to my own race, "Cast down your bucket
where you are." Cast it down among the eight
millions of Negroes whose habits you know,
80 whose fidelity and love you have tested in days
when to have proved treacherous meant the
ruin of your firesides. Cast down your bucket
among these people who have, without strikes
and labour wars, tilled your fields, cleared
85 your forests, built your railroads and cities,
and brought forth treasures from the bowels
of the earth, and helped make possible this
magnificent representation of the progress of
the South. Casting down your bucket among
90 my people, helping and encouraging them
as you are doing on these grounds, and to
education of head, hand, and heart, you will
find that they will buy your surplus land, make
blossom the waste places in your fields, and
95 run your factories. While doing this, you can be
sure in the future, as in the past, that you and
your families will be surrounded by the most
patient, faithful, law-abiding, and unresentful
people that the world has seen. As we have
100 proved our loyalty to you in the past, in nursing
your children, watching by the sick-bed of
your mothers and fathers, and often following
them with tear-dimmed eyes to their graves,
so in the future, in our humble way, we shall
105 stand by you with a devotion that no foreigner
can approach, ready to lay down our lives, if
need be, in defense of yours, interlacing our
industrial, commercial, civil, and religious
life with yours in a way that shall make the
110 interests of both races one. In all things that
are purely social we can be as separate as
the fingers, yet one as the hand in all things
essential to mutual progress.

The Analysis

What is Washington's point of view? Is he an angry man demanding change? Is he an outraged man warning of rebellion? Is he a timid man begging indulgence? No, he is none of these. Booker T. Washington's point of view is that of the inspirational Southern preacher who urges blacks and whites to rally round the same economic flag. He employs three principal rhetorical strategies in this part of his speech.

1. Throughout, there is an appeal to sentiment; this is particularly noteworthy in the first paragraph.

2. Next, there is the central image of the bucket, which could be considered part of either an extended metaphor or an allegory; this is first addressed to the black population, then to white people.

3. Finally, to support the imagery, Washington uses analogy (e.g., "there is as much dignity in tilling a field as in writing a poem"), scare tactics (e.g., the references to people of foreign birth), and interesting deductive reasoning. Washington purports that the continual loyalty and hard work of blacks in the past proves that they will be loyal, hard-working collaborators in the future. While the claim is reasonable, the logic is not; in the past that Washington is talking about, the blacks were slaves. For the most part, they had no choice but to be hard-working and loyal.

Now, keep all the above information in mind as you read the following sample essay, which was written in 40 minutes under actual test conditions.

A Student Essay

Born into slavery and liberated by the Emancipation Proclamation, Booker T. Washington is widely regarded as one of the most influential African American figures in the history of the United States. In 1881, he started the Tuskegee Normal and Industrial Institute, and soon became recognized, admired, and respected for his wisdom. Because a number of well-placed business leaders and political figures turned to him for advice, he delivered his most famous speech "The Atlanta Compromise Address" in 1895. It is an explication of his beliefs that his fellow African Americans and other former slaves should make the best of what they have and strive to excel in the positions and jobs they already occupy rather than continually fighting for something. Furthermore, he argues that the people of the white race also do not see what they have around them. A moving speech, the impact of the "Atlanta Compromise" was so powerful partially because of Washington's skill as an orator and partially because of his strong rhetorical strategies of appeal to ethos, allegory, and repetition, and style and tone.

One of the most memorable quotes from the "Atlanta Compromise" is "cast down your buckets where you are." In this short allegory about a lost ship without drinking water being found by another ship and saved by using what was around them, Washington conveys his central idea that African Americans can help themselves and save themselves by using what resources they already have. The lost ship, in thinking that it is surrounded by salty water, does not even attempt to try the water before the second ship suggests the idea. Similarly, Washington implies that simply because they do not think they have anything to work with, the African Americans who were once slaves do not try to see what can be done with what they have. The impact of the allegory of the two ships is strengthened by Washington's repetition of the phrase "cast down your bucket where you are." However, in repeating it, he applies it to not only the African Americans, but also to "those of the white race." In that context, he states that the white Americans could look to the African Americans for help with the "prosperity of the South" instead of looking to "those of foreign birth and strange tongue and habits." Again, he implores both sides to look around and make use of what is already present.

The idea of the speech is set up in the introductory paragraph, wherein Washington states that the recognition of the race of the "American Negro" at the Exposition will do much to "cement the friendship of the two races." It is in this paragraph and these phrases that Washington turns to the strategy of an appeal to ethos. By asserting that the Exposition will help further the friendship between the white Americans and the African Americans, he subtly suggests that this end, this friendship, is what the organizers of the exposition should want (a moral want). This appeal is utilized again in the final paragraph of the passage. In asking the white Americans to cast down their buckets, Washington also asks them to remember that the African Americans "have proved [their] loyalty to [the white Americans] in the past." Thus, he seems to be saying it would be immoral for the white Americans to turn away from proved loyalty when they are in search of help and employees.

However, the most compelling element of Washington's speech is his tone and style. When reading the passage, one can almost imagine Washington delivering his oration. His tone and style are uplifting, optimistic, and emphatic, much like the tone of a passionate Southern preacher. His own emotions seem to be invested in every word. With phrases like "it is at the bottom of life that we must begin, and not at the top," or "there is as much dignity in tilling a field as in writing a poem," Washington lends nobility and a right to pride to the common labor that most African Americans performed at the time. When he speaks of casting down the bucket "in agriculture, in mechanics, in commerce, in domestic service, and in the professions," he assures both the African Americans and the white Americans that hard labor is not something to be looked down on. Neither, he implies, is the struggle to rise above your station a condemnable action. Nevertheless, he always comes back to the point that one must first make use of what is already present and readily available before searching for something else.

A wise and powerful man and speaker, Booker T. Washington often knew just what to say to convey his ideas and opinions. Even more important, he knew how to phrase and present what was important. In "The Atlanta Compromise Address," Washington successfully utilizes the strategies of appeal to ethos, repetition, allegory, style, and tone to impart his message of using what one had to improve oneself. In simplified terms, "The Atlanta Compromise" is a speech based on carpe diem, the idea of seizing what one has and using it to one's advantage.

What do you think? This essay would probably earn a score of 7 or 8; it's strong, but it isn't as clear as it could be. It's obvious from the outset that the student knows about Booker T. Washington and understands the historical context of the speech. The fact that both the introduction and the conclusion evince an attempt to go beyond the bare bones is probably what would make the reader lean toward the higher score.

However, there are two glaring problems in this essay. Although one of them would probably not affect the score, it is an unnecessary and entirely avoidable error; it has to do with the five-paragraph form. The last sentence of the introduction announces a road map for the essay: "strategies of appeal to ethos [sentiment], allegory and repetition, and style and tone." That's fine. However, the student goes on to address the three examples in a different order: First the student addresses allegory and repetition, then discusses appeal to sentiment, and, finally, gets to style and tone. Luckily, most AP readers would overlook this, but it's better to be safe than sorry—keep your organization consistent. There is another problem that readers would probably not overlook. Do you remember the two tasks that we set for our reading? One was to look for rhetorical strategies. The other was to establish a clear point of view. The student never addresses point of view in a coherent manner and in the only mention of it seems to confuse it with tone.

Let's look at another example of an analytical/expository essay, to get more practice.

SAMPLE ESSAY #2—GIVING IT ANOTHER TRY

Okay, let's go through another essay. For this one, make sure you try writing the essay on your own before you read the student essay—you should get as much practice as you can before test day.

THE DIRECTIONS

ENGLISH LANGUAGE AND COMPOSITION

SECTION II

Total Time—2 hours

Question 1

(Suggested time—40 minutes. This question counts as one-third of the total essay score.)

In 1676, Madame de Sévigné wrote the letter below. Read it carefully; then write an essay in which you identify the writer's purpose and analyze how she uses language to achieve that purpose. Pay particular attention to organization, point of view, and diction.

THE FIRST TIME YOU READ THE PROMPT

Write down the type of essay you'll need to write, and describe your "job" in writing this essay on the lines below.

_____

_____

_____

_____

_____

THE SECOND TIME YOU READ THE PROMPT

Next, circle the hints in the prompt.

There isn't much to circle, is there? There are only two items: the fact that the writer is a woman (Madame), and the historical context of the letter (seventeenth-century France under Louis XIV); if you know that "de" indicates nobility, then you have another clue to the point of view—the writer, indeed, belongs to the privileged nobility.

Here is the letter.

THE PASSAGE

The Brinvilliers Affair is still the only thing talked about in Paris. The Marquise confessed to having poisoned her father, her brothers,

Line and one of her children. The Chevalier Duget
5 had been one of those who had partaken of a poisoned dish of pigeon pie, and when the Brinvilliers woman was told three years later that he was still alive, her only remark was: "That man surely has an excellent constitution."
10 It seems she fell deeply in love with Sainte Croix, an officer in the regiment of her husband, the Marquis, who lived in their house. Believing that Sainte Croix would marry her if she were free, she attempted to poison her husband.
15 Sainte Croix, not reciprocating her desire, administered an antidote and, thus, saved the poor Marquis' life.

And now, all is over. The Brinvilliers woman is no more. Judgment was given yesterday,
20 and this morning her sentence was read to her; she was to make a public confession in front of Notre Dame, after which she was to be executed, her body burned, and her ashes scattered to the winds. She was threatened with
25 torture, but she said that it was unnecessary and that she would tell all. Accordingly, she recounted the history of her whole life, which was even more horrible than anyone had imagined, and I could not hear of it without
30 shuddering.

At six in the morning she was led out, barefoot, and clad only in a loose garment, with a halter round her neck. From Notre Dame she was taken away in a wagon, in which I saw her
35 lying on straw, with the doctor on one side of her and the executioner on the other; the sight of her struck me with horror. I am told that she mounted the scaffold with a firm step and died as she had lived, resolutely, and without fear or
40 emotion.

She asked her confessor to place the executioner so that she need not gaze on Degrais, who, you will remember, tracked her to England and ultimately arrested her
45 at Liège. After she had mounted the ladder to the scaffold, she was exposed to the public for a quarter of an hour, while the executioner prepared her for execution. This raised a murmur of disapproval among the people, and
50 it was a great cruelty. It seems that some say she was a saint, and after her body had been burned, the people crowded near to search for bones as relics, but little was to be found, as her ashes were thrown into the fire. And, it may be
55 supposed, that we now inhale what remains of her. It is to be hoped that we shall not inhale her murderous instincts also.

List at least two, but no more than four, aspects of language that Madame de Sévigné's uses to serve her purpose.

_____

_____

_____

_____

_____

By the way, you are not expected to ascertain the "correct" purpose of the letter; the limited amount of text offered implies various points of view. Does Madame de Sévigné condemn the crime? Does she feel sorry for the criminal? The key is to point out that, above all else, the letter's purpose is to relate an event. Beyond that, you would only be conjecturing.

Here's a sample essay by the same student who wrote the previous one. This time there is no doubt: The essay falls clearly into the 8 to 9 range. The student addresses the difficult prompt well, follows the road map, provides relevant examples from the text, and supports it all with strong, organized writing.

A STUDENT ESSAY

In the 1600s, life was by no means easy for women. They were expected to cater to any whim their husband might have, and they were treated like property. Whenever a woman outstepped the boundaries society had established for her, and her crime was serious enough, she was humiliated and punished publicly. In her 1676 letter, Madame de Sévigné writes of the Brinvilliers affair and incites questions regarding the treatment of women in her time.

Society of the seventeenth century, especially the upper echelons of France, was mostly occupied with the scandalous doings of others in their class. Each affair was picked apart, discussed, and passed from ear to eager ear. Naturally, details tended to be embellished and exaggerated, and each individual's opinions and emotions wormed their way into the retelling. In her description of the Brinvilliers affair, Madame de Sévigné includes many of her own feelings upon witnessing and hearing of the fiasco. Watching the Marquise de Brinvilliers' be taken from Notre Dame to the scaffold, Sévigné declares that "the sight of [the Marquise] struck [her] with horror." Expressing her condemnation of the criminal, Sévigné writes that "it seems that some say [the Marquise] was a saint," implying that Sévigné herself does not share in that opinion. The Marquise's life story affected Madame de Sévigné in such a way that she shuddered. Further evidence of Sévigné disdain is evident in her hope that the Marquise's "murderous instincts" will not be inhaled by the people along with her ashes. Nevertheless, a certain reluctant admiration is evident in Sévigné's declaration that the Marquise "died as she had lived, resolutely, and without fear or emotion." Despite the Marquise's transgressions, one must respect a woman who displayed such strength in the face of the poor treatment they received from men, society, and even other women.

Though she has included some personal sentiments and observations, the majority of Sévigné's letter is dedicated to a fairly objective account of the proceedings of the Brinvilliers affair. She begins by explaining how the entire affair began—"The Marquis [...] poisoned her father, brothers [...] one of her children," and her husband because she believed that "Sainte Croix would marry her if she were free." Tracked to England by Degrais and arrested in Liege, the Marquise was brought back to France and sentenced. Her punishment included a public confession, an execution, and a cremation. Sévigné's narrative continues with details of the public punishment and humiliation of the Marquise. In a matter-of-fact manner, Sévigné relates the unfortunate end that the Marquise de Brinvilliers met with after her crimes against her family.

In the most obvious manner, Madame de Sévigné paints the Brinvilliers affair as a shocking event—she simply states that "the Brinvilliers affair is still the only thing talked about in Paris." The fact that the Marquise's proper first name is never mentioned lends the air and quality of an unmentionable scandal to the whole affair. One can imagine this straightforward letter being read in a shocked tone of voice, an underlying excitement and eagerness evident in the speaker's voice due to the very "deliciously scandalous" nature of the event. Her crime was so abominable that her persecutors even threatened her with torture to procure her confession. Sévigné's diction, quite candid, underscores the shocking quality of the Brinvilliers affair.

Madame de Sévigné effectively portrays society's treatment of women who have overstepped their limits in the seventeenth century. Her hinted-at emotions relay Sévigné's condemning opinion of the Marquise, while simultaneously they convey reluctant admiration. Both her narrative and her diction underline the fact that the Brinvilliers affair was a major scandal. However, overall, one is imparted with the sense that this treatment is ultimately unjust.

Hopefully, you can see that this essay is clear, precise, and well written. Is it perfect? No, but keep in mind that you do not have to write the perfect essay to earn a high score.

In this chapter, we talked about what goes into writing the analysis essay on the AP English Language and Composition exam and looked at a couple of very well-written examples. Keep the method for approaching these essays that we outlined in this chapter in mind when you are doing the sample exams at the end of this book (and, of course, on the real exam).

In the next chapter, we move on to the argumentative essay.

5

The Argumentative
Essay

FIRST, A WORD...

When you get to the argumentative essay on the AP English Language and Composition exam, you will be asked to take a stand and present your point of view on a topic. This should be an essay that you look forward to! You are not only allowed to use the first person singular ("I"), but also required to use it. Plus, there is no correct position—all that matters is how effectively you substantiate your position. If you like to debate topics, this is the part of the free-response section where you should really shine.

As you may recall from the last chapter, when you read the prompt for the first time, you should identify the type of essay you are required to write and figure out which tasks you're being asked to accomplish. Every argumentative essay prompt in recent history has contained the following phrase: "refute, support, or qualify." In other words, you should have no trouble distinguishing between an analytical/expository essay and an argumentative one.

SAMPLE ESSAY #1 — HERE'S HOW IT'S DONE

Here's a sample argumentative essay prompt. The passage that follows this prompt is typical of argumentative essays you'll see on the test—they're much shorter than the analytical essays.

THE DIRECTIONS

ENGLISH LANGUAGE AND COMPOSITION

SECTION II

Total time—2 hours

Question 1

(Suggested time—40 minutes. This question counts as one-third of the total essay section score.)

Read and think carefully about the following quotation, taken from *Utilitarianism*, by John Stuart Mill. Then write an essay in which you refute, support, or qualify the author's claim. Make sure to use appropriate evidence from literary, historical, or personal sources to develop your argument.

THE FIRST TIME YOU READ THE PROMPT

Remember, as you read the prompt for the first time you should underline the directions it gives you. Your prompt should now look as follows:

Read and think carefully about the following quotation, taken from *Utilitarianism*, by John Stuart Mill. Then write an essay in which you <u>refute, support, or qualify the author's claim.</u> Make sure to use appropriate <u>evidence from literary, historical, or personal</u> sources to develop your argument.

Since you know that the argumentative essay prompt always contains the phrase "refute, support, or qualify," you know right away that this is an argumentative essay. Notice that we also underlined the phrase "evidence from literary, historical, or personal." When you read the passage for the first time and begin to formulate a response, the kind of evidence that pops into your mind should determine what stand you take on the argument. Remember that no reader knows or cares what you really think about an issue. This is an AP test, not a testimonial. You'll want to take the stand that's easiest for you to defend at that particular moment, based on the ideas that come to you.

THE SECOND TIME YOU READ THE PROMPT

Your second reading of the prompt can be fairly superficial; at this point there shouldn't be too much more information for you to glean. If you've taken a lot of history courses, then you may have studied John Stuart Mill, and this would give you some information about context. If not, then at least the title should be a tip-off about the content of the passage.

THE PASSAGE

The creed which accepts as the foundation of morals, Utility, or the Greatest Happiness Principle, holds that actions are right in proportion as they tend to promote happiness, wrong as they tend to produce the reverse of happiness. By happiness is intended pleasure, and the absence of pain; by unhappiness, pain, and the privation of pleasure. To give a clear view of the moral standard set up by the theory, much more requires to be said; in particular, what things it includes in the ideas of pain and pleasure; and to what extent this is left an open question. But these supplementary explanations do not affect the theory of life on which this theory of morality is grounded—namely, that pleasure, and freedom from pain, are the only things desirable as ends; and that all desirable things (which are as numerous in the utilitarian as in any other scheme) are desirable either for the pleasure inherent in themselves, or as means to the promotion of pleasure and the prevention of pain.

THE ANALYSIS

In this case, the author's thesis is clearly stated in the topic sentence: "… actions are right in proportion as they tend to promote happiness, wrong as they tend to produce the reverse of happiness." In the next sentence, Mill defines happiness ("pleasure") and unhappiness ("pain or the privation of pleasure"). This is not an analytical/expository essay, so you do not have to take apart the entire passage; initially your goal is merely to identify the author's claim. After you do this, your next step is to refute, support, or qualify that claim.

If possible, you should refute the claim made by the author of the passage. If done well, essays that refute the author's claim will be the most interesting for the reader. However, if you take a clear, firm stand, in either direction—either for the author's claim or against it—you'll be off to a good start. The most important things are that you have clearly decided how you feel about the issue and that you have the examples to back up your claim.

In this passage, Mill has made an ethical claim: Good actions are those that give oneself pleasure (and, thus, happiness); bad actions are those that give oneself pain or deprive oneself of pleasure (causing unhappiness). What examples (from literary, historical, or personal sources) come to mind that either refute or support the thesis? Quickly jot down three to five of them on the lines below.

_____

_____

_____

_____

_____

Now review your ideas. Which are the easiest to develop? Which do you feel most strongly about? Do you have two or three that will allow you to refute the author's claim? If so, then go for it. If not, do you have two or three examples that will allow you to support the claim? Then go in that direction. In virtually all cases, you should be able to think of evidence for or against the claim. However, if you're caught without very strong evidence that points in either direction, then you'll have to qualify the author's claim. Whatever you decide to do, make your position perfectly clear in the introduction of your essay.

Let's look at an essay that was written by a student under actual testing conditions.

A Student Essay

In John Stuart Mill's work <u>Utilitarianism,</u> the author advances a theory of morality that associates "the promotion of pleasure and the prevention of pain" with ethical correctness. While the pursuit of happiness can sometimes lead to a path of moral righteousness, Mill's claim is flawed in that it assumes hedonism will inherently bring positive results. By championing any action that produces pleasure, Mill condones humanity's greed, lust, and selfishness; three traits that are clearly immoral. As history and literature have demonstrated, pursuing goals motivated purely by self-interest does not lead to ethically responsible outcomes. Furthermore, the greatest achievements often arise when people readily eschew pleasure to attain a nobler end.

During the second half of the nineteenth century, a number of technological advances made the American economy blossom and helped to make the nation a world power. Eager to enjoy the pleasures made possible by great wealth, entrepreneurs and businessmen sought to increase profits and lower costs in any possible way. Workers were paid abysmally low wages, conditions were highly unsafe, and monopolies were commonplace. Though the heads of "Big Business" clearly adhered to Mill's "Greatest Happiness Principle," their actions were highly unethical. Their pleasure came at the expense of the poor and created a polarized society. In contrast, patriots seeking independence from England a century before, gladly relinquished the "absence of pain" afforded by accepting the status quo. Despite the great "privation of pleasure" brought about by the Revolutionary War, the patriots achieved their lofty goal of freedom, a morally desirable outcome. Evidently, seeking happiness does not necessarily entail finding "what is right and good."

F. Scott Fitzgerald's portrait of the Roaring Twenties, <u>The Great Gatsby</u>, examines hedonism and reaches a conclusion much different than Mill's. Jay Gatsby pursues pleasure in the form of rekindling a relationship with a former love, Daisy. Following utilitarian principles, seeking the desirable outcome should be an ethically sound choice. However, it instead leads Gatsby to engage in questionable business and to court a married woman, two clear violations of ethical standards. Clearly, morality based on pleasure is an unsound principle.

This essay is a little bit short—another example would have made it stronger—but it does the job remarkably well. It would most likely receive a score of 8. The introduction is slightly long, but notice how well this student addresses the two tasks set forth. Right away, the student states the author's claim: "...the author advances a theory of morality that associates the 'promotion of pleasure and the prevention of pain' with ethical correctness...." Later in the paragraph, the student takes a clear stand that refutes Mill's claim: "As history and literature have demonstrated, pursuing goals motivated by mere self-interest does not lead to ethically responsible outcomes." The student gives the reader a road map for the rest of the essay; first the student uses a historical example (second half of the nineteenth century), and follows with a literary example (*The Great Gatsby*). Had a personal example been included, this essay would have scored a perfect 9.

DON'T FORGET TO WRITE IN THE PRESENT TENSE

Little things, such as underlining the title of the book, reinforce the impression that this writer knows how to write. As was the case in the two sample essays from the previous chapter, this writer does an excellent job of handling verb tenses. Particularly important is the use of the present tense when addressing the author, text, and claim: "the author advances," "it assumes," "achievements often arise," and so on. The student uses the past tense only when presenting historical facts in the second paragraph, with "advances made," "entrepreneurs and businessmen sought," and "monopolies were." One of the most common grammatical errors that students make in AP English essays is using improper verb-tense shifts. You should be writing in the present tense throughout the essay—and you should shift to the past tense only if you are relating historical facts.

SAMPLE ESSAY #2—GIVING IT ANOTHER TRY

Let's try another one. Again, now that you're comfortable with the process for writing the argumentative essay, try writing this one on your own before you look at the student's essay.

THE DIRECTIONS

ENGLISH LANGUAGE AND COMPOSITION

SECTION II

Total time—2 hours

Question 1

(Suggested time—40 minutes. This question counts as one-third of the total essay section score.)

Read carefully the passage below from "The Collective Wisdom," by Herbert Spencer (1820–1903). Then in a carefully written essay support, refute, or qualify Spencer's assertion that the House of Commons acted foolishly in denying the water rights.

THE FIRST TIME YOU READ THE PROMPT

Remember, as you read the prompt for the first time you should underline the directions it gives you. Your prompt should now look as follows:

Read carefully the passage below from "The Collective Wisdom," by Herbert Spencer (1820–1903). <u>Then in a carefully written essay support, refute, or qualify Spencer's assertion</u> that the House of Commons acted foolishly in denying the water rights.

THE SECOND TIME YOU READ THE PROMPT

Remember, your second reading of the prompt can be fairly superficial; at this point there shouldn't be too much more information for you to glean. Circle the dates that Herbert Spencer lived, circle the House of Commons, and get right to the passage.

THE PASSAGE

On the edge of the Cotswolds, overhanging the valley of the Severn, occur certain springs, which, as they happen to be at the end of
Line the longest of the hundred streams which
5 join to form the Thames, have been called by poetical fiction "the sources of the Thames." Names, even when poetical fictions, suggest conclusions; and conclusions drawn from words instead of facts are equally apt to influence
10 conduct. Thus it happened that, when, recently, there was formed a company for supplying Cheltenham and some other places from these springs, great opposition arose. The *Times* published a paragraph headed, "Threatened
15 Absorption of the Thames," stating that the application of this company to Parliament had "caused some little consternation in the city of Oxford, and will, doubtless, throughout the valley of the Thames;" and that "such a
20 measure, if carried out, will diminish the water of that noble river a million of gallons per day." A million is an alarming word—suggests something necessarily vast. Translating words into thoughts, however, would have calmed
25 the fears of the *Times* paragraphist. Considering that a million gallons would be contained by a room fifty-six feet cube, the nobility of the Thames would not be much endangered by the deduction. The simple fact is that the current of
30 the Thames, above the point at which the tides influence it, discharges in twenty-four hours eight hundred times this amount.

When the bill of this proposed water company was brought before the House
35 of Commons for second reading it became manifest that the imaginations of members were affected by such expressions as the "sources of the Thames," and "a million gallons daily," in much the same way as the
40 imaginations of the ignorant. Though the quantity of water proposed to be taken bears to the quantity which runs over Teddington were about the same ratio that a yard bears to a half a mile, it was thought by many members
45 that its loss would be a serious evil. No method of measurement would be accurate enough to

detect the difference between the Thames as it now is, and the Thames minus the Cerney springs; and yet it was gravely stated in the
50 House that, were the Thames diminished in the proposed way, "the proportion of sewage to pure water would be seriously increased." Taking a minute out of twelve hours would be taking as large a proportion as the Cheltenham
55 people with to take from the Thames. Nevertheless, it was contended that to let Cheltenham have this quantity would be "to rob the towns along the banks of the Thames of their rights." Though, of the Thames flowing by
60 each of these towns, some 999 parts out of 1,000 pass by unused, it was held that a great injustice would be committed were one or two of these 999 parts appropriated by the inhabitants of a town who can now obtain daily but four gallons
65 of foul water per head.

But the apparent inability thus shown to think of causes and effects in something like their true quantitative relations was still more conspicuously shown. It was stated by
70 several members that the Thames Navigation Commissioners would have opposed the bill if the commission had not been bankrupt, and this hypothetical opposition appeared to have weight. If we may trust the reports, the
75 House of Commons listened with gravity to the assertion of one of its members, that, if the Cerney springs were diverted, "shoals and flats would be created." Not a laugh nor a cry
80 of "Oh! oh," appears to have been produced by the prophecy that the volume and scouring power of the Thames would be seriously affected by taking away from it twelve gallons per second! The whole quantity which these
85 springs supply would be delivered by a current moving through a pipe one foot in diameter at the rate of less than two miles per hour. Yet, when it was said that the navigability of the Thames would be injuriously affected by this
90 deduction, there were no shouts of derision. On the contrary, the House rejected the Cheltenham Water Bill by a majority of one hundred and eighteen to eighty-eight.

Phew! After writing your own essay, take a look at the essay on the next page, which was written by a student under actual time constraints.

A STUDENT ESSAY

In "The Collective Wisdom," Herbert Spencer suggests that "conclusions drawn from words instead of facts are equally apt to influence conduct." Under this premise, Spencer goes on to examine a decision made by the House of Commons to reject the Cheltenham Bill that granted water rights to several towns along the so-called "source springs" of the Thames. In his essay, Spencer correctly asserts that the House of Commons' opposition to the bill was quite foolish by taking a closer look at the "facts" (or rather, "words") that were presented to the members of the committee.

First, the House of Commons voted against the water rights bill based on some deceiving information about its impact on the Thames' water volume. The Times published an article that cited a million gallon loss of water per day, were the bill to be passed in the House. To most people, including the members of the House of Commons, a million gallons per day sounds like quite a lot of water. However, Spencer provides the reader with some comparison to make the situation clearer. Apparently, a million gallons is not much of a problem for the Thames since it discharges at about 800 times this amount in a single day. In fact, Spencer also notes that there would be methods accurate enough to measure the difference in volume between the river with and without its "source springs." In this case, the House of Commons was influenced by the seemingly large quantity of "a million gallons per day," which was not presented in an appropriate context.

Second, the House of Commons was given another set of misleading statistics regarding the bill's supposed impact on the purity of the Thames. A report in the House stated that "the proportion of sewage to pure water would be seriously increased" if the springs were tapped by the surrounding towns. Again, Spencer helps the reader to see the ignorance of the House's decision by shedding some light on the situation with a more logical comparison. The towns in question only use about one part out of 1,000 parts of water each day from the springs, so 999 out of 1,000 parts pass by unused. Therefore, the ratio of sewage to pure water is quite insignificant and definitely not as dangerous as the report makes it seem.

The central idea of Spencer's essay is that the House of Commons acted with ignorance when they rejected the Cheltenham Water Bill without seeking the appropriate context for certain facts and figures. Spencer qualifies this as acting "foolishly" since the members of the committee did not consider the whole picture when making their decisions. One assumes that members of the House of Commons would have acted with the intelligence of a legislative body instead of the ignorance of the general public; however, Spencer's essay suggests that this is not always the case, especially when "words" instead of facts are the basis for judgment.

This student essay is strong enough for a distinguished mark—probably a 7—but certainly not an 8 or a 9. The student takes a clear stand and writes strongly. The only snafu comes in the following thesis statement:

> In his essay, Spencer correctly asserts that the House of Commons' opposition to the bill was quite foolish <u>by taking a closer look at the "facts" (or rather, "words") that were presented to the members of the committee.</u>

The phrase "Spencer correctly asserts" is clear and appropriate, but note the ambiguity caused by the position of the prepositional phrase (underlined). Was the opposition quite foolish because the House took a closer look at the facts? Clearly, this is not what the student means. By placing the preposition phrase close to the noun it modifies (Spencer), the introduction would gain clarity—and clarity translates into points.

> <u>By taking a closer look at the "facts" (or rather, "words") that were presented to the members of the committee,</u> Spencer correctly asserts that the House of Commons' opposition to the bill was quite foolish.

Also notice that we have eliminated the phrase "in his essay." Don't get into the habit of including superfluous words in the introduction, such as: "in the novel *Pride and Prejudice*," "in the play *A Doll's House*," "in the novella *Heart of Darkness*," and so on. The reader knows that the student is talking about Spencer's essay, so does the phrase add anything? No. If words do not add, then they subtract. Sometimes, students make even worse errors by using phrases such as "in the <u>novel *A Doll's House*</u>" or "in the play, <u>*A Doll's House.*</u>" The first is an egregious error that calls into question the student's knowledge of either the work in particular or literature in general, and the second is an error in usage.

The rest of the sample essay is very good, but the reader would probably like to see the student bring more original thought to bear on the subject. First and foremost, the student makes the mistake of limiting proof to Spencer's thoughts without providing personal thoughts. Essentially, Spencer is taking a stand on what we consider a modern issue: ecology. The student should have brought this issue to the fore and integrated it into the essay.

It would also have been helpful if the student had highlighted some of the rhetorical fallacies used by Spencer in his essay. For example, on the one hand Spencer accuses the *Times* of using scare tactics, and a supporter of Spencer's free use stand could compare this with current radical ecologists' ploys. On the other hand, one could argue that Spencer himself is guilty of using straw man arguments by simplifying the conservationists' position, or that his *ad hominem* attack on the *Times* reporter ("the paragraphist") reveals that Spencer is not limiting himself to facts. A student writing against Spencer's stand could bring in a rhetorical fallacy of his or her own: the slippery slope argument—if one begins by permitting the diversion of the Cerney Springs, then one is opening the door to the kind of ecological rape of watersheds that, in fact, occurred in England over the course of the next hundred years.

By taking a "personal" stand (not necessarily what the student truly believes, by the way) on this ecological dispute, and even without explicitly naming the rhetorical fallacies, this student would have improved the grade by at least one point.

MOST OF ALL, HAVE FUN

When you get to this essay on this exam, attack it with optimism. Relax and concentrate on what you want to say, rather than what you think the reader wants to hear. As long as you take a clear stand, use appropriate specific examples, and write reasonably well, you'll do fine.

Now that we've learned about writing the argumentative essay, let's take a look at how to tackle the synthesis essay. Remember that you can skip this chapter if you're taking the test in 2006.

6

New for 2007 — The Synthesis Essay

WHY ARE THEY DOING THIS TO ME?

If you're reading this chapter, then you're taking the AP English Language exam in the year 2007, and the analytical/expository and argumentative essays have a new friend: the synthesis essay. This new essay came about because college professors begged the AP English Language and Composition test writers to develop an essay that would test students' abilities to read and evaluate multiple sources and integrate appropriate ones into a coherent, cogent essay. In essence, professors wanted to know that students who use the AP English Language and Composition exam for credit or placement out of freshman English know the rudiments of research paper–style writing.

The good news is that, to allow enough time for students to both read the sources and write about them, the folks at ETS decided to allot an extra 15 minutes for this essay. Instead of the 40 minutes you get to write the other essays, you will have 55 minutes to craft the perfect synthesis essay. At the writing of this book, not a single previously administered synthesis essay question has been released. However, there is enough information out there for us to predict with confidence what these questions will look like.

When you get to the Essay section, you won't have to be a rocket scientist to figure out which essay is the synthesis essay. For one thing, it will have four to seven passages, and at least one of them will be an image. The directions will tell you that the suggested time for writing this essay is 55, and not 40, minutes. That said, be careful: The AP writers will ask you to use the sources in either one of two ways: either to *explain* something or to *argue* a point. Thus, the extra reading aside, what this really means is that you'll be either writing another analytical/expository or another argumentative essay.

In one sense, this new essay broadens the scope of your analysis because there is so much more to read and because you'll have images, as well as text, to consider. In another sense, this essay narrows your possibilities because if you have to argue a point, you will be able to use only the examples that the AP test provides—you won't be able to draw substantially from other knowledge of history or literature or from your personal experiences.

SAMPLE ESSAY #1 — HERE'S HOW IT'S DONE

On the synthesis essay, it's more important than ever that you get a clear grasp of the prompt. Unless you know what you're looking for, you will not be able to deal with the mass of material that you must read and digest. If you know what to look for, then you can skim the parts that do not pertain to your thesis—and underline just the good stuff.

What follows is another sample question. Since these questions are so long, in this chapter we'll break it into parts.

THE DIRECTIONS

ENGLISH LANGUAGE AND COMPOSITION

SECTION II

Total time—2 hours, 15 minutes

Question 1

(Suggested time—55 minutes. This question counts as one-third of the total essay section score.)

Read or examine carefully the sources that follow; you should keep in mind the validity of the documents, as well as their relevance to the prompt. Then write a well-organized essay in which you include citations from at least four of the sources, including a reference to an image. You have an extra 15 minutes on this section to study the sources and to organize your thoughts.

Basing your answer on the information below about the Dreyfus Affair, support, refute, or qualify the assertion that, over time, even the most despicable historical wrongs are made right.

THE FIRST TIME YOU READ THE PROMPT

As always, do your first reading of the prompt and underline the key instructions and other terms. First you should have underlined the words "support, refute, or qualify." Then you should have underlined the part of the passage that stated you had to use citations from four sources and refer to one image. Before you begin writing, you must double-check to make sure, in your outline, you planned to use at least the required number of sources. The number of sources will always be spelled out in the instructions; normally you will not be required to use all of the sources provided. Finally, you should have underlined the thesis: "Over time, even the most despicable historical wrongs are made right."

THE SECOND TIME YOU READ THE PROMPT

In this case, a second reading of the prompt probably won't help you much, unless you have already studied the Dreyfus Affair; if you have, then you have a leg up on everyone else.

IT'S TIME TO READ—SORT OF

How closely you read the passages should depend on how well you know the context of the topic. If you are not familiar with the Dreyfus Affair you will have to read the passage carefully enough to understand the basics; in addition, you should have your pen in hand and be ready to underline anything that supports or refutes the thesis. Once you've made up your mind about what position you'll take, you are free to underline only the points that substantiate your position.

As a general rule, you should examine all of the sources. Put a mark through the ones you do not intend to use. Do not assume that all the sources are relevant; it is unlikely that you will use them all, but you should use as many as you can—and of course at least as many as they require.

As you plan your essay, remember your task. In this case, no one is asking you to explain the Dreyfus Affair. Your goal is simply to make a convincing case for or against the notion that "over time, even the most despicable historical wrongs are made right." Stick to your task.

The sources for this question can be found on the following pages.

THE SOURCES

Source 1

From "The Dreyfus Affair: The Sequel," by Chaz Lerdthraril

Nearly 2,000 people, invited by France's Central Consistory of Jews, listened to General Jean-Louis Mourrut deliver a speech about Captain Alfred Dreyfus, who more than a century ago was sentenced to life imprisonment on infamous Devil's Island. Mourrut admitted that the French army had been wrong. On the one hand, Jean Kahn, President of the Central Consistory of Jews, was moved by the speech: "The general said things before us that never had been said by a military man. That is, indisputably, progress." On the other hand, the satirical *Le Canard Enchainé* contained this jibe: "The army got it! Incredible! Dreyfus was innocent!" Although Mourrut's speech did not really constitute an apology, just admitting that the army had been wrong was an unexpected twist to a lingering tragic affair.

At the close of the nineteenth century, the Dreyfus Affair engendered a political maelstrom that ripped through French society. The French were divided into "Dreyfusards," who saw Captain Dreyfus as an innocent victim of both anti-Semitism and an army conspiracy, and conservative "Anti-Dreyfusards," who considered any questioning of the army as traitorous and who regarded Jews as untrustworthy. Nearly twelve years passed before Dreyfus was called back from Devil's Island and given a new trial—one that would pit justice for an individual against the grandeur, glory, and greatness of the French army. Even though a preponderance of proof existed to prove that Dreyfus was not guilty of treason, the result of the verdict was never in doubt. Dreyfus was again found guilty; however, almost immediately after the trial, he was accorded a presidential pardon. In spite of the outlandish treatment and humiliation, the poor captain returned to the army. As an almost farcical compensation for a dozen years in a penal colony, the army promoted Dreyfus to the rank of major and awarded him the Legion of Honor.

Until Morrut's speech, the army had officially maintained that Dreyfus was guilty—or, at least, not innocent. The army seems to have pardoned Dreyfus, but it is doubtful that such an action will, once and for all, put this divisive affair to rest.

UN DINER EN FAMILLE

Surtout ne parlons pas de l'affaire Dreyfus

"Above all, let's not talk about the Dreyfus Affair!"

They talked about it.

Source 3

On January 13, 1998, Jacques Chirac, President of the French Republic, answered the "open letter"(*J'accuse*...!) that Emile Zola addressed to President Félix Faure exactly one hundred years earlier.

Just a century ago, France was experiencing a grave and deep crisis. The Dreyfus Affair was tearing French society apart, dividing families, dividing the country into two opposing camps violently confronting each other. Because Captain Dreyfus had to remain guilty as charged at all costs, his subsequent trials became nothing but a pathetic farce. After having been stripped of his rank and having seen his military sword broken, he was going to suffer, on Devil's Island, for the conspiracy deliberately plotted against him in the secrecy of some office.

In spite of the unyielding efforts by Captain Dreyfus' family, his case could have been filed away forever. A dark stain, unworthy of our country and our history, a colossal judicial error and a shameful state compromise! But a man stood up against lies, malice and cowardice. Outraged by the injustice against Captain Dreyfus, whose only crime was to be a Jew, Emile Zola cried out his famous "I Accuse...!" Published on January 13, 1898 by *L'Aurore,* this text struck minds like lightning and changed the fate of the Affair within a few hours. Truth was on the march.

That day, Emile Zola was appealing to the President of the French Republic. Today we are celebrating the centennial of this letter which has entered History. Today, I would like to tell the Dreyfus and Zola families how much France is grateful to their ancestors to have been able to give all its meaning to the values of liberty, dignity and justice.

Let us not ever forget that the man who was rehabilitated to shouts of "Long live Dreyfus!" answered with a strong voice: "No! Long live France!" In spite of his humiliation, his exile, his sufferings, wounded in his heart and in his flesh, harmed in his dignity, Captain Dreyfus was able to forgive. Magnificent forgiveness, magnificent answer: love of country against intolerance and hate.

Let us not ever forget the courage of that great writer who, taking every risk, jeopardizing his peace and quiet, his fame and even his own life, dared to take up his pen and put his talent to the service of truth. Emile Zola, high literary and moral character, had understood that his responsibility was to enlighten and his duty was to speak up when others kept silent. Like Voltaire before him, he has become since then the incarnation of the best of the intellectual tradition.

Captain Dreyfus' tragedy took place a century ago. However, after so many years, it still resonates strongly in our hearts. Zola's text has remained in our collective memory as "a great moment in the conscience of humanity."

Half a century after the Vichy regime, we know that dark forces, intolerance, injustice can insinuate themselves up to the highest levels of the State. But we also know that France, in moments of truth, can find again the best of herself: great, strong, united and vigilant. This is without a doubt what Emile Zola and Alfred Dreyfus are telling us, after all these years. It is because they had faith in our common values, those of our Nation and our Republic, and because they so deeply loved France, that these exceptional men were able to reconcile her with herself.

Let us not ever forget this masterful lesson of love and unity.

Jacques Chirac
President of the French Republic
January 13, 1998
(Translation: Jean-Max Guieu, Georgetown University)

Source 4

In 1898, renowned French novelist Emile Zola wrote an open letter to the president of France; the excerpt below is from that letter. Zola was later accused and convicted of libel; he was forced to flee to England and lost most of his fame and fortune when he left France.

I accuse Lieutenant Colonel du Paty de Clam of having been the diabolical creator of the judicial error, unconsciously, I'm sure, and then to have defended his nefarious creation for three years by the most bold-faced and culpable machinations.

I accuse General Mercier of having been an accomplice, at least through feebleness of mind, of one of the greatest iniquities of the century.

I accuse General Billot of having had in his hands certain proof of Dreyfus' innocence and of having suppressed it, of having been guilty of crimes against humanity and against justice, for political ends and in order to protect an already compromised chiefs of staff. (…)

I accuse the three handwriting experts, Belhomme, Varinard, and Couard, of having made untruthful and fraudulent reports, unless a medical examination can prove that an illness has impaired their eyes and judgment. (…)

I have only one passion, which is the light of truth, in the name of humanity, which has suffered so greatly and which has a right to happiness. My enflamed protest is no more than the loud voice of my soul. So let them dare take me to court, and let the investigation take place in broad daylight!

Source 5

After his attempt at vengeance fails miserably, Ludvik, a character in Milan Kundera's *The Joke*, meditates on the workings of history—both personal and universal.

Yes, suddenly I saw it clearly: most people deceive themselves with a pair of faiths: they believe in eternal memory (of people, things, deeds, nations) and in redressibility (of deeds, mistakes, sins, wrongs). Both are false faiths. In reality the opposite is true: everything will be forgotten and nothing will be redressed. The task of obtaining redress (by vengeance or by forgiveness) will be taken over by forgetting. No one will redress the wrongs that have been done, but all wrongs will be forgotten.

Source 6

From "The Dreyfus Affair Again," by Bradford R. Pilcher—February 7, 2002 (israelinsider.com)

It is then with some irony that a second, albeit far more minor, Dreyfus Affair has recently occurred. Just this past week, that statue of Dreyfus was vandalized. A yellow Star of David, like Hitler once forced the Jews to wear, was painted over the statue's plaque. The words, "Dirty Jew" accompanied it.

An act of anti-Semitic vandalism is, sadly, not uncommon in France. Since the outbreak of the Al-Aqsa Intifada, worldwide anti-Semitism has seen a marked increase. France has been one of the centers of that upswing, so much so that even top government officials and diplomats find themselves in anti-Jewish gaffes.

France, where Dreyfus was tried and the Vichy collaborated, has been exposed as a nation where anti-Semitism has not been defeated. Instead, its anti-Semitism has been left under the rug to grow like a mold, ready to lash out when the moment is right. Still these recent events speak to more than just France. They speak to the world, and particularly the Jews' role in it.

The Analysis

That's quite a lot of reading! If you want to use your extra 15 minutes effectively, you must read selectively. You may have noticed that the overwhelming majority of examples that you can glean from the sources refutes the thesis that historical wrongs are made right over time. France could not make up for what it did to Dreyfus and to Zola. One can presume that even the family divisions depicted in the cartoon called *A Family Dinner* caused lasting harm. Also, notice that in the last source, the author points out that such wrongs as anti-Semitism, which played a key role in the Dreyfus Affair, do not appear to have disappeared over time.

You're ready to refute the claim. Hopefully you underlined some great examples and jotted down a quick outline for how you'll go about using them. Now, it's time to write a strong synthesis (argumentative) essay.

When you're finished writing your essay, take a look at the essay below. This is a sample of an essay that was written by a real student in the allotted 55 minutes. As you read it, evaluate how well it addresses the prompt and whether it integrates enough sources well.

A Student Essay

Throughout history, institutions of authority have made policies later judged to have been mistakes. From Galileo's imprisonment half a millennium ago, to the Japanese internment camps of this past century, wrongs committed by those in power are rarely, if ever, redressed. The nature of certain historical misdeeds is such that no formal apology, admission of error, or financial compensation could ever erase the damage. The six million Jews lost in the Holocaust can never be brought back to life; the careers ruined by the fervor of McCarthyism can never be restored. Clearly, as exemplified by the Dreyfus affair, even the passage of time cannot amend the greatest historical wrongdoings. The consequences of this scandal prove too immense and the attempts at restitution too weak to make right the French government's wrong.

In the case of Captain Dreyfus himself, the suffering he endured robbed him of twelve years of his life after his sentence of "life imprisonment on infamous Devil's Island." Even though he eventually returned to the army to great success, the injustice done to him could not be undone. As for Emile Zola, a famous writer and supporter of Dreyfus, his piece "J'Accuse," an open condemnation of the government's despicable conduct—led to a libel conviction. That forced Zola "to flee to England [where] he lost most of his fame and fortune." This career-ending blow as a result of defending Dreyfus can hardly be reversed. History will never know what the brilliant Zola could have accomplished had the government not persecuted him. On a more global scale, the implications of the Dreyfus affair reached far beyond those immediately involved. As depicted in the cartoon "A Family Dinner," the tension between Dreyfusards and traditionalists tore families apart, creating rifts impossible to repair. The extent of the damage caused by France's mishandling of the Dreyfus affair makes it all the more unsurprising that feeble attempts at making amends have been entirely inadequate.

Firstly, the French government did not acknowledge its wrongs until it was far too late to help anyone who actually suffered as a result of their error. The military offered a statement that "did not really constitute an apology" "more than a century" after the incident, lending credence to the adage "too little, too late." Similarly, Emile Zola's letter to the French president only received a response a century later, and even then, the president's reply centered far more on glorifying the French state than rectifying the heartache the French government caused. Finally, the Dreyfus affair was unable to inspire the change in attitudes that could be considered a justification for the suffering it brought about. Anti-Semitism is still a rampant problem in France, where it has been "left under the rug to grow like a mold ready to lash out when the moment is right." Evidently, no efforts at erasing past wrongdoings can truly nullify the suffering caused by the mistakes made by authority. In the words of Milan Kundera, "nothing will be redressed."

What did you think? Clearly, this is another strong essay—probably an 8, but not quite a 9. The student's introduction is very strong, but the conclusion is simply tacked on to the last body paragraph. The student's stand is clear: "Wrongs committed by those in power are rarely, if ever, fully redressed. The nature of certain historical misdeeds is such that no formal apology, admission of error, or financial compensation could ever erase the damage." The sentence could be improved if the "if ever" in the thesis statement had been omitted; it seems like a qualification. Also, the final sentence seems to narrow the thesis to only the Dreyfus Affair, which is a mistake.

Although the student uses appropriate sources and integrates them well, the result would have been even stronger had the sources been cited better. For example, in the first body paragraph, the student inserts the quotation "life imprisonment on infamous Devil's Island" but fails to tell the reader the source of the citation. The student should have done one of two things. One solution would have been to add a brief parenthetical citation so that the reader can keep track of which sources were used: "life imprisonment on infamous Devil's Island" (Source 1). Another solution would be to integrate an identifying characteristic (most often the title or the author) into the text of the essay: "life imprisonment on infamous Devil's island," as Chaz Lerdthraril relates.

The student does this well later, in the paragraph on Emile Zola and families: "As depicted in the cartoon 'A Family Dinner,' the tension between Dreyfusards and traditionalists tore families apart, creating rifts impossible to repair." In fact, that sentence is so good that a reader would latch onto it and use it to justify a high grade. Readers like to see when even, under the stress of test conditions, students can show flashes of absolute mastery over written expression.

Although the sample essay neither exhausts the possibilities of the sources nor truly follows a clear organizational plan, it should garner a score of at least 8. Remember, you don't need to be perfect. And to score high on the test overall, all you really need to do is to keep all three of your essays in the 6 to 7 range. By following our strategies and using the essays that you've seen as models, you can do that.

MOVING ON...

In this and the two preceding chapters, you've seen some pretty solid examples of essays. In the next parts of this book, you learn (or review) the important aspects of formal training in rhetoric and composition that will prepare you to craft essays that equal—or exceed—the ones that you've examined so far.

PART ◆ IV

AP English Language

7

Words and Their Use

THE GOOD NEWS AND THE BAD NEWS ABOUT THE AP ENGLISH LANGUAGE AND COMPOSITION EXAM

THE GOOD NEWS

While the title of this exam allows people to differentiate between this test and the AP English *Literature* and Composition exam; the title is somewhat misleading. The AP English *Language* and Composition exam is not a language exam—at least not in the sense that you may think. For example, it is possible not to know the difference between a gerund and a present participle—or even a gerund and a giraffe—and still score a 5 on this exam.

In the Multiple-Choice section of the exam, test writers will attempt to evaluate your ability to analyze how writers use language to explain or to argue; in the Free-Response, or Essay, section they will expect you to use language to explain or to argue. Naturally, you'll want to avoid making egregious errors in grammar or usage on the test, but as you study don't get hung up on the rules of language. If you're considering taking the AP exam, your language skills are probably sufficient for the task. Now, you may be wondering what *is* tested on the exam, then. The answer is *composition*, and we'll spend Part V of this book reviewing all you need to know about composition to be fully prepared for the test.

THE BAD NEWS

Now for the bad news. Despite the test's lack of emphasis on the rules of language, there are some aspects of language that we must examine here to make sure you're ready for test day. We'll start by discussing diction, style, tone, and point of view. We'll move on to circumlocution and euphemism, and discuss irony and satire. Finally, we will review the many types of figurative language and go through some drills that will prepare you for the types of questions you'll see on all of these topics. Let's begin!

DICTION

The basic definition of **diction** is "word choice." Generally, the diction questions you'll see on the test will ask you to evaluate why an author's choice of words is particularly effective, apt, or clear. However, as we explained in Part II, in the Multiple-Choice section, more often than not it is the test writer's diction that you have to crack. While knowledge of grammar and usage is almost irrelevant for this exam, a broad vocabulary is a necessity.

After common sense, vocabulary is the most important tool that you can use on the Multiple-Choice section of the exam. For this reason, we've included a Hit Parade in Part VI of this book—a list of terms and their definitions that you should know cold before you sit down to take the test. To ensure that you'll remember these terms for the exam, you may want to make flashcards as you work through this book.

Let's look at a question that emphasizes the importance of studying vocabulary as you prepare for the test.

The style of the paragraph on the previous page
can best be described as

(A) pedantic
(B) lyrical
(C) terse
(D) ludic
(E) edifying

While it's possible that none of the answers stands out to you as the correct choice, if you knew what pedantic meant, you could rule it out, since pedantic means "narrowly, stodgily, and often ostentatiously learned," and it isn't possible that you think that of the writing in this book. Likewise, a Princeton Review book and lyricism (intense, intimate display of emotion) make for an unlikely pair, so you can use Process of Elimination and get rid of that choice too. The test writers slipped ludic (pertaining to game, playful) in there in case you know some Latin (*ludus*), and finally terse (concise, without superfluous detail) shows up regularly on this exam but probably doesn't describe the writing in this book very well. Given that the last choice can mean both enlightening and informative, (E) is the best answer.

But as you can see, if you knew none of these words, the question may as well have read as follows:

The style of the paragraph above can best be
described as

(A) pompom
(B) banana
(C) dog
(D) tire iron
(E) Susan

And then which would seem like the correct answer?! Obviously, vocabulary is important, so study that Hit Parade.

Let's try another question that illustrates the importance of a relatively wide vocabulary to scoring well on this exam.

> If survival is an art, then mangroves are artists of the
> beautiful: not only that they exist at all—smooth-barked,
> glossy-leaved, thickets of lapped mystery—but that they
> *Line* can and do exist as floating islands, as trees upright and
> 5 loose, alive and homeless on the water.
> I have seen mangroves, always on tropical ocean
> shores, in Florida and in the Galapagos. There is the red
> mangrove, the yellow, the button, and the black. They are
> all short, messy trees, waxy-leaved, laced all over with
> 10 aerial roots, woody arching buttresses, and weird leathery berry pods. All this tangles from a black muck soil, a
> black muck matted like a mud-sopped rag, a muck without any other plants, shaded, cool to the touch, tracked at
> the water's edge by herons and nosed by sharks.

> The style of the passage on the previous page is characterized by
>
> (A) extended metaphors
> (B) historical allusions
> (C) vividness of diction
> (D) technical language
> (E) colloquial expressions

The best answer is (C); vividness of diction. The speaker's language is very descriptive and paints a very clear picture of the mangrove. Here's a list of the vocabulary you needed to know to answer this question: metaphor, allusion, diction, and colloquial.

As we explained in Part II, if you understand the passage but don't know the meaning of any of the answers, it's still possible to get the right answer. However, it's easier and faster to get the right answer if you do know the meanings of the words that make up the answer choices. Let's continue our review of important language terms.

SYNTAX

Another language term that you should be familiar with for the AP English Language exam is syntax. **Syntax** is the ordering of words in a sentence; in other words, it describes sentence structure. Syntax is not a topic that excites many high school students—or teachers—and therefore is not discussed very much. However, *syntax* is a word that finds it way onto AP English Language exams on a regular basis. Don't worry: You don't need to be an expert on this subject, but you should know how manipulating syntax can enhance an author's meaning, tone, or point of view. Let's look at another example from *Candide*, this time from the famous opening of Chapter 3.

> Never was anything so gallant, so well outfitted, so brilliant, and so finely disposed as the two armies. The trumpets, fifes, reeds, drums, and cannon made such harmony as never was heard in Hell.

The first sentence poses as a fairly simple sketch of a glorious battle scene. The second begins in the same fashion, but its words are arranged in a way that maximizes the effect of surprise that comes at the end of the sentence. The cannons are slipped in as the final member of a list of military musical instruments; the formation of the list creates an expectation that the final element will fit nicely into the set. It doesn't, but we don't have time to register our surprise because we're immediately distracted by a new setup with the phrase "such harmony as never was heard...." We expect harmony to be something beautiful, and we already begin to supply the final word (Earth? Heaven?) when—surprise—we are jolted by the word that Voltaire chose instead: hell. The syntax in this sentence is brilliant.

Here's another slightly different example. In the following example, Candide through his servant and side-kick, Cacambo, is asking about the proper etiquette for greeting the King of Eldorado.

> When they drew near to the royal chamber, Cacambo asked one of the officers in what manner they were to pay their respects to His Majesty; whether it was the custom to fall upon their knees, or to prostrate themselves upon the ground; whether they were to put their hands upon their heads, or behind their backs; whether they were to lick the dust off the floor; in short, what was the usual ceremony for such occasions.

The syntax of this long sentence is very carefully constructed; Voltaire uses all of the parallel clauses that begin with "whether" to achieve great comic effect. At first, the text is fairly straightforward—after all, going down on one's knees before a king would have been fairly standard for a European reader of the eighteenth century; however, with each clause, the groveling etiquette becomes more extreme, and the final image—of licking the dust off the floor—pushes the concept beyond the believable. The syntax of this sentence is structured in a way that allows us to see the absurdity of *all* forms of ceremonial deference. In fact, in this story the enlightened King of Eldorado simply embraces both Cacambo and Candide.

Related to syntax are style, tone, and point of view. As you will read in the next section, these elements work together with syntax to create a "profile" of the speaker, which tells us how the speaker or author feels about the subject at hand.

STYLE, TONE, AND POINT OF VIEW

You can count on seeing some combination of the terms *style*, *tone*, and *point of view* in both multiple-choice and essay questions on this exam, so let's make sure you're familiar with their definitions.

Style is the manner of expression. It describes how the author uses language to get his or her point across (e.g., pedantic, scientific, and emotive).

Tone is the mood or the sentiments revealed by the style. Tone describes how the author seems to be feeling (e.g., optimistic, ironic, and playful).

Point of view is the stance revealed by the style and the tone of the writing. The author's point of view expresses his or her position on the topic discussed. Point of view can be tricky—sometimes, especially in works of fiction, it is difficult to determine point of view, and, thus, you may be left with nothing more to say than "first-person narrator" or "third-person omniscient narrator."

Consider this passage.

> Our left fielder couldn't hit the floor if he fell out of bed! After striking out twice (once with the bases loaded!), he grounded into a double-play. My grandmother runs faster than he does! In the eighth inning, he misjudged a routine fly ball, which brought in the winning run. What a jerk! Why didn't the club trade him last week when it was still possible? What's wrong with you guys?

The *style* is simple, direct, unsophisticated, truculent, and even crass. The style helps evoke a simple sentiment: anger. The *tone* is angry, brash, emotional, and even virulent.

The *point of view* is clear; the author appears to be a disgruntled spectator who doesn't like the player at all and wants the team to get rid of him.

Okay. You may not have needed any help with that passage, but let's take a look at another that's more like something you'd see on test day.

Serendipities by Umberto Eco

So what was the big argument all about in the time of Columbus? The sages of Salamanca had, in fact, made calculations more precise than his, and they held that the earth, while assuredly round, was far more vast than the Genoese navigator believed, and therefore it was mad for him to attempt to circumnavigate it in order to reach the Orient by way of the Occident. Columbus, on the contrary, burning with a sacred fire, good navigator but bad astronomer, thought the earth smaller than it was. Naturally, neither he nor the learned men of Salamanca suspected that between Europe and Asia there lay another continent. And so you see how complicated life is, and how fragile are the boundaries between truth and error, right and wrong. Though they were right, the sages of Salamanca were wrong, and Columbus, while he was wrong, pursued faithfully his error and proved to be right—thanks to serendipity.

Style: What can you say about the style of this passage? At the beginning, the writing is scholarly, but toward the end the author addresses the reader personally ("And so you see…"), and the passage takes on a looser, more personal style.

Tone: The tone is ambiguous. For example, why does the writer assiduously avoid using the term "professors"? We have "the sages of [the University of] Salamanca" and "the learned men of [the University of] Salamanca"—is there a reason for this *periphrasis* (circumlocution)? Is the author being respectful, or, rather, is he using a tone of mocking condescension? Also consider the phrase "burning with a sacred fire, good navigator but bad astronomer." Although the words appear innocent and "factual" enough, what's behind the trite cliché of the first part and the humor lurking in the second part? And doesn't the title, *Serendipities*, call forth a light, playful tone? Perhaps—but it is difficult to pin down the author; it's almost as if he were deliberately playing a scholarly game of hide and seek.

Point of view: Style and tone provide us with clues about the point of view of the author. He appears to be questioning the "truths" of the past, and cautioning us against believing too much in the "truths" of the present. The point of view appears to be that of an erudite man who is considering history with a critical eye and is suggesting that serendipity (chance) might play as great a role as any other force in shaping history.

As we've said before, the questions on the AP English Language and Composition exam will test your ability to analyze writing as we analyzed the passage above. More often than not, identifying elements of style and tone will help you uncover what the test writers might call "the purpose of the writer" or "the author's attitude," and in some cases, get you one step closer to choosing the right answer on a test question.

Now that you're comfortable using these terms, let's try a sample question with an excerpt from Fyodor Dostoyevsky's *Notes from Underground.*

The long and the short of it is, gentlemen, that it is better to do nothing! Better conscious inertia!

The tone of the speaker is best characterized as

(A) ironic
(B) nihilistic
(C) reflective
(D) optimistic
(E) accusatory

You probably immediately eliminated (C) and (D) because the passage did not sound particularly reflective or optimistic. The author is not accusatory (E) either. Choice (B) may have confused you a bit; nihilism refers to a belief in nothing. (Again notice the importance of vocabulary!) The speaker's tone can indeed by described as "nihilistic," so the correct choice is (B).

FIGURATIVE LANGUAGE AND RHETORIC

Figurative language is strictly defined as speech or writing that departs from literal meaning to achieve a special effect or meaning. The terms covered later in this section are terms you should know cold before taking the exam. Multiple-choice questions may use them in answer choices, and you are certainly expected to use them in your free-response essays.

AVOIDING THE RHETORIC

First of all, what *is* rhetoric? **Rhetoric** is the art of speaking or writing effectively. As we stated at the beginning of this chapter, you don't need to be an expert in rhetoric to ace the AP English Language and Composition exam; however, you do need to have some understanding of how language works. With the exception of technical manuals (like the one that helped you assemble your entertainment center), few texts are written such that all of their language is meant to be taken literally. Take, for example, the end of one of Abraham Lincoln's inaugural speeches.

> With malice toward none, with charity for all, with firmness in the right as God gives us to see the right, let us strive on to finish the work we are in, to bind up the nation's wounds, to care for him who shall have borne the battle and for his widow and his orphan, to do all which may achieve and cherish a just and lasting peace among ourselves and with all nations.

Are we supposed to take "to bind up the nation's wounds" literally? Of course not. Lincoln has personified our country to make the suffering of particular individuals relatable to all the people of the nation. And what about "him who shall have borne the battle"? Clearly, Lincoln is using the singular (a man) to represent the collective mass of soldiers, and when he adds "his widow and his orphan," we understand that "shall have borne the battle" really means "shall have died in battle." Lincoln personalizes the suffering of this group of people by instead speaking of individual sacrifice, which he knows is far more likely to strike a profound emotional chord in his listeners.

Despite the effectiveness of Lincoln's speech, you should keep in mind that many other perfectly convincing arguments and explanations are conveyed primarily through literal language. On this exam, there's no need for you to strain yourself attempting to use figurative language in the free-response section. But it will be very helpful for you to review the common terms associated with figurative language that we've listed below because you will be obliged to analyze texts that contain figurative language on this test.

With all this in mind, here is a list of some common terms related to figurative language; we've put them in order of their decreasing relevance to the test.

IMAGERY

For the purposes of this exam, you may consider **imagery** to be synonymous with figurative language. However, in a more restricted sense, imagery is figurative language that is used to convey a sensory perception (visual, auditory, olfactory, tactile, or gustatory).

HYPERBOLE

Hyperbole is overstatement or exaggeration; it is the use of figurative language that significantly exaggerates the facts for effect. In many instances, but certainly not all, hyperbole is employed for comic effect.

> Example: If you use too much figurative language in your free-response essays, the AP readers will crucify you!

Clearly, this statement is a gross exaggeration; while the readers may give you a poor grade if you use figurative language that doesn't suit the purposes of your essay, they will not kill you.

UNDERSTATEMENT

Understatement is figurative language that presents the facts in a way that makes them appear much less significant than they really are. Understatement is almost always used for comic effect.

> Example: After dinner, they came and took into custody Doctor Pangloss and his pupil Candide, the one for speaking his mind and the other for appearing to approve what he heard. They were conducted to separate apartments, which were extremely cool and where they were never bothered by the sun.

Taking the last sentence literally would lead you astray. The understatement in this case ("They were conducted to separate apartments, which were extremely cool and where they were never bothered by the sun") should be taken to mean that the poor men were thrown into horribly dark, dank, and cold prison cells.

SIMILE

A **simile** is a comparison between two unlike objects, in which the two parts are connected with a term such as *like* or *as*.

> Example: The birds are like black arrows flying across the sky.

You can easily identify a simile—and distinguish it from a metaphor—because of the use of *like* or *as*.

METAPHOR

A **metaphor** is a simile without a connecting term such as *like* or *as*. Here's an example of a metaphor.

> Example: The birds are black arrows flying across the sky.

Birds are not arrows, but the commonalities (both are long and sleek, and they travel swiftly through the air—and both have feathers) allow us to easily grasp the image.

EXTENDED METAPHOR

An extended metaphor is precisely what it sounds like—it is a metaphor that lasts for longer than just one phrase or sentence. A word of caution for the exam, however; do not use extended metaphors in your own AP essays, for many scholars (and many AP graders) believe that the extended metaphor is a poor expository or argumentative technique.

Example: During the time I have voyaged on this ship, I have avoided the cabin; rather, I have remained on deck, battered by wind and rain, but able to see moonlight on the water. I do not wish to go below decks now.

As surprising as this may seem, this passage is not about nautical navigation. The ship's voyage is the central metaphor (representing the course of life); the writer extends the metaphor by relating elements of figurative language: cabin, deck, wind and rain, moonlight, water, and decks. The cabin is a safe place, but it's a place where you can't experience much; on deck, you're exposed to the elements, but you can experience beauteous sights. Having made the difficult, dangerous, but rewarding choice of staying on deck, it would be a personal defeat, a kind of surrender to wish for the safety, comfort, and limited horizons of the cabin later in life.

Symbol

A **symbol** is a word that represents something other than itself.

Example: The Christian soldiers paused to remember the lamb.

In this case, the rough, tough soldiers did not stop to think about the actual animal; the lamb is a traditional Christian symbol for Jesus Christ.

Sometimes, it is difficult to distinguish between metaphor and symbol. Remember that a metaphor always contains an implied comparison between two elements. Recall the metaphorical image of the birds and the arrows: The birds remain birds, and the arrows remain arrows—the metaphor serves to give us an image of the flight of the birds by suggesting a visualization of arrows. However, in the case of a symbol, the named object really doesn't count. There is no lamb; *lamb* is merely an object that's meant to conjure up another object or element.

Denotation and Connotation

Denotation refers to a word's primary or literal significance, while connotation refers to the sometimes vast range of other meanings that a word suggests. Context determines which connotations may be appropriate for a word. Some literary critics argue that it is impossible to distinguish between denotation and connotation. Who, they ask, is to determine which meaning to assign as a primary significance? Let's move on and look at an example.

Example: I am looking at the sky.

The denotation of the underlined word should be as clear as a cloudless sky (the space, often blue, above the Earth's surface). However, there can be connotations associated with the word. The sky is often associated with heaven; it can also evoke the idea of freedom or vast openness. Because of connotation, one can't help but believe that the sky evokes in the writer a sense of longing for freedom from work, the computer, or the AP English Language and Composition exam.

Oxymoron

An **oxymoron** is an apparent contradiction of terms.

Example: I advise you to make haste slowly.

What would you do if someone said this to you? At first, you might think that this is simply a foolish, contradictory statement, and you might ignore the advice. However, it is possible to make sense of the apparent contradiction, which is in fact an oxymoron. In essence, the sentence advises you to go as fast as you can, while going slowly enough to do things right.

PARADOX

The **paradox** is an apparent contradiction of ideas or statements and, therefore, is closely related to the oxymoron. Think of a paradox as an oxymoron on a larger scale.

> Example: The only way to overcome death is to die.

This paradox pops up in various contexts; it is not a contradiction, for some would say that only after death is it possible to pass on to eternal life (in heaven, for instance), and *eternal* life precludes (another) death. Thus, one dies (physically) but then lives (spiritually) forever.

It is possible to have a paradox that offers no real hope of resolution. For instance, there is the Cretan Liar Paradox (dating from Greek times), which goes like this: "All Cretans are liars; I am a Cretan."

PERSONIFICATION

Personification is the figurative device in which inanimate objects or concepts are given human qualities. It can enhance our emotional response because we usually attribute more emotional significance to other humans than to things or concepts.

> Example: He had been wrestling with lethargy for days, and every time that he thought that he was close to victory, his adversary escaped his hold.

This figurative wrestling match, in which lethargy is personified as the opponent to the author of this sentence, brings the struggle to life—human life. If you don't believe me, think about the literal alternative: He tried to stop being lethargic, but he was not successful. This doesn't sound very lively.

RHETORICAL QUESTION

A **rhetorical question** is a question whose answer is obvious; these types of questions do not need to be answered—and usually aren't. Rhetorical questions attempt to prove something without actually presenting an argument; sometimes they're used as a form of irony, in which something is stated, but its opposite is meant.

> Example (no irony): With all the violence on TV today, is it any wonder kids bring guns to school?

Since I've already determined that you agree (even if you don't), then I don't have to substantiate my remark—especially if I keep speaking (or writing) and don't let you get in a word edgewise.

> Example (with irony): Aren't AP exams great fun?

Here, there is an assumption that you would answer in the negative, although there is no way for you to respond—unless you write us a letter. Rhetorical questions allow a writer to make a point without further support whether it's a straightforward remark or one with a touch of irony.

BOMBAST

Bombast (adjective = bombastic) is language that is overly rhetorical (pompous), especially when considered in context. Generally speaking, graduation speeches contain bombast; pedantic people (those who use their learning ostentatiously) tend to use bombast. Occasionally, a passage on the AP English Language and Composition exam will contain bombast.

We are here in these hallowed halls, accompanied
by genial kin and erudite mentors, surrounded by
Corinthian columns and the three wisdom of the ages,
to celebrate the conjunction of fare the well and many
happy returns and to proffer advice worthy of Athena
to these prodigal sons and daughters as they depart our
august institution. You happy survivors are not gradu-
ates, but champions who have been assailed on all sides
by demons of mathematics, dragons of science, and
inhuman beasts of humanities, but who have emerged
victorious from each and every battle. In this respect, one
is reminded of Thucydides, who writes: "So long as a
vessel was coming up to charge another boat, the men on
the decks rained darts, arrows and stones upon her, but
once alongside, the heavy infantry tried to board each
other's vessel, fighting hand to hand. In many quarters
it happened, because of the restricted space, that a vessel
was charging an enemy on one side and being charged
herself on another, and that two or even more ships
were entangled all around one, obliging the helmsmen
to attend to defense here, offense there, not to one thing
at a time, but to many things on all sides, while the huge
commotion caused by the number of ships crashing
together not only spread terror, but also made the orders
of the boatswains inaudible." I urge you to remember
Attica, and to remember the Spartan way, for…

The passage above is marked by pretentious and inflated speech; it is a perfect example of bombast. I certainly hope that your commencement speaker does not concoct a bombastic speech such
as this one!

Pun

A **pun** is a play on words. In general, a pun either plays on the multiple meanings of a word or replaces one word with another that is similar in sound but very different in meaning. Puns are almost
always used for comic effect.

> Example: In *Star Wars*, why did the Evil Empire leave the Catholic nuns alone?
> Force of habit.

If you know anything about *Star Wars*, you know that the "force" is the power of good, and you'll
get the play on words here.

Metonymy and Synecdoche

Both *metonymy* and *synecdoche* are terms that mean the use of figurative language in which characteristics are substituted for the things with which they are associated.

In **metonymy,** one term is substituted for another term with which it is closely associated.

> Example: The sailors drank a glass of hearty red.

Red is a color; sailors cannot drink it. However, metonymically, the color represents wine (red
wine), which sailors over the age of twenty-one may drink.

Synecdoche is a form of metonymy that's restricted to cases where a part is used to signify the
whole.

> Example: All hands on deck!

The hands (part of each sailor) represent the sailors (the whole).

If you have an aversion for learning rhetorical terms, then for the purposes of this exam you can feel free to forget the definition of synecdoche; you can get away with using the term *metonymy* for any situation in which a characteristic of a certain thing is used to represent the thing.

THEME

A **theme** is a general idea contained in a text; the theme may be stated explicitly or only suggested. A theme is not just an idea; it is *an idea that is developed,* often over the course of a chapter or an entire book. Usually, one can identify a central theme and several minor ones. Sometimes both are overtly stated, as in the example that follows:

> Many scholars agree that the central theme in *Huckleberry Finn* is the conflict between nature and civilization. But clearly, the book contains other themes, such as the worth of honor and the voyage of self-discovery.

Read the following passage, and see if you can identify a central theme.

> We now touch on civilization's most sensitive spot; it is an unpleasant task to raise one's voice against the folly of the day, against chimeras that have caused a downright
>
> *Line* epidemic.
>
> 5   To speak against the absurdities of trade today means to expose oneself to anathemas, just as much as if one had spoken against the tyranny of the popes and the barons in the twelfth century. If it were a matter of choosing between two dangerous roles, I think it would be
>
> 10 less dangerous to offend a sovereign with bitter truths than to offend the mercantile spirit that now rules like a despot over civilization—and even over sovereigns!
>
>   And yet a superficial analysis will prove that our commercial systems defile and disorganize civilization
>
> 15 and that in trade, as in all other things, we are being led further and further astray.
>
>   The controversy on trade is barely half a century old and has already produced thousands of books, and yet the participants in the controversy have not seen that the
>
> 20 trade mechanism is organized in such a way that it is a slap in the face to all common sense. It has subordinated the whole of society to one class of parasitic and unproductive persons: the merchants. All the essential classes of society—the proprietor, the farmer, the manufacturer,
>
> 25 and even the government—find themselves dominated by a non-essential, contingent class, the merchant, who should be their subordinate, their employed agent, removable and accountable, and who, nevertheless, directs and obstructs at will all the avenues of circulation.

It should not surprise you that the title of the essay that this passage is excerpted from is "On Trade." In his essay, the French socialist Charles Fourier develops a central theme: Merchants, through trade, have both corrupted society and become its tyrant.

Many of the passages in the Multiple-Choice and Free-Response sections of the AP exam are long enough to permit you to identify at least one central theme, and you will almost certainly be asked to do so.

APHORISM

An **aphorism** is a concise, pithy statement of an opinion or a general truth.

> Example: Life is short, the art [of medicine] is long, opportunity fleeting, experimentation dangerous, reasoning difficult.

That aphorism is attributed to Hippocrates, the "Father of Medicine." Note that his statement is more sophisticated than the "commonplace wisdom" of a saying like "Haste makes waste."

MALAPROPISM

Malapropism is the unintentional use of a word that resembles the word intended but that has a very different meaning.

> Example: The girl used a fire distinguisher to put out the blaze.

The AP English Language and Composition readers often collect malapropisms to share with friends and colleagues as they read through the free-response essays; it isn't in your best interest to provide them with any good laughs, so try to avoid them.

CIRCUMLOCUTION AND EUPHEMISM

Circumlocution has two meanings, and you should be familiar with both of them. For the purposes of this exam, we'll say that one meaning of circumlocution is "talking around a subject" and that the other is "talking around a word." Now let's take a closer look at some examples of circumlocution.

It is entirely possible that you have used circumlocution when addressing your parents. For instance, instead of simply asking them straight out if you may borrow the car, have you ever said something such as "I understand that you guys are going to stay in tonight and watch a DVD, right? If so, since I've already seen that movie, I was thinking about maybe going downtown. It's a nice summer evening and all that, but it's still too far to walk, and I'll be with Nina, anyway, and she'd never agree to walk downtown. We were thinking that she could drive, but, unfortunately, Nina's parents are going out, so she can't take their car. I know that I forgot to put gas in your car the last time that I drove to the mountains, but I learned my lesson. That won't happen again." You may even have gone on speaking for longer. You might never have gotten to the point where you actually asked to borrow the car, but your parents understood what you wanted and put you out of your misery by saying something such as "We already told your sister that she could use the car tonight."

That kind of circumlocution is an example of the first meaning of circumlocution—"talking around the subject."

On the AP English Language and Composition exam, you're more likely to encounter the second type of circumlocution—"talking around a word"—that is, using several words or a phrase in place of a specific word (or specific words). You may have noticed that sometimes it is more effective to be wordy than to be precise. For example, some people consider their automobiles cars, and, not surprisingly, they refer to these objects as cars. Other people, however, use evocative circumlocutions when referring to their heap of metal—one of which is "cruisin' machine" (and the other of which is "heap of metal.") The point is that circumlocution is often an effective means for communicating points of view. Take a look at the following sentence.

> Candide was court-martialed, and he was asked which
> he liked better, to run the gauntlet six and thirty times
> through the whole regiment, or to have his brains blown
> out with a dozen musket-balls.

In this sentence, we read that in a spirit of compassion and justice, the military court is giving Candide a choice: He may choose to be either beaten to death or executed by firing squad. The wording of the second choice, in particular, provides a wonderful example of the evocative power of well-used circumlocution. While using the phrase "execution by firing squad" would have allowed both the author and the reader to remain distant from the event and dispassionate, the circumlocution that the author employed with "to have his brains blown out with a dozen musket-balls" vividly describes the horror and brutality of the event. In this sentence, Voltaire succeeds in relating his feelings about the court-martial without commenting on it.

A **euphemism** is a word or words that are used to avoid employing an unpleasant or offensive term. Again, you probably (hopefully) use euphemisms all the time. In both fiction and nonfiction, the most common euphemisms have to do with sex. In these cases, the author knows what he or she means, you know what he or she means, and the author knows that you know what he or she means. Let's look at another example from Voltaire's *Candide*. In this passage, Voltaire uses euphemism for comic effect.

> One day when Mademoiselle Cunegunde went to
> take a walk in a little neighboring wood that was called
> a park, she saw—through the bushes—the sage Doctor
> Pangloss giving a lecture in experimental philosophy to
> her mother's chambermaid, a little brown wench, very
> pretty and very accommodating.

Voltaire knows that his readers know what is really going on here. This particular example of euphemism is used for comic effect rather than direct avoidance of the word *sex*. One may expect Pangloss to limit his sagacity to philosophical matters, but clearly his "lecture in experimental philosophy" is most prosaic.

IRONY AND SATIRE

When reading the passages on the AP English Language exam, you cannot always take what you see at face value; in fact, when reading you must always be on the lookout for slightly or very veiled meanings behind the words.

ISN'T IT IRONIC?

Irony: Most people use the term without really knowing its definition. If you don't believe this, ask one of your friends to define irony and see what kind of answer you receive. The two basic types of irony that you'll need to be familiar with for this test are verbal irony and situational irony.

VERBAL IRONY

Verbal irony refers to the process of stating something but *meaning* the opposite of what is stated. Verbal irony can refer to irony that's used in spoken language as well as in print. In spoken language, intonation is often a clue to ironic intent; however, in writing, it is not possible to imply things through intonation, so there's always a danger that the irony may be missed; in essence, the writer who employs irony risks communicating the exact opposite of what is intended. For example, let's say that you write, "This Princeton Review book is really interesting." Unless your listener or reader hears your remark in context, he or she won't know if this is high praise for this book, or if you're bored silly and have chosen to express your sentiment more forcefully by using verbal irony.

Consider the following passage. The philosopher Pangloss has just given a rather personalized history of venereal disease, a veritable uncontrollable—and uncontrolled—plague in eighteenth-century Europe.

> "O sage Pangloss," cried Candide, "what a strange genealogy is this! Is not the devil at the root of it all?"
> "Not at all," replied the great man, "it was unavoidable, a necessary ingredient in the best of worlds."

The student Candide shows sincere respect for Pangloss when he addresses him as "sage Pangloss;" Candide has no ironic intent. However, the same cannot be said of the narrator—who for all intents and purposes is Voltaire. In *Candide*, one of Voltaire's principal aims is to excoriate (to censure scathingly) the "philosophers of optimism," of whom Pangloss is a caricature. He does this through the frequent use of verbal irony; in the passage above, his use of "great man" is ironic—even though Candide's tone is not. After all, neither the narrator nor the careful reader views Pangloss as a great man—he is just the opposite.

In essence, to fully appreciate the passage, we must read in stereo, simultaneously picking up on Candide's serious tone and the narrator's ironic tone. This is a pretty complicated case of verbal irony. Got it? Let's move on.

Sarcasm is simply verbal irony used with the intent to injure. It's often impossible to discern between irony and sarcasm, and, more often than not, sarcasm is in the mind of the beholder. Let's say that your close friend and soccer teammate missed a wide-open goal from ten feet away, and you smiled and shouted, "Nice shot!" Presumably your friend, used to your jests, would interpret your quip as playful irony. If the opposing team's goalie said the same words, however, it is far more likely that your friend would take the remark as sarcasm—and reply with a not-so-kind word or two. In written form, irony and sarcasm can be considered to be fairly synonymous—but just think of sarcasm as malicious. Here is an example from Heinrich Ibsen's *Hedda Gabbler*.

> Brack: There's a possibility that the appointment may be decided by competition—
> Tesman: Competition! By Jove, Hedda, fancy that!
> Hedda: [*motionless in her chair*] How exciting, Tesman.

Of course, it is easier to see the sarcasm when you are familiar with the play, but it is sufficient for you to know that Tesman is the rather boring, plodding husband and that Hedda is an unfulfilled wife. The stage direction ("motionless in her chair") helps us see that her words are at least full of irony; if you add the bitter, malignant intent, which the husband misses but we do not, then you have sarcasm.

Situational Irony

Situational irony refers to a situation that runs contrary to what was expected.

Perhaps last year you told your friends that you didn't care what grade you might earn on the AP English Language and Composition exam and that you wouldn't lift a finger to prepare for the exam. But here you are, dutifully reading away, carefully studying, and feeling more confident that you'll be successful on the test. How ironic! Here's another example. What if you lived on the East Coast and made fun of California all the time, vociferously (vehemently, insistently) claiming that there was no way that you could ever live there. Then, what if you found yourself enjoying your ninth year of residence in the Sunshine State with no plans to leave? This is situational irony.

SATIRE

In **satire,** something is portrayed in a way that's deliberately distorted to achieve comic effect. Implicit in most satire is the author's desire to critique what is being mocked. Voltaire's *Candide* is principally a satire of optimism, the philosophy that, given that the first "cause" was perfect (God's creation of the world), all causes and effects must naturally be part of this original perfect plan. The French satirist takes on many other causes, however, and one of his favorite targets is the part of religion that he considers no more than fanatical superstition. Here is what happens after Candide and Pangloss are caught in the infamous earthquake of Lisbon, Portugal.

> After the earthquake, which had destroyed three-
> fourths of the city of Lisbon, the sages of that country
> could think of no better manner to preserve the kingdom
> Line from complete ruin than to entertain the people with an
> 5 *auto-da-fe*, it having been decided by the University of
> Coimbra that burning a few people alive over low heat
> and with great ceremony is an infallible way to prevent
> earthquakes.
> In consequence, they had seized a Biscayan for marry-
> 10 ing his godmother and two Portuguese for taking out the
> bacon of a larded chicken they were eating; after dinner,
> they came and took into custody Doctor Pangloss and
> his pupil Candide, the one for speaking his mind and
> the other for appearing to approve what he heard. They
> 15 were conducted to separate apartments, which were
> extremely cool and where they were never bothered
> by the sun. Eight days later, they were each dressed in
> a *sanbenito* and their heads were adorned with paper
> *mitres*. The *mitre* and *sanbenito* worn by Candide were
> 20 painted with upside down flames and with devils that
> had neither tails nor claws, but Doctor Pangloss's devils
> had both tails and claws, and his flames were right side
> up. In these clothes they marched in the procession and
> heard a very pathetic sermon, which was followed by an
> 25 anthem accompanied by bagpipes. Candide was flogged
> to the beat of the music while the anthem was being
> sung; the Biscayan and the two men who would not eat
> bacon were burned, and Pangloss was hanged, which is
> not a common custom at these solemnities. The same day
> 30 there was another earthquake, which created the most
> dreadful havoc.

After the real earthquake of 1755, there were real *auto-da-fes* ("acts of faith"), where "evil" inhab-
itants of Lisbon were sacrificed to appease God, who, ostensibly (to all outward appearances), had provoked the earthquake to punish the city. The "evils" that are being punished say more about the ridiculous prejudices of the persecutors than they do about the so-called evil victims. The two Por-
tuguese who refrained from eating the bacon are guilty of nothing—but they are taken for Jews; the man who married his godmother, who, presumably, is not tied to him by blood, is guilty of no more than infringing on a technicality of the religious code (Catholicism, in this case).

Note that the satire is heightened by Voltaire's use of verbal irony ("the sages"), situational irony (right after the ceremony there is a second earthquake), and a comical circumlocution ("burning a few people alive over low heat and with great ceremony" is a circumlocution for *auto-da-fe*). Satire can be effective in both fiction and nonfiction, and *Candide*, a philosophical story that combines both, is thought to be one of the most brilliant satires of all.

Most critics, however, relegate satire—and satirists—to a secondary sphere in the universe of writing; satire makes for good entertainment, but mocking others does not measure up to the conviction of cogent writing. Had Voltaire been nothing more than a satirist, he would not have been remembered as a brilliant *philosophe*, but as a clever joker—if he were remembered at all. Although Voltaire's satire in *Candide* is quite brilliant, some other examples of satire are a little easier to figure out. Let's look at a sample question based on a passage from Jonathan Swift's *Gulliver's Travels*.

> For about seventy moons past there have been two struggling parties in this empire, under the names of *Tramecksan* and *Slamecksan,* from the high and low heels
> *Line* of their shoes, by which they distinguish themselves. It
> 5 is alleged, indeed, that the high heels are most agreeable to our ancient constitution; but, however this be, his majesty has determined to make use only of low heels in the administration of the government, and all offices in the gift of the crown, as you cannot but observe; and particu-
> 10 larly that his majesty's imperial heels are lower at least by a *drurr* than any of his court (*drurr* is a measure about the fourteenth part of an inch). The animosities between these two parties run so high, that they will neither eat, nor drink, nor talk with each other. We compute the
> 15 *Tramecksan*, or high heels, to exceed us in number; but the power is wholly on our side. We apprehend his imperial highness, the heir to the crown, to have some tendency towards the high heels; at least we can plainly discover that one of his heels is higher than the other, which gives
> 20 him a hobble in his gait.

The above passage is an example of

(A) an analysis of court customs
(B) a satire of British footwear
(C) a study of British eccentricities
(D) a satire of the British court
(E) a nonsensical account of life at court

Well, the correct answer must be either (B) or (D) because this section is all about satire. The correct answer is (D). The passage serves to satirize the Whig-Tory discord (the Whigs dominated politics during much of the eighteenth century) and the relationship of the "parties" (the Whigs and Tories were not really political parties as we know them today) and the King. Unless you recognize that the passage is satirical, you will not have a good grasp of what is going on—which will lead to major problems with all of the multiple-choice questions on that passage.

The next chapter is the Hit Parade, so move on to that chapter, and start learning those words!

8

The Hit Parade—
Words, Words, Words

A great way to improve your reading and essay-writing skills is to improve your vocabulary. The more words you know on the day of the test, the easier it will be. It's as simple as that. For this reason, it's important that you get to work on your vocabulary immediately. We suggest that you mark any words you don't know in the chapter and make flashcards for yourself.

THE HIT PARADE

The Hit Parade list consists of the words that show up most often on the AP English Language and Composition exam. Each word on the list is accompanied by its definition, a pronunciation guide, and a sentence that uses the word. Your vocabulary-building program should start with these words.

LEARN THE WORDS IN GROUPS

This Hit Parade has been arranged by groups of related words. Learning groups of related words can help you better remember each word's meaning. After all, even if you don't remember the exact meaning of a word, you may remember what group it's from. This will give you an idea of the word's meaning, which can help you use POE to get to an answer.

Make each group of words a part of your life. Rip out one of the group lists, carry it around with you, and use the words throughout your day. For example, on Monday you may feel like using words of *disdain* (see the "If you can't say anything nice" list), but on Friday you may wish to be more *affable* (see the "Friendly" list).

DON'T MEMORIZE THE DICTIONARY

Only a tiny percentage of all the words in the English language are ever used on the exam. Generally speaking, it tests the kinds of words that an educated adult—your English teacher, for example—would know without having to look up. It tests the sorts of words that you encounter in your daily reading, from a novel in English class to the newspaper.

HOW TO MEMORIZE NEW WORDS

Here are three effective methods for learning new words.

- **Flashcards:** You can make your own flashcards out of 3 x 5 index cards. Write the word on one side and its definition on the other. Then quiz yourself on the words, or practice with a friend. You can carry a few cards around with you every day and work on them in spare moments, like when you're riding on the bus.

- **The Image Approach:** The image approach involves letting each new word suggest a wild image to you, then using that image to help you remember the word. For example, the word *enfranchise* means, "to give the right to vote." Women did not become enfranchised in the United States until 1920, when the Nineteenth Amendment to the Constitution guaranteed them the right to vote in state and federal elections. The word *franchise* may suggest to you a McDonald's franchise. You could remember the new word by imagining people lined up to vote at a McDonald's. The weirder the image, the better you'll remember the word.

- **Mnemonics:** Speaking of "the weirder, the better," another way to learn words is to use mnemonics. A mnemonic is a device or trick, such as a rhyme or song, that helps you remember something. "In fourteen hundred ninety-two Columbus sailed the ocean blue" is a mnemonic that helps you remember a date in history. The funnier or stranger you make your mnemonic, the more likely you are to remember it. Write down your mnemonics (your flashcards are a great place for these).

Although you may not be able to think of a mnemonic for every Hit Parade term, sometimes you'll end up learning the word just by thinking about the definition and a suitable mnemonic long enough.

Look It Up

Well-written general publications—like the *New York Times* and *Sports Illustrated*—are good sources of vocabulary. You should read them on a regular basis. When you come across a new word, write it down, look it up, and remember it. You can make flashcards for these words as well.

Before you can memorize the definition of a word you come across in your reading, you have to find out what it means. You'll need a real dictionary for that. ETS uses two dictionaries in writing the AP English Language and Composition exam: the *American Heritage Dictionary* and the *Webster's New Collegiate Dictionary*. You should own a copy of one or the other. (You'll use it in college too—it's a good investment.)

Keep in mind that most words have more than one definition. The dictionary will list these in order from the most to least common meanings of the word. ETS will also often trip you up by testing the second, third, or even fourth definition of a familiar-sounding word. For example, the word *pedestrian* shows up repeatedly on the exam. When ETS uses it, however, it never means a person on foot—the definition of *pedestrian* you're probably most familiar with. ETS uses it to mean common, ordinary, banal—a *secondary* definition.

Very often, when you see easy words on hard AP English Language and Composition exam questions, ETS is testing a second, third, or fourth definition that you may not be familiar with.

Here we go!

Are You Talkin' to Me?

assertion   uh SUR shun
a declaration or statement
We could not believe John's assertion that he had never seen *Star Wars*.

clarity   KLAR uh tee
clearness in thought or expression
Carol spoke with such clarity that her two-year-old understood exactly what she wanted him to do.

cogent   KO jent
convincing; reasonable
Christina's argument was so cogent that even her opponents had to agree with her.

coherent   ko HEER ent
logically connected
The old prospector's story was not coherent; he rambled on about different things that had nothing to do with one another.

cohesive   ko HEE siv
condition of sticking together
Eric's essay was cohesive because each point flowed nicely into the next point.

didactic   dy DAK tik
intended to instruct
The tapes were entertaining and didactic because they amused and instructed the children.

discourse   DIS kors
verbal expression or exchange; conversation
Their discourse varied widely; they discussed everything from Chaucer to ice fishing.

eloquence   EH lo kwens
the ability to speak vividly or persuasively
Cicero's eloquence is legendary; his speeches were well-crafted and convincing.

emphasize   EM fuh size
to give special attention to something, to stress
During English class, our instructor emphasized the importance of learning vocabulary.

fluid   FLOO id
easily flowing
The two old friends' conversation was fluid; each of them was able to respond quickly and easily to what the other had to say.

implication   im pli KAY shun
the act of suggesting or hinting
When your mother asks, "Were you raised in a barn?" the implication is that you should close the door.

lucid   LOO sid
easily understood; clear
Our teacher does a good job because he provides lucid explanations of difficult concepts.

rhetoric   RET uh rik
the art of using language effectively and persuasively
Since they are expected to make speeches, most politicians and lawyers are well versed in the art of rhetoric.

I'll Be the Judge of That

arbiter   AHR bih ter
a judge who decides a disputed issue
An arbiter was hired to settle the Major League Baseball strike because the owners and players could not come to an agreement.

biased   BYE ist
prejudiced
Judges should not be biased but should rather weigh the evidence fairly before making up their minds.

exculpate   EKS kul payt
to free from guilt or blame
When the gold coins discovered in his closet were found to be fake, Dr. Rideau was exculpated and the search for the real thief continued.

impartial   im PAR shul
not in favor of one side or the other, unbiased
The umpire had a hard time remaining impartial; his son was pitching for the home team, and this made it difficult to call the game fairly.

incontrovertible   in kon truh VERT uh bul
not able to be denied or disputed
The videotape of the robbery provided incontrovertible evidence against the suspect—he was obviously guilty.

integrity   in TEG rit ee
trustworthiness; completeness
The integrity of the witness was called into question when her dislike for the defendant was revealed—some jurors suspected that she was not being entirely truthful.

objectivity   ahb jek TIV ih tee
treating facts without influence from personal feelings or prejudices
It is important that judges hear all cases with objectivity, so that their personal feelings do not affect their decision.

penitent   PEN ih tunt
expressing remorse for one's misdeeds
His desire to make amends to the people he had wronged indicated that he was truly penitent, so the parole board let him out of the penitentiary.

plausible   PLAWZ ih bul
seemingly valid or acceptable; credible
Keith's excuse that he missed school yesterday because he was captured by space aliens was not very plausible.

substantiated   sub STAN shee ay tid
supported with proof or evidence; verified
The fingerprint evidence substantiated the detective's claim that the suspect had been at the scene of the crime.

vindicated   VIN duh kayt id
freed from blame
Mrs. Layton was finally vindicated after her husband admitted to the crime.

You're so Vain

condescending   kon de SEND ing
treating people as weak or inferior
Robert always looked down on his sister and treated her in a condescending manner.

contemptuous   kun TEMP choo us
feeling hatred; scornful
She was so contemptuous of people who wore fur that she sprayed red paint on them.

despotic   des PAHT ik
exercising absolute power; tyrannical
He was a despotic ruler whose every law was enforced with threats of violence or death.

dictatorial   dik tuh TOR ee ul
domineering; oppressively overbearing
The coach had a dictatorial manner and expected people to do whatever he demanded.

disdain   dis DAYN
(n.) contempt, scorn, (v.) to regard or treat with contempt; to look down on
I felt nothing but disdain for the person who stole my lunch—what a jerk!

haughty   HAW tee
arrogant; vainly proud
His haughty manner made it clear that he thought he was better than everyone else.

imperious   im PEER ee us
arrogantly domineering or overbearing
She had a very imperious way about her; she was bossy and treated everyone as if they were beneath her.

patronizing   PAY truh ny zing
treating in a condescending manner
Patrick had such a patronizing attitude that he treated everyone around him like a bunch of little kids.

When the Going Gets Tough

convoluted   kon vuh LOO tid
intricate; complex
The directions were so convoluted that we drove all around the city and got lost.

cryptic   KRIP tik
difficult to comprehend
The writing on the walls of the crypt was cryptic; none of the scientists understood it.

futile   FEW tul
having no useful purpose; pointless
It is futile to try to explain the difference between right and wrong to your pet.

impede   im PEED
to slow the progress of
The retreating army constructed barbed-wire fences and destroyed bridges to impede the advance of the enemy.

obscure   ub SKYUR
(adj.) relatively unknown, (v.) to conceal or make indistinct
Scott constantly makes references to obscure cult films, and no one ever gets his jokes.
The man in front of me was so tall that his head obscured my view of the movie.

quandary   KWAHN dree
a state of uncertainty or perplexity
Ann was in a quandary because she had no soap with which to do her laundry.

I'm a Loser, Baby

indolent   IN duh lunt
lazy
Mr. Lan said his students were indolent because they had not done their homework.

insipid   in SIP id
uninteresting; unchallenging
That insipid movie was so boring and predictable.

listless   LIST luss
lacking energy
Since he is accustomed to an active lifestyle, Mark feels listless when he has nothing to do.

torpor   TOR per
laziness; inactivity; dullness
The hot and humid day filled everyone with an activity-halting torpor.

REVOLUTION

alienated   AY lee en ay tid
removed or disassociated from (friends, family, or homeland)
Rudolph felt alienated from the other reindeer because they never let him join in their reindeer games.

alliance   uh LY uhns
a union of two or more groups
The two countries formed an alliance to stand against their common enemy.

disparity   dis PAR uh tee
inequality in age, rank, or degree; difference
There is a great disparity between rich and poor in many nations.

servile   SER vile
submissive; like a servant
Cameron's servile behavior finally ended when he decided to stand up to his older brother.

suppressed   suh PREST
subdued; kept from being circulated
The author's book was suppressed because the dictator thought it was too critical of his regime.

YOU ARE SO BEAUTIFUL

embellish   em BELL ish
to make beautiful by ornamenting; to decorate
We embellished the account of our vacation by including descriptions of the many colorful people and places we visited.

florid   FLOR id
describing flowery or elaborate speech
The candidate's speech was so florid that although no one could understand what he was talking about, they all agreed that he sounded good saying it.

opulent   AHP yuh lunt
exhibiting a display of great wealth
Dances at the king's palace are always very opulent affairs because no expense is spared.

ornate   or NAYT
elaborately decorated
The carved wood was so ornate that you could examine it several times and still notice things you had not seen before.

ostentatious   ah sten TAY shus
describing a showy or pretentious display
Whenever the millionaire gave a party, the elaborate decorations and enormous amounts of food were always part of his ostentatious display of wealth.

poignant   POYN yunt
profoundly moving; touching
The most poignant part of the movie was when the father finally made peace with his son.

OVERKILL

ebullience   ih BOOL yuns
intense enthusiasm
A sense of ebullience swept over the crowd when the matador defeated the bull.

effusive   eh FYOO siv
emotionally unrestrained; gushy
Gwyneth Paltrow was effusive in her thanks after winning the Oscar; she even burst into tears.

egregious   uh GREE jus
conspicuously bad or offensive
Forgetting to sterilize surgical tools before an operation would be an egregious error.

flagrant   FLAY grunt
extremely or deliberately shocking or noticeable
His throwing the pie at his teacher was a flagrant sign of disrespect.

frenetic   freh NEH tik
wildly excited or active
The pace at the busy office was frenetic; Megan never had a moment to catch her breath.

gratuitous   gruh TOO ih tus
given freely; unearned; unwarranted
The film was full of gratuitous sex and violence that was not essential to the story.

superfluous   soo PER floo us
extra; unnecessary
If there is sugar in your tea, adding honey would be superfluous.

IT'S GETTING BETTER

alleviate   uh LEEV ee ayt
to ease a pain or burden
John took aspirin to alleviate the pain from the headache he got after taking the SAT.

asylum   uh SY lum
a place of retreat or security
The soldiers sought asylum from the bombs in the underground shelter.

auspicious   aw SPISH us
favorable; promising
Our trip to the beach had an auspicious start; the rain stopped just as we started the car.

benevolent   buh NEH vuh lunt
well-meaning; generous
She was a kind and benevolent queen who was concerned about her subjects' well-being.

benign   buh NINE
kind and gentle
Uncle Charlie is a benign and friendly man who is always willing to help.

mollify   MAHL uh fy
to calm or soothe
Anna's apology for scaring her brother did not mollify him; he was mad at her all day.

reclamation rek luh MAY shun
the act of making something useful again
Thanks to the reclamation project, the once unusable land became a productive farm.

sanction   SANK shun
to give official authorization or approval
The students were happy when the principal agreed to sanction the use of calculators in math classes.

LIAR, LIAR, PANTS ON FIRE

dubious   DOO bee us
doubtful; of unlikely authenticity
Jerry's claim that he could fly like Superman seemed dubious—we didn't believe it.

fabricated   FAB ruh kay tid
made; concocted to deceive
Fabio fabricated the story that he used to play drums for Metallica; he had never actually held drumsticks in his life.

hypocrisy   hih POK ruh see
the practice of pretending to be something one is not; insincerity
People who claim to be vegetarian but eat chicken and fish are guilty of hypocrisy.

slander   SLAN der
false charges and malicious oral statements about someone
After the radio host stated that Monica was a space alien, she sued him for slander.

spurious   SPUR ee us
not genuine
The sportscaster made a spurious claim when he said that the San Antonio Spurs were undefeated.

SHE'S CRAFTY

astute   uh STOOT
shrewd; clever
Kevin is financially astute; he never falls for the tricks that credit card companies play.

clandestine   klan DES tin
secretive
The spies planned a clandestine maneuver that depended on its secrecy to work.

coup   KOO
a brilliantly executed plan
It was quite a coup when I talked the salesperson into selling me this valuable cuckoo clock for
five dollars.

disingenuous   dis in JEN yoo us
not straightforward; crafty
Mr. Gelman was rather disingenuous; although he seemed to be simply asking about your health,
he was really trying to figure out why you'd been absent.

ruse   ROOZ
a crafty tick
The offer of a free cruise was merely a ruse to get people to listen to their sales pitch.

stratagem   STRAT uh jem
a clever trick used to deceive or outwit
Planting microphones in the gangster's home was a clever, but illegal, stratagem.

surreptitiously   sur ep TISH us lee
done by secretive means
Matt drank the cough syrup surreptitiously because he didn't want anyone to know that he was
sick.

wary   WAIR ee
on guard
My father becomes wary whenever a salesman calls him on the phone; he knows that many crooks
use the phone so that they can't be charged with mail fraud.

wily   WY lee
cunning
Wily Coyote devised all sorts of clever traps to catch the Roadrunner.

SITTIN' ON THE FENCE

ambiguous   am BIG yoo us
open to more than one interpretation
His eyes were an ambiguous color: Some thought they were brown, and some thought they were green.

ambivalent   am BIH vuh lunt
simultaneously having opposing feelings; uncertain
She had ambivalent feelings about her dance class: On one hand, she enjoyed the exercise, but on the other hand, she thought the choice of dances could be more interesting.

apathetic   a puh THEH tik
feeling or showing little emotion
When the defendant was found guilty on all charges, her face remained expressionless and she appeared to be entirely apathetic.

arbitrary   AR bih trayr ee
determined by impulse rather than reason
The principal made the arbitrary decision that students could not wear hats in school without offering any logical reason for the rule.

capricious   kuh PREE shus
impulsive and unpredictable
The referee's capricious behavior angered the players because he was inconsistent with his calls; he would call foul for minor contact, but ignore elbowing and kicking.

equivocate   eh KWI vuh kayt
to avoid making a definite statement
On critical reading questions, I choose answers that equivocate; they use words such as *could* or *may* that make them difficult to disprove.

indifferent   in DIF rent
not caring one way or the other
The old fisherman was completely indifferent to the pain and hunger he felt; his only concern was catching the enormous marlin he had hooked.

spontaneous   spon TAY nee us
unplanned; naturally occurring
Dave is such a good musician that he can create a song spontaneously, without having to stop and think about it.

whimsical   WIM zuh kul
subject to erratic behavior; unpredictable
Egbert rarely behaved as expected; indeed, he was a whimsical soul whose every decision was anybody's guess.

Just a Little Bit

inconsequential   in kahn suh KWEN shul
unimportant
The cost of the meal was inconsequential to Quentin because he wasn't paying for it.

superficial   soo per FISH ul
concerned only with what is on the surface or obvious; shallow
The wound on his leg was only superficial, even though it looked like a deep cut.

tenuous   TEN yoo us
having little substance or strength; shaky; unsure, weak
Her grasp on reality is tenuous at best; she's not even sure what year it is.

trivial   TRIH vee ul
of little importance or significance
Alex says he doesn't like trivia games because the knowledge they test is trivial; he prefers to spend his time learning more important things.

I Will Survive

assiduous   uh SID yoo us
hard-working
Spending hours in the hot sun digging out every tiny weed, Sidney tended her garden with assiduous attention.

compelling   kom PEL ing
forceful; urgently demanding attention
By ignoring the problems in the city, the mayor gave people a very compelling reason to vote him out of office.

diligent   DIL uh jent
marked by painstaking effort; hard-working
With a lot of diligent effort, they were able to finish the model airplane in record time.

dogged   DOG id
stubbornly persevering
Her first attempts resulted in failure, but her dogged efforts ultimately ended in success.

endure   en DUR
to put up with; to survive a hardship
It was difficult to endure the incredibly boring lecture given in class the other day.

intrepid   in TREH pid
courageous; fearless
The intrepid young soldier scaled the wall and attacked the enemy forces despite being outnumbered 50 to 1.

maverick MAV uh rik
one who is independent and resists adherence to a group
In the movie *Top Gun*, Tom Cruise was a maverick; he often broke the rules and did things his own way.

obdurate AHB dur ut
stubborn; inflexible
Leanna was so obdurate that she was unable to change her way of thinking on even the most minor issues.

obstinate AHB stin ut
stubbornly adhering to an opinion or a course of action
Even though he begged them constantly, Jeremy's parents were obstinate in their refusal to buy him a Nintendo.

proliferate pro LIF er ayt
to grow or increase rapidly
Because the number of fax machines, pagers, and cell phones has proliferated in recent years, many new area codes have been created to handle the demand for phone numbers.

tenacity ten ASS uh tee
persistence
With his overwhelming tenacity, Clark was finally able to interview Brad Pitt for the school newspaper.

vitality vy TA lih tee
energy; power to survive
After a few days of rest, the exhausted mountain climber regained his usual vitality.

GO WITH THE FLOW

assimilation uh sim il AY shun
to absorb; to make similar
The unique blend of Mexican culture was formed by the assimilation of the cultures of the Native Americans and the Spanish.

consensus kun SEN sus
general agreement
After much debate, the committee came to a consensus, although they differed on minor points.

context KAHN tekst
circumstances of a situation; environment
The senator complained that his statements had been taken out of context and were therefore misleading; he said that if the newspaper had printed the rest of his speech, it would have explained the statements in question.

derived   de RYVD
copied or adapted from a source
Many AP English Language and Composition questions are derived from older questions—the details may have been changed, but the same basic concept is being tested.

incumbent   in KUM bunt
imposed as a duty; obligatory
Since you are the host, it is incumbent upon you to see that everyone is having fun.

inevitable   in EV ih tuh bul
certain to happen, unavoidable
Gaining a little extra weight during the wintertime is inevitable, especially after the holidays.

malleable   MAL ee uh bul
easily shaped or formed; easily influenced
Gold is malleable; it is easy to work with and can be hammered into very thin sheets.

subdue   sub DOO
to restrain; to hold back
It took four officers to subdue the fugitive because he fought like a madman.

WAYS OF KNOWING

acquired   uh KWY erd
developed or learned; not naturally occurring
A love of opera is an acquired taste; almost nobody likes it the first time he or she hears it.

conception   kun SEP shun
the ability to form or understand an idea
Most people have no conception of the enormous amount of genetic information present in a single living cell.

conviction   kun VIK shun
a fixed or strong belief
Although he privately held onto his convictions, threats by the church caused Galileo to publicly denounce his theory that the Earth orbited the sun.

dogmatic   dog MAT ik
stubbornly adhering to unproved beliefs
Doug was dogmatic in his belief that exercising frequently boosts one's immune system.

enlightening   en LYT uh ning
informative; contributing to one's awareness
The Rosetta Stone was enlightening because it allowed linguists to begin to translate Egyptian hieroglyphs, which had previously been a mystery.

impression   im PREH shun
a feeling or understanding resulting from an experience
It was my impression that I was supposed to throw a curve ball, but I must have been wrong because the catcher didn't expect it.

intuition   in too ISH un
the power of knowing things without thinking; sharp insight
It is said that some people have intuition about future events that allows them to predict the future.

misconception   mis kun SEP shun
an incorrect understanding or interpretation
His belief that storks bring babies was just one of his many misconceptions.

perception   per SEP shun
awareness; insight
The detective's perception of people's hidden feelings makes it easy for him to catch liars.

perspective   per SPEK tiv
point of view
People from the North and South viewed the Civil War from different perspectives—each side's circumstances made it difficult for them to understand the other side.

profound   pro FOWND
having great depth or seriousness
There was a profound silence during the ceremony in honor of those who died during World War II.

FEELING AT HOME

inherent   in HER ent
inborn; built-in
One of the inherent weaknesses of the AP English Language and Composition exam is that a multiple-choice test, by definition, cannot allow students to be creative in their answers.

innate   in AYT
possessed from birth; inborn
Cats have an innate ability to see well in the dark; they are born with this skill and do not need to develop it.

inveterate   in VET uh rit
long established; deep-rooted; habitual
Stan has always had trouble telling the truth; in fact, he's an inveterate liar.

omnipotent   om NIP uh tent
all-powerful
He liked to think that he was an omnipotent manager, but he really had very little control over anything.

proximity   prahk SIM ih tee
closeness
I try to sit far away from Roxy—I don't like sitting in proximity to her because she wears too much perfume.

On the Road Again

elusive   il OO siv
difficult to capture, as in something actually fleeting
The girl's expression was elusive; the painter had a hard time recreating it on the canvas.

emigrate   EM ih grayt
to leave one country or region and settle in another
Many Jews left Russia and emigrated to Israel after it was founded in 1948.

transient   TRAN zhunt
passing away with time; passing from one place to another
Jack Dawson enjoyed his transient lifestyle; with nothing but the clothes on his back and the air in his lungs, he was free to travel wherever he wanted.

transitory   TRAN zih tor ee
short-lived or temporary
The sadness she felt was only transitory; the next day her mood improved.

Friendly

affable   AF uh bul
easy-going; friendly
We enjoyed spending time with Mr. Lee because he was such a pleasant, affable man.

amenable   uh MEN uh bul
responsive; agreeable
Since we had been working hard all day, the group seemed amenable to my suggestion that we all go home early.

camaraderie   kahm RAH duh ree
good will between friends
There was great camaraderie among the members of the team; they were friends both on and off the field.

cordial   KOR jul
friendly; sincere
Upon my arrival at camp, I received a warm and cordial greeting from the counselors.

facetious   fuh SEE shus
playfully humorous
Although the teacher pretended to be insulting his favorite student, he was just being facetious.

UNDER THE WEATHER

impinge   im PINJ
hinder; interfere with
By not allowing the students to publish a newspaper, the school was impinging upon their right to free speech.

lament   luh MENT
express grief for; mourn
After Beowulf was killed by the dragon, the Geats wept and lamented his fate.

melancholy   MEL un kaw lee
sadness; depression
Joy fell into a state of melancholy when her Coldplay CD got scratched.

sanction   SANK shun
an economic or military measure put in place to punish another country
In 1962, the United States imposed economic sanctions on Cuba to protest Fidel Castro's dictatorship; travel and trade between the countries are severely restricted to this day.

truncated   TRUN kay tid
shortened; cut off
The file Chris downloaded from the Internet was truncated; the end of it was missing.

I WRITE THE SONGS

aesthetic   es THET ik
having to do with the appreciation of beauty
The arrangement of paintings in the museum was due to aesthetic considerations; as long as the paintings looked good together, it didn't matter who painted them or when they were painted.

anthology   an THAH luh jee
a collection of literary pieces
This anthology contains all of William Shakespeare's sonnets, but none of his plays.

contemporary   kun TEM po rer ee
current, modern; from the same time
Contemporary music is very different from the music of the 1920s.
Pocahontas and William Shakespeare were contemporaries; they lived during the same time, though not in the same place.

dilettante   dih luh TAHNT
one with an amateurish or superficial understanding of a field of knowledge
You can't trust Betsy's opinion because she's just a dilettante who doesn't understand the subtleties of the painting.

eclectic   uh KLEK tik
made up of a variety of sources or styles
Lou's taste in music is eclectic; he listens to everything from rap to polka.

excerpt   EK serpt
a selected part of a passage or scene
We read an excerpt from *Romeo and Juliet* in which Juliet says, "Romeo, Romeo, wherefore art thou Romeo?"

genre   ZHAHN ruh
describing a category or artistic endeavor
Gene enjoyed only science-fiction movies; in fact, he never went to see anything that was not in that genre.

medley   MED lee
an assortment or a mixture, especially of musical pieces
At the concert, the band played a medley of songs from its first album, cutting an hour's worth of music down to five minutes.

mural   MYUR ul
a large painting applied directly to a wall or ceiling surface
The mural on the wall of the library showed the signing of the Declaration of Independence.

narrative   NAR uh tiv
(adj.) characterized by the telling of a story, (n.) a story
Tony gave us a running narrative of the game, since he was the only one who could see over the fence.

parody   PAR uh dee
an artistic work that imitates the style of another work for comic effect
The Onion is a satirical publication that is a parody of other, nonsatirical newspapers that give real, true news.

realism   REE uh liz um
artistic representation that aims for visual accuracy
His photographs have a stark realism that conveys the true horror of the war.

virtuoso   ver choo OH so
a tremendously skilled artist
Some people say that Jason Loewenstein is a guitar virtuoso because of his amazing work in Sebadoh—others say that his music is just noise.

Cool It Now

decorous   DEK er us
proper; marked by good taste
The class was well-behaved and the substitute was grateful for their decorous conduct.

equanimity   ek wuh NIM uh tee
the quality of being calm and even-tempered; composure
She showed great equanimity; she did not panic even in the face of catastrophe.

modest   MAH dist
quiet or humble in manner or appearance
Although Mr. Phillips is well-off financially, he lives in a modest, simple home.

propriety   pruh PRY uh tee
appropriateness of behavior
Anyone who blows his nose on the tablecloth has no sense of propriety.

prudent   PROO dunt
exercising good judgment or common sense
It wouldn't be prudent to act until you've considered every possible outcome.

serene   suh REEN
calm
The quiet seaside resort provided a much-needed vacation in a serene locale.

staid   STAYD
unemotional; serious
Mr. Carver had such a staid demeanor that he remained calm while everyone else celebrated the team's amazing victory.

stoic   STOW ik
indifferent to pleasure or pain; impassive
Not one to complain, Jason was stoic in accepting his punishment.

If You Can't Say Anything Nice

condemn   kun DEM
to express strong disapproval of; denounce
Homer Simpson condemned Mayor Quimby for allowing the schoolchildren to drink spoiled milk; he was outraged and let the mayor know it.

discredit   dis CRED it
to cause to be doubted
The claim that pi is exactly equal to 3 can be discredited simply by careful measurement.

disparage   dis PAR uj
to speak of in a slighting way or negatively; to belittle
Glen disparaged Wanda's work as being careless and unoriginal.

pejorative   puh JOR uh tiv
describing words or phrases that belittle or speak negatively of someone
Teachers should refrain from using such pejorative terms as *numbskull* when dealing with students who need encouragement.

plagiarism   PLAY juh riz um
the act of passing off the ideas or writing of another as one's own
The author was accused of plagiarism when an older manuscript was discovered that contained passages that she had used, word for word, in her own book.

vilify   VIL uh fye
to make vicious statements about
Chad issued a series of pamphlets that did nothing but vilify his opponent, but his cruel accusations were not enough to win him the election.

Nasty Boys

brusque   BRUSK
rudely abrupt
Mr. Weird was a brusque teacher who didn't take time to talk to or listen to his students.

caustic   KAW stik
bitingly sarcastic or witty
He had a very caustic wit, and he seldom told a joke without offending someone.

fractious   FRAK shus
quarrelsome; unruly
Leonard was a fractious child who disagreed with everything and refused to listen.

incorrigible   in KOR ij uh bul
unable to be reformed
She is absolutely incorrigible; no matter how many times you punish her, she goes right ahead and misbehaves.

ingrate   IN grayt
an ungrateful person
It is a true ingrate who can accept favor after favor and never offer any thanks.

insolent   IN suh lunt
insulting in manner or speech
It was extremely insolent of him to stick his tongue out at the principal.

notorious   no TOR ee us
known widely and usually unfavorably; infamous
Al Capone was a notorious gangster in the 1930s; he was feared throughout America.

pugnacious   pug NAY shus
combative; belligerent
Lorenzo was a pugnacious child who settled his differences by fighting with people.

reprehensible   rep ree HEN si bul
worth of blame
It was reprehensible of the girls to spit their gum in their teacher's water bottle; they had detention for a week.

PURE EVIL

brittle   BRIT ul
easily broken when subjected to pressure
That antique vase is so brittle that it may break at any moment.

deleterious   del uh TEER ee us
having a harmful effect; injurious
Although it may seem unlikely, taking too many vitamins can actually have a deleterious effect on your health.

enmity   EN muh tee
mutual hatred or ill-will
There was a great enmity between the opposing generals, and each wanted to destroy the other.

heinous   HAY nus
hatefully evil; abominable
To murder someone in cold blood is a heinous crime.

malfeasance   mal FEEZ uns
wrongdoing, misconduct
The senator was accused of malfeasance after he was caught sneaking out of a local brothel.

malice   MAL is
extreme ill-will or spite
It was clear that he was acting with malice when he disconnected the brakes in his business partner's car.

putrid   PYOO trid
rotten
He threw his lunch in the bottom of his locker every day and it was a putrid mess by the end of the year—rotten bananas, moldy sandwiches, and curdled milk were some of the more disgusting ingredients.

rancorous   RANK er us
hateful; marked by deep-seated ill-will
They had such a rancorous relationship that no one could believe that they had ever gotten along.

toxic   TAKH sik
poisonous
Since many chemicals are toxic, drinking from random flasks in the chemistry lab could be hazardous to your health.

OLD SCHOOL

archaic   ar KAY ik
characteristic of an earlier period; old-fashioned
"How dost thou?" is an archaic way of saying, "How are you?"

hackneyed   HACK need
worn out through overuse; trite
All my mom could offer in the way of advice were these hackneyed old phrases that I'd heard a hundred times before.

medieval   med EE vul
referring to the Middle Ages, old-fashioned
His ideas about fashion were positively medieval; he thought that a man should always wear a coat and tie and a woman should always wear a dress.

obsolete   ahb suh LEET
no longer in use; old-fashioned
Eight-track tape players are obsolete because music isn't recorded in that format anymore.

BO-O-O-RING

austere   aw STEER
without decoration; strict
The gray walls and bare floors provided a very austere setting.

mediocrity   mee dee AH krit ee
the state or quality of being average; of moderate to low quality
Salieri said that he was the patron saint of mediocrity because his work could never measure up to Mozart's.

mundane   mun DAYN
commonplace; ordinary
We hated going to class every day because it was so mundane; we never did anything interesting.

ponderous   PAHN duh rus
extremely dull
The 700-page book on the anatomy of the flea was so ponderous that I could not read more than one paragraph.

prosaic   pro ZAY ik
unimaginative; dull
Rebecca made a prosaic mosaic—it consisted of only one tile.

sedentary   SEH dun tair ee
not migratory; settled
Galatea led a sedentary existence; she never even left her home unless she had to.

WHO CAN IT BE NOW?

apprehension   ap reh HEN shun
anxiety or fear about the future
My grandmother felt apprehension about nuclear war in the 1960s, so my grandfather built a bomb shelter in the backyard to calm her fears.

harbinger   HAR bin jer
something that indicates what is to come; a forerunner
When it is going to rain, insects fly lower, so cows lie down to get away from the insects; therefore, the sight of cows lying down is a harbinger of rain.

ominous   AH min us
menacing; threatening
The rattling under the hood sounded ominous because we were miles from the nearest town and would have been stranded if the car had broken down.

premonition   prem uh NISH un
a feeling about the future
Luckily, my premonition that I would break my neck skiing was unfounded; unluckily, I broke my leg.

timorous   TIM uh rus
timid; fearful about the future
Tiny Tim was timorous; he was afraid that one day he would be crushed by a giant.

trepidation   trep uh DAY shun
uncertainty; apprehension
We approached Mrs. Fielding with trepidation because we didn't know how she would react to our request for a field trip.

New Sensation

innovative   IN no vay tiv
introducing something new
The shop on the corner has become known for its innovative use of fruit on its pizzas.

naive   nah YEEV
lacking sophistication
It was naive of him to think that he could write a novel in one afternoon.

nascent   NAY sunt
coming into existence; emerging
If you study Nirvana's first album, you can see their nascent abilities that were brought to maturity by their second album.

novel   NAH vul
strikingly new or unusual
Sharon's novel approach to the problem stunned the scientific community; no one had ever thought to apply game theory to genetics.

novice   NAH vis
a beginner
Having only played chess a couple of times, Barry was a novice compared with the contestants who had been playing all their lives.

Straight Up

candor   KAN der
sincerity; openness
It's refreshing to hear Lora's honesty and candor—when asked about her English teacher, she says, "I can't stand her!"

frank   FRANK
open and sincere in expression; straightforward
When Jim lost my calculator, he was frank with me; he admitted to losing it without trying to make up some excuse.

Earth, Wind, and Fire

arid   AYR id
describing a dry, rainless climate
Since they receive little rain, deserts are known for their arid climates.

conflagration   kahn fluh GRAY shun
a widespread fire
The protesters burned flags, accidentally starting a fire that developed into a conflagration that raged out of control.

nocturnal   nok TER nul
of or occurring in the night
Owls are nocturnal animals because they sleep during the day and hunt at night.

sonorous   SAH nuh rus
producing a deep or full sound
My father's sonorous snoring keeps me up all night unless I close my door and wear earplugs.

Full On

ample   AM pul
describing a large amount of something
Because no one else wanted to try the new soda, Andy was able to have an ample sample.

comprehensive   kahm pre HEN siv
large in scope or content
The final exam was comprehensive, covering everything that we had learned that year.

copious   KO pee us
plentiful; having a large quantity
She had taken copious notes during class, using up five large notebooks.

permeated   PER mee ay tid
spread or flowing throughout
After Kathryn had her hair professionally curled, the scent of chemicals permeated the air.

pervasive   per VAY siv
dispersed throughout
In this part of town, graffiti is pervasive—it's everywhere.

prodigious   pruh DIJ us
enormous
The shattered vase required a prodigious amount of glue to repair.

replete   ruh PLEET
abundantly supplied; filled to capacity
After a successful night of trick-or-treating, Dee's bag was replete with Halloween candy.

R-E-S-P-E-C-T

exemplary   eg ZEM pluh ree
commendable; worthy of imitation
Jay's behavior was exemplary; his parents wished that his brother, Al, were more like him.

idealize   eye DEE uh lyze
to consider perfect
The fans had idealized the new star pitcher; they had such unrealistically high expectations that they were bound to be disappointed.

laudatory   LAW duh tor ee
giving praise
The principal's speech was laudatory, congratulating the students on their AP exam scores.

paramount   PAR uh mount
of chief concern or importance
The workers had many minor complaints, but the paramount reason for their unhappiness was the low pay.

venerated   VEN er ay tid
highly respected
Princess Diana was venerated for her dedication to banning land mines around the world; people today still sing her praises.

catalog   KAT uh log
(v.) to make an itemized list of
He decided to catalog his expenses for the week, hoping that this list would show him where he could cut back his spending.

facile   FAS ul
done or achieved with little effort; easy
Last night's math homework was such a facile task that I was done in ten minutes.

fastidious   fas TID ee us
possessing careful attention to detail; difficult to please
Since Kelly was so fastidious, we tried to keep her out of our group.

hierarchy   HY er ar kee
a group organized by rank
With each promotion raising him higher, Archie moved up in his company's hierarchy.

meticulous   muh TIK yuh lus
extremely careful and precise
The plastic surgeon was meticulous; he didn't want to leave any scars.

pragmatic   prag MAT ik
practical
Never one for wild and unrealistic schemes, Amy took a pragmatic approach to research.

solvent   SAHL vunt
able to pay one's debts
After five years of losing money, the business has finally solved its financial problems and become solvent.

OTHER WORDS

abstract   ab STRAKT
not applied to actual objects
"Justice" is an abstract concept because it is merely an idea.

anachronism   an A krun ism
something out of place in time or sequence
Jill was something of an anachronism; she insisted on carrying a parasol when going out in the sun and believed that a woman's place was at home in the kitchen and with the children.

anthropomorphism   an thrah puh MOR fizm
the attribution of humanlike characteristics to inanimate objects, animals, or forces of nature
Beatrix Potter is known for her children's books filled with anthropomorphism; Peter Rabbitt, Squirrel Nutkin, and Samuel Whiskers were all animal characters with very human qualities.

apology   uh PAWL uh gee
defense of an idea
Du Bellay wrote an apology in which he justified the use of French in place of Latin.

apposition   app uh ZIH shun
a grammar construction in which a noun (or noun phrase) is placed with another as an explanation
My grandmother, a fine woman of 83, enjoys riding her motorcycle at high speeds in heavy traffic on Highway 280.

archetype   AR keh type
a perfect example; an original pattern or model
Steve enjoyed stealing candy from babies, tripping elderly women in crosswalks, and pilfering money from the Save the Children charity jar; he was the archetype of pure evil.

apparatus   ap uh RAT us
equipment; a group of machines
The storeroom behind the physics lab was filled with a cumbersome apparatus that has since been replaced by a much smaller and more accurate piece of equipment.

chiasmus   ky AZ muss
an inversion in the second of two parallel phrases
John F. Kennedy's "Ask not what your country can do for you, but what you can do for your country" is an example of chiasmus.

cogent   KOH jent
convincing
Rob and Thomas were an amazing debate team; their cogent arguments always swayed the judges to vote in their favor.

gesticulating   jes TIK yeh lay ting
making gestures while speaking
The commencement speaker's gesticulating hands were quite distracting; the students had stopped listening to her words and were now counting the number of times she made awkward gestures.

hypothetical   hye puh THET ih kul
existing only as an assumption or speculation
Heather wondered why her class had to study hypothetical cases when they had actual case histories they could look at.

lexicon   LEKS uh kahn
a word book describing language with definitions; a dictionary
When his teacher wrote that his essay was "abysmal," Eddie decided to look it up in his lexicon and found that this was quite insulting.

metonymy   meh TAHN uh mee
a type of figurative language in which one term is substituted for another term with which it is closely associated
"Today, Capitol Hill (U.S. Congress) voted on the Internet Privacy bill" is an example of metonymy.

oxymoron   ahk see MORE on
an apparent contradiction of terms
Angela spent her lazy summer afternoon contemplating oxymorons: "freezer burn," "plastic glasses," and "deafening silence" were among her favorites.

panegyric   pan eh JIR ik
statement of high praise
For his senior essay, Boris wrote an eloquent panegyric to his high school; he had truly enjoyed the last four years, and he wanted his teachers to know how much he appreciated them.

paradigm   PAR a dym
an example or model
The current educational paradigm has students engaged in discovery-based learning, whereas the older model had teachers lecturing and students merely taking notes.

parallelism   PARE uh lell izm
a grammar construction in which two identical syntactic constructions are used
On Mondays, Ms. Smith spends her time *baking cakes* for local charities and *knitting socks* for the homeless.

period (periodic sentence)   PEER ee uhd
long, complex, grammatically correct sentence
While writing his essay, Sam thought he was being very articulate with his long, complex sentences. However, his English teacher disagreed; those lengthy sentences weren't periods; they were simply rambling run-ons.

pernicious   per NIH shus
causing great harm
In *Mean Girls*, the Plastics loved to spread pernicious rumors about their classmates; they effectively ruined the social lives of several students with their nasty gossip.

phenomenon   feh NAH meh nahn
an unusual, observable event
The phenomenon of lightning remained unexplained until scientists discovered electricity.

propitious   pruh PIH shus
presenting favorable circumstances; auspicious
In Chinese culture, the color red is seen as sort of propitious omen; red is thought to bring luck.

rational   RASH un ul
logical; motivated by reason rather than feeling
While Joe is more impulsive, Frank is more rational because he thinks things through rather than acting on his feelings.

sardonic   sar DAH nik
disdainfully or ironically humorous; harsh, bitter, or caustic
In Rachel's group of friends, Estelle was known as the sardonic one; sometimes her sarcastic comments really hurt the other girls.

syllogism (syllogistic reasoning)   SIH luh jih zum
a form of deductive reasoning: a major premise, a minor premise, and a conclusion
Humans are mortal (major premise); Seth is human (minor premise); Seth is mortal (conclusion).

synecdoche   sin ECK duh kee
a form of metonymy that's restricted to cases where a part is used to signify the whole
"A thousand swords came charging toward us from the nearby mountain range; we could hear the angry army as it marched closer and closer" is an example of synecdoche.

theoretical   thee oh RET ih kul
lacking application or practical application
Theoretical physics is concerned with ideas, whereas applied physics is concerned with using ideas.

PART ◆ V

AP English Composition

9

Rhetorical Fallacies

AVOIDING THE FATAL FALLACY

A **fallacy** is strictly defined as guile or trickery or a false or mistaken idea. Fallacies have the appearance of truth but are erroneous. Let's say that you really want to attend a famous university in Cambridge, Massachusetts, and you've heard that the acceptance rate for the institution is 25 percent higher for early decision applicants. However, it is a fallacy that applying early would increase your chances of being accepted. But why? Because if you have a 2.8 GPA, then that university isn't going to accept you regardless of when you apply.

You should not be surprised to hear that the fallacy we address in this book has to do with the name of the AP English Language and Composition exam. As we mentioned earlier, although "language" is contained in the title of this exam, the exam primarily tests rhetoric and composition. In other words, this exam tests how language works.

In this chapter we provide you with an overview of some common rhetorical fallacies. You should be familiar with *all* of these for the exam. Rhetorical fallacies may appear as answers on the Multiple-Choice sections. In addition, they may be relevant to your essays in the free-response questions.

COMMON RHETORICAL FALLACIES

Oftentimes, when writers have trouble making convincing "honest" arguments with the facts that they have in hand, they resort to using rhetorical fallacies. As you may expect, when you begin to write your essays in the Free-Response section of the exam, you shouldn't resort to these tactics. However, you should be able to recognize the use of these common fallacies in the reasoning of others; this will help you substantially on test day.

Ad Hominem Argument

An *ad hominem* (in Latin, "to the man") argument is any kind of fallacious argument that criticizes an idea by pointing something out about the person who holds the idea, rather than directly addressing the actual merit of the idea. There are people who learn this form of rhetorical fallacy at a very tender age and may argue thusly: "You're wrong because you're a jerk." But there are plenty of mature examples of *ad hominem* arguments, too.

> Example: Of course that writer supports gun control; she's a Democrat!

The attack shifts from the issue (gun control) to the political affiliation of the writer (Democrat).

Argument from Authority (or Argument from False Authority)

An **argument from authority** tempts us to agree with the writer's assumptions based on the authority of a famous person or entity or on his or her own character (when the writers are well-known).

> Example: It is absurd to believe that professional baseball players have used steroids because the most famous slugger of our time has repeatedly asserted that such a claim is false.

You see how it works? Or how about this: If The Princeton Review put the following quotation on the back cover of a book, how impressed would you be?

> "This is absolutely awesome—it's the best review book ever written."—John Schmuckovic

Would that convince you? Probably not. How about this quote?

> "This is absolutely awesome—it's the best review book ever written."—Shakira

Even though the rock star didn't have to take AP exams in her native Colombia, her fame may give her the authority necessary to get some students to buy the book.

APPEAL TO IGNORANCE

Appeal to ignorance is based on the assumption that whatever has not been proven false must be true (or, similarly, whatever has not been proven true must be false).

> Example #1: No one can prove that the Loch Ness monster does not exist; therefore the Loch Ness monster exists.

> Example #2: No one can prove that the Loch Ness monster exists; therefore the Loch Ness monster does not exist.

This is a fairly common form of rhetorical fallacy.

BEGGING THE QUESTION

Begging the question is a fallacious form of argument in which someone assumes that parts (or all) of what the person claims to be proving are proven facts. This circular form of reasoning is easier to grasp by example.

> Example #1: The Loch Ness monster spoke to me in my dreams, so it must exist.

Well, wouldn't you want me to prove to you *first* that the Loch Ness monster really did speak to me in my dreams before you would accept my conclusion? I hope so. It may have been the pepperoni pizza that was speaking to me in my dreams.

> Example #2: Examine the following scenario.

> Interviewer: Your resume looks impressive, but I need another reference.

> Brendan: Heidi can give me a good reference.

> Interviewer: Good, but how do I know that Heidi is trustworthy?

> Brendan: I can vouch for her.

Hasty Generalization

Sometimes a writer will deliberately lead you to a conclusion by providing insufficient, selective evidence. This is called a **hasty generalization.**

> Example: Ping-pong is an extremely dangerous sport; last year, my friend got hit in the eye with a ping-pong ball and almost lost his vision in that eye.

This rhetorical fallacy can be used very effectively. In the case of hasty generalization, often statistics that are "good"—meaning empirically true—are used to "prove" things that aren't true.

Non Sequitur

In Latin, *non sequitur* means "It doesn't follow." In English, a *non sequitur* is a statement that does not relate logically to what comes before it.

> Example: If you really wanted to earn a 5 on the AP English Language and Composition exam, you wouldn't spend so much time reading Isabel Allende's novels.

Wait a second. First of all, reading novels may help you prepare for the exam. Second, who says that you don't have plenty of time for preparing for the exam and reading—especially now that you've stopped wasting time in front of the television? In a *non sequitur*, there is no logical connection between the initial phrase and the one that follows it, so you shouldn't try to make one.

False Dichotomy

False dichotomy consists of a consideration of only the two extremes when there are one or more intermediate possibilities.

> Example: AP Calculus BC class is impossible; either you get it or you don't.

This statement sounds like a great way to explain to your parents why you just earned a less-than-stellar grade on your last calculus test, but it sets up a false dichotomy. In fact, there are various levels of understanding and thus various degrees of success in AP Calculus, and as is the case in many fields, success is a direct result of effort.

Slippery Slope

Slippery slope arguments suggest dire consequences from relatively minor causes.

> Example: If we stop requiring men to wear coats and ties in the dining room, pretty soon they'll start coming in dressed in beachwear.

Another way that the slippery slope fallacy can be expressed is by the phrase "give 'em an inch, and they'll take a mile."

Faulty Causality

Faulty causality refers to the (sometimes unintentional) setting up of a cause-and-effect relationship when none exists. In faulty causality, one event can happen after another without the first necessarily being the direct cause of the second.

> Example: Violent crime among adolescents has risen in the past decade, and that is the result of increased sales of violent video games.

As is the case with all examples of faulty causality, there is no proof for the video game argument, and it is possible to think of a dozen other convincing reasons for the rise of violent crime—a trend that we just made up.

STRAW MAN ARGUMENT

The **straw man argument** consists of an oversimplification of an opponent's argument to make it easier to attack.

(By the way, the new, more politically correct fallacy is called the straw person argument) Here's an example of how this works.

> Example: Students who want to eliminate the school uniform are exhibitionists who want to show off bare midriffs.

In fact, students who are arguing against having to wear a school uniform may be interested only in expressing their individuality; it's even possible that they would be happy in conservative clothing. However, if the author of this sentence attributes a simplistic argument to the students, who had, in reality, a more substantive motivation (individuality), it is easier to attack their position.

SENTIMENTAL APPEALS

This commonly used tactic attempts to appeal to the *hearts* of readers (or, of course, listeners) so that they forget to use their *minds*.

> Example: "The assignment that I gave you last night was much too long, but just think how pleased your parents and I will be when you score a 5 on the AP exam. Think about the pride you'll feel when tears of joy stream down our faces!"

Here, the teacher knew that arguing that the assignment was an important intellectual exercise wouldn't convince his students, even though that may have been a more valid argument. So in this case, he decided to use a sentimental appeal. Sentimental appeals are generally not valid arguments, but they work sometimes!

RED HERRING

A **red herring** attempts to shift attention away from an important issue by introducing an issue that has no logical connection to the discussion at hand.

> Example: "My opponent talks about the poor quality of military intelligence, but this is a time for decisiveness, not for weakness. We must stick together and present a common front as the other nations look on. If we do not, we could jeopardize our position as a global leader."

As you can see, this is very similar to a sentimental appeal, although the political speaker is (apparently) still appealing to minds, rather than sentiments. In this case, the speaker shifts the discussion from the topic under debate (military intelligence) to a different issue (our role as a super power).

SCARE TACTICS

The aptly named **scare tactic** is used to frighten readers or listeners into agreeing with the speaker; often, when scare tactics are used, the speaker has no logical argument on which to fall back.

Example: "My opponent talks about the need to explore stem cell research, but this would bring about an end to ethical uses of technology, and, before long, scientists will be creating superraces—the Nazi dream of an Aryan Nation will ensue!"

Here the speaker mentions Nazis to frighten the listeners; there is no logical (or at least, logically presented) link between exploring stem cell research and the creation of an Aryan Nation. The example may seem to you like a combination of scare tactics and slippery slope; this combination is sometimes seen when a slippery slope argument is used to scare readers or listeners.

BANDWAGON APPEALS

Bandwagon appeals have a different name in school settings; there, they are known as "peer pressure." A bandwagon appeal encourages the listener to agree with a position because everyone else does. The logic goes something like this: If everybody else is doing it, it must be all right.

Example: It's time for our county to repeal the ban on strip mining—every other county in the state has already done so!

Notice that the speaker (or writer) avoids having to explain the merits of the issue and explain why the ban is inappropriate.

DOGMATISM

Dogmatism does not allow for discussion because the speaker presumes that his or her beliefs are beyond question; essentially, the "logic" runs thusly: I'm correct because I'm correct.

Example: We are members of the Wombat Party and, as such, know that we are right when we assert that Wombats are the best!

There is no way to rebut the claim.

EQUIVOCATION

Equivocation is telling part of the truth, while deliberately hiding the entire truth; typically, this is similar to lying by omission.

Example: There is a Pink Panther movie in which Inspector Clouseau enters a quaint European hotel and, upon spying a cute little dog, asks the owner, "Does your dog bite?" The manager responds, "No," and Clouseau attempts to pet the dog, which growls and bites him. "You told me that your dog does not bite!" exclaims Clouseau. "That's not my dog," responds the owner.

Setting the comedy aside for a moment, the owner of the chalet gave an equivocal answer. Presumably, he was telling the truth when he responded that his dog does not bite, but that truth hid the more relevant truth—the dog he was with at the time does, in fact, bite. It is possible that you have indulged in equivocation. Let's say that you're about to leave the house, but your mom stops you and says, "You're not going to Marina's party tonight, are you? I heard that her parents are out of town and there's not going to be any supervision." "No mom, I'm not going there." Your mom smiles in relief and lets you go. You're relieved too because you are going to Dave's party, where there will be no supervision because his parents are out of town. You did not exactly lie because you truly are not going to Marina's party; however, you did lie because you are going to the same kind of party somewhere else, and it is the *kind* of party that your mom objects to, not its specific location.

FAULTY ANALOGY

A **faulty analogy** is an illogical, misleading comparison between two things.

> Example: Why should we invade that country? Let me explain it to you like this. What if you looked out the window and saw a 20-dollar bill in the street? Wouldn't you go outside and take it?

This analogy is *really* faulty! A better analogy would be: What if you saw a person in the street with a 20-dollar bill? Wouldn't you go outside and try to steal it from the person? Analogy is always a weak form of argumentation; a faulty analogy exploits this weakness to mislead listeners (or readers), when true logic may not convince them.

As we mentioned earlier, make sure you have memorized all of these rhetorical fallacies before test day. After you've studied them carefully (make flashcards if you need to, using the examples we gave you), try the following questions.

SAMPLE QUESTIONS

In each question, choose the most fitting rhetorical fallacy.

1. If such actions were not illegal, then they would not be prohibited by law.

    (A) faulty causality
    (B) begging the question
    (C) appeal to ignorance
    (D) argument from authority
    (E) *ad hominem*

2. We all knew he would think abortion is wrong! He's a priest!

    (A) faulty causality
    (B) hasty generalization
    (C) *ad hominem*
    (D) false dichotomy
    (E) dogmatism

3. "Recently, I've been thinking that there is some merit in the Republican's tax-cut plan. I suggest that we come up with something like it because if we Democrats are going to survive as a party, we have got to show the people that we are as tough-minded as the Republicans, since that is what the public wants."

    (A) red herring
    (B) straw man argument
    (C) slippery slope
    (D) equivocation
    (E) *non sequitur*

4. "We should have a car wash to raise money for Senior Prom. The three classes before us have all done it!"

   (A) begging the question
   (B) argument from authority
   (C) red herring
   (D) scare tactics
   (E) dogmatism

5. The mill must be polluting the river because there has been a recent increase in bird deaths around there.

   (A) straw man argument
   (B) appeal to ignorance
   (C) faulty analogy
   (D) *non sequitur*
   (E) slippery slope

Rhetorical fallacies, when used with savvy, can be very convincing. It is worth knowing about them to do well on the AP English Language and Composition exam and to become a critical reader and listener—and not to become the victim of clever rhetorical tactics.

In the next chapter, we will discuss rhetorical modes, or patterns of exposition. This is an important topic because it will outline ready-made tactics and methods for writing your free-response essays.

The answers to the above questions are: (B), (C), (A), (B), and (D). If you didn't get them right, go back and review those rhetorical terms.

10

Rhetorical Modes and Patterns of Exposition — Basic Modes

WHAT ARE RHETORICAL MODES?

The rhetorical modes (or patterns) contained in this chapter are worth studying for two reasons. First, they will provide you with ready-made approaches for writing your essays on the exam, and second, the multiple-choice questions on the test also often include some of the terminology.

As you prepare for the exam by taking practice tests, you'll see that 40 minutes is not much time in which to write a sophisticated essay, and the shortcuts you'll learn in this chapter will be invaluable in helping you write a great essay in the allotted time. However, you do not need to cram and memorize all the material in this section. If you read and understand the explanations and just make sure you retain the basics, you'll be comfortable enough with the process to do well on the exam.

Another important point to remember is that, more often than not, rhetorical modes are used in combination. Breaking them up into individual components is a somewhat arbitrary process—but for our purposes, it makes the material easier to understand. Let's begin.

EXAMPLE OR ILLUSTRATION

Our first rhetorical mode consists of using specific examples to illustrate an idea. Now, this may seem like a pretty simple idea, but one of the most common mistakes students make when writing their AP English Language and Composition essays is to use too many or poor examples. Remember that all examples are not created equal. If you use poor illustrative examples, your ideas will be communicated much less clearly and effectively than if you'd used solid, appropriate ones. In writing these essays, your principal goal is clarity.

Read the following passage, and as you do so, evaluate the effectiveness of the examples that it uses.

> Pangloss is correct when he claims that everything is for the best in the best of all possible worlds. First of all, we are seeing more and more technological innovation every year. Computer technology, in particular, has helped us in many ways, and breakthroughs in medicine have helped raise the life expectancy significantly. Furthermore, in most cities, there are bustling restaurants and great nightlife. Finally, travel has become affordable for most people, and paradises like Aruba and Hawaii await us all!

I'm sure you agree that the examples are not convincing, but I hope that you also understand that they are not even appropriate. Implicit in the examples chosen is the reduction of the best of all possible worlds to the writer's own tiny corner. A better approach would be something as follows:

> Pangloss is correct when he claims that everything is for the best in the best of all possible worlds. First of all, the challenges that we have faced or are facing have inspired some of our most important scientific advances. Great famines have led scientists to exciting new agricultural discoveries, such as drought-resistant crops; great droughts have inspired engineers to develop cost-effective desalination plants. In essence, the evils in the world have been necessary stimulants for changes for the better. Furthermore, advances in medicine are no

> longer restricted to the wealthy nations of the world, and there is
> reason to hope that coordinated efforts to help developing countries
> will become more effective; take, for example, the international relief
> efforts to help the people whose homes were destroyed by the recent
> tsunami. Not only will the victims have better and safer homes now,
> but also the cooperation among the developed nations will translate
> into a better, safer world. Indeed, everything is for the best.

While the second essay is impractical and naive, at least it does its best to substantiate an untenable position. Without any doubt, the examples in the second passage are much more appropriate for the argument than those that were used in the first passage.

Just as it is important to choose relevant, convincing examples to substantiate your own ideas, it is essential to constantly evaluate the examples that others use in their attempts to explain or to convince.

Tricksters, dogmatists, and charlatans usually illustrate their positions with scanty, inappropriate details. Be critical.

LAUNDRY LIST FOR EXAMPLE (ILLUSTRATION)

- Use examples that your reader (the person who reads your essays) will identify with and understand. Do not assume that the AP reader has seen the latest teen cult film or knows any pop culture icons younger than Britney Spears.

- Draw your examples from "real life," "real" culture (literature, art, classical music, and so on), and well-known folklore.

- Make sure the example really does illustrate your point. Don't use a fancy example just to show off your knowledge; find ones that really work!

- Introduce your examples using transitions, such as, *for example, for instance, case in point*, and *consider the case of.*

- A single example that is perfectly representative can serve to illustrate your point.

- A series of short, less-perfect (but still relevant.) examples, can, by their accumulation, serve to illustrate your point.

- The ideal approach is to construct a well-developed, representative example supported by several shorter examples.

- Remember that you are in control of what you write. As you brainstorm, discard examples that may disprove your point. Your AP essays will have little or nothing to do with your beliefs or with a balanced examination of an issue. You will be defending a point of view (argumentative essay) or explaining something (expository essay)—don't feel like you have to be fair to all sides of an argument; your aim is to get your point across.

- Quality is more important than quantity; poorly chosen examples detract significantly from your presentation.

SAMPLE QUESTION

Write a thoughtful and carefully constructed essay in which you use specific examples to defend, challenge, or qualify the assertion that Hollywood movies are a reflection of a decaying society.

DRILL: REFLECT ON HOW YOU COULD USE EXAMPLES TO ADDRESS THE FOLLOWING TOPICS

As you read each of the topics listed below, make a list of five examples you could use to support them. Are your examples all relevant? Do they support just this side of the argument? Treat each as the basis for your thesis statement in a practice free-response question.

TOPIC 1:   High schools unwittingly encourage students to cheat.

TOPIC 2:   Studying the humanities is important.

TOPIC 3:   Respecting diversity reveals much about a person.

CLASSIFICATION

How do you classify things? Well, you probably start by dividing up whatever you have into groups according to certain characteristics. For example, if you wanted to explain "new music" to someone, you might divide the artists into groups by type (female vocalists, male vocalists, and bands) and classify the groups by genre (heavy metal, punk rock, alternative, and so on.). This would make the material easier for someone to understand because it would be organized. In other words: *We classify to more easily analyze and explain.*

There is almost always more than one way to classify things. Right now, you may group your teachers as being either cool or uncool. Later, it's more likely that you'll classify them according to what they helped you learn: The new categories may be teachers who inspired you, teachers who taught you the most, teachers who taught you about life, and teachers who should not have been teachers.

When you place things into categories on the AP English Language and Composition exam, avoid creating classifications that overlap. For example, it would not make sense to classify your favorite foods in the following way: sweets, barbequed meats, vegetables, and chocolates; logically, the last group is a smaller subset of the first group.

All of this boils down to the following: Classification is nearly the same thing as organization. And organization is important. As you know by now, the directions in the Free-Response section of the AP English Language and Composition exam request that you write "a well-organized essay." It may seem obvious that the test writers would request this of you—but then you'd be surprised how poorly organized many of the AP essays that students write are. Classify before you write.

Aristotle liked to classify, and he did so quite often. Some of classifications have stood the test of time, including the one you see below, which is the beginning of Part 6 of an essay entitled "Categories."

> Quantity is either discrete or continuous (…). Instances of discrete quantities are number and speech; instances of continuous quantities are lines, surfaces, solids, and, besides these, time and place.
>
> *Line*
>
> 5   In the case of the parts of a number, there is no common boundary at which they join. For example: two fives make ten, but the two fives have no common boundary,

but are separate; the parts three and seven also do not
join at any boundary. Nor, to generalize, would it ever
10 be possible in the case of number that there should be
a common boundary among the parts; they are always
separate. Number, therefore, is a discrete quantity.

The same is true of speech. That speech is a quantity
is evident: for it is measured in long and short syllables.
15 I mean here that speech which is vocal. Moreover, it is a
discrete quantity for its parts have no common boundary. There is no common boundary at which the syllables
join, but each is separate and distinct from the rest.

A line, on the other hand, is a continuous quantity, for
20 it is possible to find a common boundary at which its
parts join. In the case of the line, this common boundary
is the point; in the case of the plane, it is the line, for the
parts of the plane have also a common boundary. Similarly you can find a common boundary in the case of the
25 parts of a solid, namely either a line or a plane.

Space and time also belong to this class of quantities. Time, past, present, and future, forms a continuous
whole. Space, likewise, is a continuous quantity; for the
parts of a solid occupy a certain space, and these have a
30 common boundary; it follows that the parts of space also,
which are occupied by the parts of the solid, have the
same common boundary as the parts of the solid. Thus,
not only time, but space also, is a continuous quantity,
for its parts have a common boundary.

Here, Aristotle's division of quantity into two categories (discrete and continuous) makes sense.
The examples that he uses to illustrate the nature of his categories reveal a great deal about his interests: time, space, language, and mathematics. This is a well-organized passage; the categories are
well-defined and Aristotle has clearly explained why the members of each category have been put
in their categories.

Laundry List for Classification

- Remember that when you're asked to analyze and explain something, classification
  will be very useful.

- Make sure you have a central idea (thesis).

- Sort your information into meaningful groups. Are there enough elements in each
  group to allow you to write a convincing, useful paragraph? Sometimes you'll find
  that you need to combine categories.

- Make sure you have a manageable number of categories—three or four. Remember
  that you have only about 40 minutes to plan and execute each essay.

- Make sure the categories (or the elements in the categories) do not overlap.

- Before writing, make sure the categories and central idea (thesis) are a good fit.
  Sometimes you'll want to modify your thesis statement based on the categories that
  you've found.

- As you write, do not justify your classification unless this is somehow necessary to address a very bizarre free-response question. Justify your thesis, not your categories.

SAMPLE QUESTION

Write a short essay in which you analyze the different methods a teacher uses to convey information to his or her class.

DRILL: REFLECT ON HOW YOU COULD USE CLASSIFICATION TO ADDRESS THE FOLLOWING TOPICS

As you read each of the topics, think about how you would organize your essay in terms of classification. Come up with a possible thesis (central idea), and plan how you could categorize the information you have on these topics into three or four meaningful divisions.

TOPIC 1: Television commercials

TOPIC 2: Movies

TOPIC 3: Students

TOPIC 4: Cars

COMPARISON AND CONTRAST

You compare and contrast every day. When you note similarities between objects, people, characteristics, and even actions, you're making comparisons. When you note the differences, you're using a rhetorical mode called contrast.

It is very likely that you will have to use comparison and contrast when writing at least one of your essays for the Free-Response section of the AP test. Sometimes you'll use this mode merely *to explain*—especially when you're comparing something unfamiliar with something well known; other times, you will use comparison and contrast *to argue* in favor of one of the two elements.

Keep in mind that to compare and contrast two elements, they need to have enough commonalities to justify comparison or contrast. It may be interesting to compare and contrast a baseball team from the National League and another from the American League, but it would be less pertinent (although potentially very entertaining) to compare and contrast one of those baseball teams with your neighbor's poker club.

To write a successful compare-and-contrast essay for the AP English Language and Composition exam, you must first select the points of comparison (and contrast) and present them. Does this sound familiar? In other words, you must start by *classifying* them.

The most common mistake people make when comparing and contrasting is to present a discussion of one of the elements first (in one paragraph), and then discuss the other element afterward (in a second paragraph). Do not do this. Instead, we'll show you an example of a good method for comparing and contrasting:

Comparison and contrast of my favorite classes	
AP English	**AP Art History**
Involves essay writing, which I love Teacher writes intriguing questions Most writing done in class	Involves essay writing Teacher writes intriguing questions Most writing done out of class
Interesting reading A variety of books No pictures in books	Interesting reading A textbook Lots of pictures in book
Teacher is old Teacher tells bad jokes Teacher is grumpy	Teacher is young Teacher is funny Teacher is good-natured

Ideally, when you turned this into an essay you would not write the first half of your essay about AP English, and the second half about AP Art History. Using the information you collected in the outline above, ideally you would spend your first paragraph discussing the role of writing in both classes, spend your second paragraph discussing aspects of the reading in the two classes, and spend your third paragraph discussing the teachers. Integration is key in comparison and contrast.

Here is a real example, taken from Charles Darwin's *The Descent of Man*, of a passage that uses comparison and contrast.

My object in this chapter is to show that there is no fundamental difference between man and the higher mammals in their mental faculties. Each division of the
Line subject might have been extended into a separate essay
5 but must here be treated briefly. As no classification of the mental powers has been universally accepted, I shall arrange my remarks in the order most convenient for my purpose; and will select those facts which have struck me most, with the hope that they may produce some effect
10 on the reader (…).

As man possesses the same senses as the lower animals, his fundamental intuitions must be the same. Man has also some few instincts in common, as that of self-preservation, sexual love, the love of the mother for
15 her new-born offspring, the desire possessed by the latter to suck, and so forth. But man, perhaps, has somewhat fewer instincts than those possessed by the animals which come next to him in the series. The orangutan in the Eastern islands and the chimpanzee in Africa, build
20 platforms on which they sleep; and, as both species follow the same habit, it might be argued that this was due to instinct, but we cannot feel sure that it is not the result of both animals having similar wants, and possessing similar powers of reasoning (…).

25 The lower animals, like man, manifestly feel pleasure and pain, happiness and misery. Happiness is never better exhibited than by young animals, such as puppies, kittens, lambs, etc., when playing together, like our own children. Even insects play together, as has
30 been described by that excellent observer, P. Huber, who saw ants chasing and pretending to bite each other, like

so many puppies. The fact that the lower animals are excited by the same emotions as ourselves is so well established, that it will not be necessary to weary the
35 reader by many details. Terror acts in the same manner on them as on us, causing the muscles to tremble, the heart to palpitate, the sphincters to be relaxed, and the hair to stand on end. Suspicion, the offspring of fear, is eminently characteristic of most wild animals (…).

Interestingly, Darwin extends this rhetorical mode of comparison and contrast over entire chapters of his famous work. Notice the rhetorical statements of comparison he uses (for example, "the lower animals, like man" or "like our own children"); Darwin does not leave it up to us to draw comparisons—he points out virtually all of them with examples. Speaking of examples (the first rhetorical mode that we discussed), notice that in the case of this passage, the two rhetorical modes of examples and comparison/contrast are used together.

Laundry List for Comparison and Contrast

- When comparing and contrasting A and B, find common elements (which will become your examples) from both.

- Do not write about A in one paragraph and B in another.

- Do your best to combine common elements into a limited number of groups—three, if possible—and write a paragraph about each group.

- Do not attempt to justify your groups or your examples; simply present them.

Sample Question

Write an essay in which you compare and contrast the careers and lifestyles of professional musicians and doctors. Be sure to include examples.

Drill: Reflect on How You Could Use Comparison and Contrast to Address the Following Topics

For each topic, make a list like the one above (AP English versus. AP art history). First, write down several similarities and differences. Then organize these similarities and differences in a logical manner; try to sort them out so that you have about three or four central ideas, which would translate into about three or four separate compare and contrast paragraphs. Do not attempt to answer the question by addressing one choice and then the other in separate paragraphs.

TOPIC 1: Two of your friends

TOPIC 2: Two teachers at your school

TOPIC 3: Two singers or bands

TOPIC 4: New York and Los Angeles (even if you haven't been to either)

TOPIC 5: The experience of traveling to the mountains and the experience of traveling to the ocean

ANALOGY

Although analogies are not that useful in argumentative writing, they *are* useful in expository writing—this means that analogies will be useful when you write your expository essay for this test.

Think of an **analogy** as a comparison used to explain something.

Analogies are sometimes used to explain things that are difficult to understand by comparing them with things that are easier to understand. Let's say that you want to explain how a well-run corporation works. You might explain that it functions like a football team. In both cases there are owners or stockholders. In the corporation, there's a CEO, who is similar to the coach of a football team. The CEO directs the managers (or vice presidents), just as the coach directs the assistant coaches; these work directly with the employees—the players. When an employee doesn't heed directions, the success of the enterprise is put at risk, just like when a player fails to execute a block or a tackle. The most important thing about using analogies is that you choose one that will be readily understood by your audience. In this case, if the reader knows nothing about football, this analogy may do more harm than good.

You can also use an analogy to explain something that's abstract by comparing it with something that's concrete. Throughout history, people have used analogies to explain their god or gods. Christians explain their god, for example, through analogy. They say that their god is like a father who loves his children and, thus, both punishes and rewards them. The only difference is that they consider their god's judgment to be perfect. They believe that their god is like a father in that both are good, but that the difference is that their god is *perfectly* good.

The most famous philosophical analogy serves as the basis for Plato's "allegory of the cave." The analogy purportedly evolves from a conversation between Socrates and Glaucon.

Imagine human beings living in an underground cave;
here they have been from their childhood, and they
have their legs and necks chained so that they cannot
Line move and can only see before them, being prevented by
5 the chains from turning round their heads. Above and
behind them, a fire is blazing at a distance, and between
the fire and the prisoners there is a raised way; and there
is a low wall built along the way, like the screen which
marionette players have to hide them and over which
10 they show the puppets.

Men are passing along the wall (and screened by the
wall) and are carrying all sorts of things and animals
made of wood and stone and various materials that appear over the wall. Some of them are talking, others are
15 silent.

Like ourselves, they see only their own shadows, or
the shadows of one another, or the shadows of the things
and animals, which the fire throws on the opposite wall
of the cave.

20 And if the human beings were able to converse with
one another, would they not suppose that they were
naming what was actually before them (even though
they were seeing only shadows of those things)?

And suppose further that the prison had an echo
25 which came from the other side, would they not be sure
to fancy when one of the passers-by spoke that the voice
which they heard came from the passing shadow?

To them, I said, the truth would be literally nothing but
the shadows of the images.

This is only part of the analogy, but you probably get the idea. Socrates uses this analogy to explain that we think that we see things just as they really are in our world, but that we are seeing only reflections of a greater truth, an abstraction that we fail to grasp. The cave is our world; the shadows are the objects and people that we "see." We are like the prisoners, for we are not free to see what creates the shadows; the truth, made up of ideal forms, is out in the light.

LAUNDRY LIST FOR ANALOGY

Use analogy for expository writing (explanation).

- Do not use analogy for argumentative writing (argumentation).
- Use analogy to explain something difficult to understand or that is abstract.
- Make sure your audience will readily understand your "simple" or concrete subject.

SAMPLE QUESTION

Write an essay in which you explain the process of applying to college. Use analogy when appropriate.

DRILL: REFLECT ON HOW YOU COULD USE ANALOGY TO ADDRESS THE FOLLOWING TOPICS

As you read each topic, think of it as the basis for the thesis of an expository essay. Come up with a simpler subject that you can use as an analogy for this more complex topic. Write down a basic plan for an essay.

TOPIC 1: The way your school functions

TOPIC 2: The benefits of honesty

MOVING ON...

In this chapter we discussed three rhetorical modes: example, classification, and comparison and contrast (analogy falls under this last category). Make sure you are familiar with the laundry lists in this chapter. If you get into good habits now when using these rhetorical modes, you'll be much better off on test day!

Further proving how useful these modes will be, we guarantee that both your expository and argumentative essay questions will fit into some combination of these modes.

Of course, remember to plan your essay before you begin writing. It often helps to write your thesis statement along with this plan so that you can keep in mind whether the parts of your plan are relevant to your central idea. This will ensure that you write the best organized, most coherent essay you can.

Now that we've covered the three basic rhetorical modes, let's move on to review a few complex modes.

11

Rhetorical Modes and Patterns of Exposition — Complex Modes

In this chapter, we'll discuss a few more—and more complex—rhetorical modes, including process analysis, cause-and-effect, definition, description, narration, and induction and deduction. As was the case with the rhetorical modes you learned about in the last chapter, it will be extremely beneficial to you to know all you can about these modes on test day. It will not only help you recognize when these modes are used in the sample passages, but also enable you to use them in your essays.

So let's jump right in.

PROCESS ANALYSIS

Process analysis is a rhetorical mode that's used by writers when they want to explain either how to do something or how something was done. When your science teacher hands you instructions for a lab, she is giving you a rather dry sheet of process analysis that says, "first do this; then do that; then examine the data; then explain such-and-such." When you write your lab report, you're also indulging in process analysis, saying, "first we did this; then we did that; then we examined the data; then we determined such-and-such." If you like to follow recipes when you cook, then you've already been exposed to process analysis. However, process analyses used in writing generally aren't as dry as recipes or how-to manuals; they usually have a few examples to spice them up a little.

Process analysis can be an effective way of relating an experience. Take, for example, this now famous passage about "Dumpster diving."

Line
5

10

15

20

25

I learned to scavenge gradually, on my own. Since then I have initiated several companions into the trade. I have learned that there is a predictable series of stages a person goes through in learning to scavenge.

At first the new scavenger is filled with disgust and self-loathing. He is ashamed of being seen and may lurk around, trying to duck behind things, or he may try to dive at night. (In fact, most people instinctively look away from a scavenger. By skulking around, the novice calls attention to himself and arouses suspicion. Diving at night is ineffective and needlessly messy.)

Every grain of rice seems to be a maggot. Everything seems to stink. He can wipe the egg yolk off the found can, but he cannot erase the stigma of eating garbage out of his mind.

That stage passes with experience. The scavenger finds a pair of running shoes that fit and look and smell brand new. He finds a pocket calculator in perfect working order. He finds pristine ice cream, still frozen, more than he can eat or keep. He begins to understand: people do throw away perfectly good stuff, a lot of perfectly good stuff.

At this stage, Dumpster shyness begins to dissipate. The diver, after all, has the last laugh. He is finding all manner of good things which are his for the taking. Those who disparage his profession are the fools, not he.

He may begin to hang onto some perfectly good things for which he has neither a use nor a market. Then he

begins to take note of the things which are not perfectly
30 good but are nearly so. He mates a Walkman with broken earphones and one that is missing a battery cover.
He picks up things which he can repair.

At this stage he may become lost and never recover.
Dumpsters are full of things of some potential value
35 to someone and also of things which never have much
intrinsic value but are interesting. All the Dumpster div-
ers I have known come to the point of trying to acquire
everything they touch. Why not take it, they reason,
since it is all free.

From ON DUMPSTER DIVING (THE THREEPENNY
REVIEW) by Lars Eighner

Here's a good example of process analysis in writing. Although the material is organized in chronological stages, the author inserts explanatory examples and personal commentary that make the passage more lively. In this passage, the author is not instructing the reader on how to scavenge for food
in Dumpsters; rather, he is explaining the psychological evolution of a homeless scavenger—based
on his own experience—and illustrating the excesses of a consumerist society.

Remember that process analysis is a rhetorical mode that serves to organize something in a step-
by-step manner, and it can serve both scientific and literary needs.

LAUNDRY LIST FOR PROCESS ANALYSIS

- Sequence is chronological and usually fixed; think of recipes.

- When you use this device, make sure the stages of the process are clear, by using
  transitions (e.g., *first, next, after two days, finally*).

- Make sure your terminology is appropriate for the reader. For example, the person
  who will read your essays probably does not know much about the embryonic
  development of frogs, so you should avoid using too-specialized terms like *Spemann
  organizer* or *Nieuwkoop center.*

- Verify that every step is clear; an error or omission in an intermediate step may
  make the rest of the process analysis very confusing. If you were describing how to
  braid hair, and wrote the following instructions: "First, comb or brush your hair so
  that it is untangled and manageable to work with. Next, take the far-right section of
  hair and put it over the middle section and under the far-left section."—this could
  be confusing to your reader because you never said to divide the hair into three sections before starting the actual braiding process.

SAMPLE QUESTION

Write a short essay in which you describe the process of how you selected the colleges to which you
applied (or are going to apply to).

DRILL: REFLECT ON HOW YOU COULD USE PROCESS ANALYSIS TO ADDRESS THE FOLLOWING TOPICS

Try making a numbered list with a few examples. Make sure you have included all the necessary steps and have used appropriate language and terminology for your reader. Remember to use transition words when you write the essay.

TOPIC 1:   How decisions are made at your school.

TOPIC 2:   How to get through your high school successfully.

TOPIC 3:   How to choose and keep close friends.

CAUSE AND EFFECT

You just saw how process analysis is a useful rhetorical mode for explaining how to do things or how things were done; the rhetorical mode known as **cause-and-effect** explains *why things should be* or *should have been done*. In a sense, cause-and-effect explains the processes responsible for the process. You've probably received at least some rudimentary process analysis about how to use a computer at some point (first, turn on the computer; then launch your browser; log on to your IM; select someone else who is logged in….), but you probably don't know *why* all that works.

Some cause-and-effect relationships are easy to describe. For instance, read the example below from *Candide*'s Dr. Pangloss.

> "It is demonstrable," said Pangloss, "that things cannot
> be otherwise than as they are; for as all things have been
> created for some end, they must necessarily be created
> for the best end. Observe, for instance, the nose is formed
> for spectacles; therefore we wear spectacles. The legs
> are visibly designed for stockings; accordingly we wear
> stockings. Stones were made to be hewn and to construct
> castles; therefore My Lord has a magnificent castle, for
> the greatest baron in the province ought to be the best
> lodged. Swine were intended to be eaten; therefore we
> eat pork all the year round."

In this passage, Pangloss is using a series of cause-and-effect relationships to prove his point, that "things cannot be otherwise than as they are." This rhetorical mode is everywhere, however. You see examples of this rhetorical mode all around you.

For example, if you were writing about the poor average AP English Language and Composition test scores at your school, you could go about it in two ways. On the one hand, you could examine some *immediate* causes: Ms. What's-Her-Name retired and was replaced by a teacher who had no experience teaching and no background in English, we didn't have a good review book for the exam, or the exam is administered in Room Z during school band practice. On the other hand, you could also examine some *underlying* causes for the poor exam scores: The superintendent of schools changed hiring policies (so a terrible teacher was hired); last year, funds for buying books were diverted to buying new lockers for the football team (so we had no good review book); and the room that the school band normally practices in was flooded when a pipe broke.

On this exam, the causes and effects that you choose to explore will depend on what you're asked to explain. You may have to use cause-and-effect in your essays and possibly in combination with one or more other rhetorical modes; you may also see a few questions in the Multiple-Choice section that deal with how the author uses cause-and-effect to make a point. When making critical decisions, writers will often consider both the immediate and the long-term effects; when analyzing an important event, writers will often examine both the immediate and the underlying causes.

LAUNDRY LIST FOR CAUSE-AND-EFFECT

- Do not confuse the relating of mere circumstances with a cause-and-effect relationship. For example, it is not logical to assume that socialism in Chile necessarily caused socialism in Argentina.

- Turn your causal relationships into causes-and-effects by using carefully chosen examples. Remember that not all causal relationships are causes-and-effects. However, careful use of evidence and examples can turn causal relationships into causes-and-effects.

- Make sure to carefully address each step in a series of causal relationships; if you don't, you risk losing your reader. Imagine the attendance secretary when she hears, "I'm sorry I'm late. We had a fire, so I had to find my cat." A better (clearer) explanation would have been: "I'm sorry I'm late. This morning at 4:00 A.M. there was an electrical fire in the garage; fortunately, there was an alarm that woke my dad, who put out the fire, but when he opened the garage door, my cat ran outside. I think it was frightened so it ran up a tree. I decided to climb up the tree and get the cat but I fell, and my mother had to take me to the emergency room."

SAMPLE QUESTION

Write an essay in which you examine the possible causes and effects of violence in the United States today.

DRILL: REFLECT ON HOW YOU COULD USE CAUSE-AND-EFFECT TO ADDRESS THE FOLLOWING TOPICS

TOPIC 1: Academic dishonesty in high schools

TOPIC 2: The fear of terrorism in the United States

TOPIC 3: The changing face of ethnic America

DEFINITION

You are probably familiar with definitions; you see them every time you look up a word in the dictionary. Hopefully when you write, you try to make sure your reader understands the words that you use.

When writing your essays for the AP English Language and Composition exam, if you happen to leave a key term unexplained or explained vaguely, even a carefully crafted essay will fall apart. This is especially true of very specialized terminology and obscure words. For example, if you are explaining a wonderful new tradition at your school and define it by synonym, you may write, "Basically, it's a Mexican *feis*." If your readers are Irish, this would be all right; if your readers were from just about anywhere else, you would need to define *feis* by putting it in a **category** (defining it in terms everyone will understand): "a *feis* is a competition for Irish dance, song, and instrumental music." Then, you could explain your project: "We want to do the same thing with traditional Mexican dance, song, and music."

For the AP exam, we have to consider *definition* in its meaning as a rhetorical mode. In this case, a paragraph—or an entire essay—is devoted to the definition of a term. Here, for example, is a paragraph that defines *feis* (pronounced "fesh").

> A *feis* is a day of competition in Irish dancing, music, and song. Perhaps you were wondering where all the Irish dancers from *Lord of the Dance* came from. All first performed at a *feis* and honed their skills through competitions at various levels. A *feis* is a living legacy of Irish culture; it is where beginners, trying to remember their left from right, unknowingly dance the ancient steps of Ireland and pass this legacy on to the next generation. On the more practical side, a *feis* is to Irish performers what a soccer game is to athletes the world over. Competitions are organized by ability (Beginner, Advanced Beginner, Novice, Open, Preliminary Championships, and Championships) and by age (Under 6, Under 7, etc). At a typical *feis*, there might be as many as 2,500 dancers.

The passage begins with a straightforward definition, but the definition is extended and rhetorical modes are mixed. You noted, I'm sure, the *analogy* to a soccer game; then, there is an inchoate (imperfectly formed) stab at *classification* (the divisions in the competition). You could even argue that the mention of *Lord of the Dance* serves as a kind of *example*. The rhetorical mode of *definition* can be used simply to explain a word or concept, but typically the author using it also wants to interest the reader in what's being explained.

Let's take a look at another good example of definition.

> The *Palio* is a horse race that's held twice each year in Siena, Italy: on July 2nd in honor of the Madonna of Provenzano, and on August 16th in honor of the Assumption of the Virgin. But saying that the Palio is just another horse race would be like calling the Superbowl just another football game. The Palio is not just a race. It is blood, sweat, and tears; it is part competition and part festival. According to some, it is the world's craziest horse race; according to others, it is Italy's most honored tradition. One thing is clear to everyone, however: the Palio represents the tradition, culture, and soul of Siena. The actual race lasts only about a minute, but those moments represent an entire year's worth of anticipation and preparation.

Again, the passage begins with a simple definition; but here, too, we have an example of another rhetorical mode—analogy (to the Superbowl).

However, the author of this passage uses an important additional tactic, known as *definition by negation*. You should be aware of this rhetorical device and use it where appropriate. In the passage above, the negation is partial—the Palio is, indeed, a race, but it is not "just a race." Most negations work in that manner; definition by negation is usually used to impress upon the reader the importance of the item under discussion or create a distinction between the item under discussion and the item with which it is being "negatively" compared. For instance, you may write, "Shakira is not a pop singer; she's a phenomenon, a true diva, a multitalented musical ambassador of Colombia." Perhaps this statement is true, but she's still a pop singer.

You may be able to use definition as a mode in your free-response essays, but most likely, you will see definition used in the passages in the Multiple-Choice sections. For example, you may be asked to answer a question that deals with how an author uses definition to analyze a topic.

LAUNDRY LIST FOR DEFINITION

- Keep your reason for defining something in mind as you're writing.
- Define key terms according to what you know of your audience, in other words, the readers of the essays; you don't want to bore your reader by defining terms unnecessarily, nor do you want to perplex your reader by failing to define terms that may be obscure to your audience. Keep in mind that for you, your readers are the AP English Language and Composition exam graders.
- Explain the background (history) when it is relevant to your definition.
- Define by negation when appropriate.
- Combine definition with any number of other rhetorical modes when applicable.

SAMPLE QUESTION

Write an essay in which you use definition to analyze the role of integrity in your life.

DRILL: REFLECT ON HOW YOU COULD USE DEFINITION TO ADDRESS THE FOLLOWING TOPICS

First define each word by category; then, define each word by negation.

WORD 1: Hip-hop

WORD 2: Success

WORD 3: Love

WORD 4: Cool

DESCRIPTION

Description can help make expository or argumentative writing lively and interesting and hold the reader's interest, which is vital, of course. Think of how many essays those test graders have to read every day; as we mentioned in the techniques chapters, a large part of scoring well on the Free-Response section is keeping your audience interested.

Oftentimes description serves as the primary rhetorical mode for an entire essay—or even an entire book. It's typically used to communicate a scene, a specific place, or a person to the reader. Although writers tend to concentrate most on the visual aspects of descriptions, descriptions can be used to appeal to any of the reader's senses.

It is important to keep in mind that sometimes description can be objective; in these cases, the author is not describing something in a sentimental or otherwise subjective way—he or she is merely stating the facts. As an example of this, take a look at Charles Darwin's depiction of Valparaiso, the chief seaport in Chile, in *Voyage of the Beagle*.

> The town is built at the very foot of a range of hills, about 1,600 feet high, and rather steep. From its position, it consists of one long, straggling street, which runs parallel to the beach, and wherever a ravine comes down, the houses are piled up on each side of it. The rounded hills, being only partially protected by very scanty vegetation, are worn into numberless little gullies, which expose a singularly bright red soil. From this cause, and from the low whitewashed houses with tile roofs, the view reminded me of St. Cruz in Tenerife. In a northwesterly direction there are some fine glimpses of the Andes, but these mountains appear much grander when viewed from the neighboring hills: the great distance at which they are situated can then more readily be perceived.

This type of objective description tends to be dryer than more subjective description. The degree of objectivity exhibited above probably doesn't thrill you—nor will it thrill the AP readers.

Fortunately, unlike most other rhetorical modes, description allows for a significant degree of subjectivity. In most descriptions, the writer attempts to communicate personal impressions of something or someone, and to do so it is necessary to draw on the powers of figurative writing; simile, metaphor, and personification are the most common.

Here is another description of a city: Nathaniel Hawthorne's impressions of Florence. The description comes not from one of Hawthorne's novels, but from one of the notebooks that he kept during his travels in Europe.

> By and by, we had a distant glimpse of Florence, showing its great dome and some of its towers out of a side-long valley, as if we were between two great waves of the tumultuous sea of hills, while, far beyond, rose in the distance the blue peaks of three or four of the Apennines, just on the remote horizon. There being a haziness in the atmosphere, however, Florence was little more distinct to us than the Celestial City was to Christian and Hopeful, when they spied at it from the Delectable Mountains.
>
> Florence at first struck me as having the aspect of a very new city in comparison with Rome; but, on closer acquaintance, I find that many of the buildings are antique and massive, though still the clear atmosphere, the bright sunshine, the light, cheerful hues of the stucco, and—as much as anything else, perhaps—the vivacious character of the human life in the streets, take away the sense of its being an ancient city.
>
> As we returned home over the Arno River, crossing the Ponte di Santa Trinitá, we were struck by the beautiful scene of the broad, calm river, with the palaces along its shores repeated in it, on either side, and the neighboring bridges, too, just as perfect in the tide beneath as in the air above—a city of dream and shadow so close to the actual one. God has a meaning, no doubt, in putting this spiritual symbol continually beside us.

Along the river, on both sides, as far as we could see, there was a row of brilliant lamps, which, in the far distance, looked like a cornice of golden light; and this also shone as brightly in the river's depths. The lilies of the evening, in the quarter where the sun had gone down, were very soft and beautiful, though not so gorgeous as thousands that I have seen in America. But I believe I must fairly confess that the Italian sky, in the daytime, is bluer and brighter than our own, and that the atmosphere has a quality of showing objects to better advantage. It is more than mere daylight; the magic of moonlight is somehow mixed up with it, although it is so transparent a medium of light.

This is a much more personal vision of a city. Hawthorne uses one simile to give us a better visual image of the countryside around Florence ("as if we were between two great waves of the tumultuous sea of hills"), and another to communicate the effect of the gas lamps ("like a cornice of golden light"); and he employs a metaphor ("a city of dream and shadow") to evoke his impression of the reflections in the river. In fact, virtually all of the description serves to communicate or explain *Hawthorne's* impressions of the city; here, the writer wishes to evoke and is not interested in scientific exactitude.

Keep in mind that this rhetorical device allows you a certain amount of freedom of language, but it also allows you certain liberties in organization. In Hawthorne's passage, for example, the author put down in writing his impressions in whatever order they came to him. In more objectively written descriptions, however, it often makes sense to think *spatially* when writing a visual description. You might describe a scene from left to right or front to back, for example; you might start a description of a person with the head (and end with the feet).

In the following passage, Fyodor Dostoyevsky gives us both a spatial description and a barrage of sensory impressions.

In the first place, on entering this house, one passes into a very bare hall, and thence along a passage to a mean staircase. The reception room, however, is bright, clean, and spacious, and is lined with redwood and metalwork. But the scullery you would not care to see; it is greasy, dirty, and odoriferous, while the stairs are in rags, and the walls so covered with filth that the hand sticks fast wherever it touches them. Also, on each landing there is a medley of boxes, chairs, and dilapidated wardrobes; while the windows have had most of their panes shattered, and everywhere stand washtubs filled with dirt, litter, eggshells, and fish bladders. The smell is abominable. In short, the house is not a nice one.

As to the disposition of the rooms, I have described it to you already. True, they are convenient enough, yet every one of them has an atmosphere. I do not mean that they smell badly so much as that each of them seems to contain something which gives forth a rank, sickly-sweet odor. At first the impression is an unpleasant one, but a couple of minutes will suffice to dissipate it, for the reason that everything here smells—people's clothes, hands, and everything else—and one grows accustomed to the rankness. Canaries, however, soon die in this house. A naval officer here has just bought his fifth. Birds cannot live long in such an air. Every morning, when fish or beef is being cooked, and washing and scrubbing are in progress, the house is filled with steam. Always, too, the kitchen is full of linen hanging out to dry; and since my room adjoins that apartment, the smell from the clothes causes me not a little annoyance. However, one can grow used to anything.

Note that Dostoyevsky's description first takes us through the ground floor and leads us up the staircase. Unlike the previous passages, this one appeals to our tactile ("so covered with filth that the hand sticks") and, even more prominently, olfactory senses. Choice of detail is important, and the choice of fish bladders, for example, conveys wonderfully the disgusting sights and smell. This is great writing—not only is the description effective, but it's also humorous, thanks to the short comment at the end of each paragraph.

LAUNDRY LIST FOR DESCRIPTION

- When possible, call on all five senses (visual, auditory, olfactory (smell), gustatory (taste), and tactile)

- Place the most striking examples at the beginnings and ends of your paragraphs (or essay) for maximum effect.

- Show, don't tell.

- Use concrete nouns and adjectives; nouns, not adjectives, should dominate.

- Concentrate on details that will convey the sense you're trying to get across most effectively. (Remember the fish bladders!)

- Employ figures of speech, especially similes, metaphors, and personification, when appropriate.

- When describing people, try to focus on distinctive mannerisms; if possible, you should go beyond physical appearance.

- Direct discourse (using dialogue or quotations) can be revealing and useful.

- A brief illustrative anecdote is worth a thousand words. Instead of simply using a general statement ("My friend Kai is a very generous person"), use an example ("My friend Kai is known for his generosity; the whole school knows about the time that he spent an entire weekend helping elderly women get home with their heavy groceries").

- To the extent possible, use action verbs. You could write, "The delightful aroma of chocolate chip cookies baking in the oven *crept around the corner and filled the den* with its sweetness" instead of just "The baking chocolate chip cookies *smelled* sweet."

SAMPLE QUESTION

Write an essay in which you describe your local shopping mall. Remember that you are not limited to physical descriptions.

DRILL: REFLECT ON HOW YOU COULD USE DESCRIPTION TO ADDRESS THE FOLLOWING TOPICS

First decide the general feeling you'd like to convey, and second begin to list some specifics; don't forget examples or anecdotes. When describing people, go beyond just the physical.

TOPIC 1:   A party

TOPIC 2:   Your parents

TOPIC 3:   A shopping mall

TOPIC 4:   A natural disaster (seen from personal experience or on television)

TOPIC 5:   Your favorite place to relax

TOPIC 6:   The campus of your school

NARRATION

A narrative is a story, in which pieces of information are arranged in chronological order. You probably know that, but what you may not know is that narration can be an effective expository technique.

Decades after her experience in a Japanese internment camp, Jeanne Wakatsuki Houston decided to narrate her experiences before, during, and immediately after imprisonment. She did not want to tell the story just for the story's sake; she wanted to relay her experience to the public to exorcize personal demons and to raise public awareness about this period in history. Here is a passage from this *personal narrative*. The passage describes the period after the Wakatsuki family had lost their house in Ocean Park, California, when they were forced into detention.

> My own family, after three years of mess hall living, collapsed as an integrated unit. Whatever dignity or feeling of filial strength we may have known before December 1941 was lost, and we did not recover it until many years after the war, not until after Papa died and we began to come together, trying to fill the vacuum his passing left in all our lives.
>
> The closing of the camps, in the fall of 1945, only aggravated what had begun inside. Papa had no money then and could not get work. Half of our family had already moved to the East Coast, where jobs had opened up for them. The rest of us were relocated into a former defense workers' housing project in Long Beach. In that small apartment there never was enough room for all of us to sit down for a meal. We ate in shifts, and I yearned all the more for our huge round table in Ocean Park.
>
> Soon after we were released I wrote a paper for a seventh-grade journalism class, describing how we used to hunt grunion before the war. The whole family would go down to Ocean Park Beach after dark, when the grunion were running, and build a big fire on the sand. I would watch Papa and my older brothers splash through the moonlit surf to scoop out the fish, then we'd rush back to the house where Mama would fry them up and set the sizzling pan on the table, with soy sauce and

horseradish, for a midnight meal. I ended the paper with
this sentence: "The reason I want to remember this is
because I know we'll never be able to do it again."

You may be asked to use personal narrative when writing your essays on the AP English Language and Composition test; and you will certainly be asked to *analyze* narratives that employ this rhetorical mode.

Additionally, sometimes you'll see questions on the essay section of the AP exam that will ask you to relate someone else's experience to illustrate a point. In essence, you'll be asked to write a narrative in the third person, but choose wisely. For example, if you're asked to "relate an experience where someone you know (directly or indirectly) overcame incredible obstacles to reach a goal," you wouldn't want to narrate the story of your cat, who managed to catch an elusive mouse.

In the following passage, Booker T. Washington uses narrative to explain how his view on education developed. Watch for changes between the first- and third-person style of narration.

When a mere boy, I saw a young colored man, who had spent several years in school, sitting in a common cabin in the South, studying a French grammar. I noted the poverty, the untidiness, the want of system, and thrift that existed about the cabin, notwithstanding his knowledge of French and other academic subjects. Another time, when riding on the outer edges of a town in the South, I heard the sound of a piano coming from a cabin of the same kind. Contriving some excuse, I entered and began a conversation with the young colored woman who was playing, and who had recently returned from a boarding-school, where she had been studying instrumental music among other things. Despite the fact that her parents were living in a rented cabin, eating poorly cooked food, surrounded with poverty, and having almost none of the conveniences of life, she had persuaded them to rent a piano for four or five dollars per month. Many such instances as these, in connection with my own struggles, impressed upon me the importance of making a study of our needs as a race, and applying the remedy accordingly.

Some one may be tempted to ask, Has not the negro boy or girl as good a right to study a French grammar and instrumental music as the white youth? I answer, Yes, but in the present condition of the negro race in this country there is need of something more. Perhaps I may be forgiven for the seeming egotism if I mention the expansion of my own life partly as an example of what I mean. My earliest recollection is of a small one-room log hut on a large slave plantation in Virginia. After the close of the war, while working in the coal-mines of West Virginia for the support of my mother, I heard in some accidental way of the Hampton Institute.

When I learned that it was an institution where a black boy could study, could have a chance to work for his board, and at the same time be taught how to work and to realize the dignity of labor, I resolved to go there. Bidding my mother good-by, I started out one morning to find my way to Hampton, though I was almost penniless and had no definite idea where Hampton was. By walking, begging rides, and paying for a portion of the journey on the steam-cars, I finally succeeded in reaching the city of Richmond, Virginia. I was without money or friends. I slept under a sidewalk, and by working on a vessel next day I earned money to continue my way to the institute, where I arrived with a surplus of fifty cents. At Hampton I found the opportunity—in the way of buildings, teachers, and industries provided by the generous—to get training in the class-room and by practical touch with industrial life, to learn thrift, economy, and push. I was surrounded by an atmosphere of business, Christian influence, and a spirit of self-help that seemed to have awakened every faculty in me, and caused me for the first time to realize what it meant to be a man instead of a piece of property.

While there I resolved that when I had finished the course of training I would go into the far South, into the Black Belt of the South, and give my life to providing the same kind of opportunity for self-reliance and self-awakening that I had found provided for me at Hampton.

Notice that in the first paragraph, the narration slips briefly into the third person—Washington is telling the story of the girl, not his own. Likewise, Washington presents the story of the boy studying French from his point of view. In these two instances, Washington switches from first to third person with ease, so that the transition is optimally effective and unnoticeable. The second paragraph effortlessly transitions to a personal anecdote, which is continued in the third paragraph. The final paragraph justifies the narrative: Washington's life story leads to his commitment to establish his own institute—called the Tuskegee Normal and Industrial Institute—deep in the South.

Laundry List for Narration

- When possible, structure the events in chronological order.

- Make your story complete: make sure you have a beginning, middle, and end.

- Provide a realistic setting (typically at the beginning). Notice how Booker T. Washington provides a setting in this passage with just a few details: "a young colored man," "a common cabin in the South," "the poverty, the untidiness, the want of system, and thrift that existed about the cabin."

- Whenever possible, use action verbs; for example, write "the fighters *tumbled* to the ground," rather than "there *were* fallen soldiers on the ground."

- Provide concrete and specific details.

- Show, don't tell. This is another way of saying that you should use anecdotes and examples whenever possible.

- Establish a clear point of view; if it's clear who is narrating and why, then it will be easier to choose relevant details.

- Include appropriate amounts of direct discourse (dialogue or quotations).

SAMPLE QUESTION

"A college education is not necessary for success." Relate an experience of someone you know (directly or indirectly) that defends, challenges, or qualifies this statement.

DRILL: REFLECT ON HOW YOU COULD USE NARRATION TO ADDRESS THE FOLLOWING TOPICS

Think of a personal experience (or an experience of someone you know) that is relevant to the topic. Determine how you would best describe this experience. Come up with a few anecdotes or examples.

TOPIC 1: The dangers when eating becomes an obsession

TOPIC 2: Hardship is a necessary part of our education

INDUCTION AND DEDUCTION

You will probably find that the rhetorical modes of induction and deduction are most useful when you're writing the argumentative essay, although they will be helpful on the expository essay too.

Induction is a process in which specific examples are used to reach a general conclusion. If you took the AP European History exam and did not like the experience and followed by taking the AP Calculus exam and did not like the experience, you might arrive at the following general conclusion: AP exams are always an unpleasant experience. If, when you were young, you found that you didn't like broccoli, asparagus, or cabbage, your parents might have concluded that you didn't like vegetables. In both cases, the conclusion would be of questionable value because there is not enough evidence to justify the generalization.

Assume that you want to argue that your English teacher is in a bad mood every time the Boston Red Sox lose a game to the New York Yankees. You could substantiate that generalization by recalling certain tantrums that he threw and comparing those days with the dates of Red Sox losses. This would substantiate your claim but not prove it, especially if you didn't even know if your teacher saw the games. After all, what if something else happened to coincide with the games and was the real cause of his bad temper, such as traffic jams on the way home from school?

We tend to believe in generalizations arrived at through induction, whether they can actually be proved. The Food and Drug Administration, for example, has to follow the inductive reasoning of scientists; just because a certain drug produced the desired results—and didn't produce an undesirable result, such as death—20,000 experimental cases does not prove that the same results will occur when 20,000,000 people take the drug.

Deduction involves the use of a generalization to draw a conclusion about a specific case. For example, if you read in the morning paper that all schools in your county would be closed that day because of inclement weather, you could conclude that you won't have to go to school. You just used deductive reasoning.

LAUNDRY LIST FOR INDUCTION AND DEDUCTION

- Induction proceeds from the specific to a generalization. For example, your classmate Ricky plays on the school's football and basketball teams, and he has ice hockey posters all over his bedroom at home. You could conclude that Ricky likes all sports in general.

- Make sure you have sufficient evidence to support your claim.

- Deduction is the process of applying a generalization to a specific case. For example, your cousin Jennifer told you that she hates dancing and loud music. From this, you could safely say that she probably wouldn't want to come with you to the hot new nightclub opening this weekend.

- Make sure your generalization has sufficient credibility before applying it to specific cases. For example, it would be an unfair generalization to assume that all baseball players use or have used anabolic steroids.

SAMPLE QUESTION

Write a short essay in which you analyze the following statement: *Contemporary films are a reflection of today's values.*

DRILL: REFLECT ON HOW YOU COULD USE INDUCTION TO SUBSTANTIATE THE FOLLOWING THESES

THESIS 1: Academic honesty is alive and well.

THESIS 2: High schools don't really care about their mission to educate.

THESIS 3: Computer games have beneficial effects.

THESIS 4: Children generally demonstrate more wisdom than their parents.

In this chapter we looked at a few more rhetorical modes that will be extremely useful to you on test day. Remember that these can be used in combination with each other *and*, further complicating matters, in combination with the modes in the previous chapter. Hopefully, these modes have given you some ideas about how you can structure your essays into coherent works that the test readers will understand and maybe even enjoy.

Here we are at the end of the review section of the book. You are now ready to take the practice tests; you may be dreading these now, but we know that once you begin, you'll see that you know a lot more than you think you do! If you've worked through the book up to this point and complete these practice exams, you'll certainly be ready for test day.

Good luck!

PART VI

The Princeton Review AP English Language and Composition Practice Tests and Explanations

12

Practice Test 1

ENGLISH LANGUAGE AND COMPOSITION

Three hours are allotted for this examination: 1 hour for Section I, which consists of multiple-choice questions, and 2 hours for Section II, which consists of essay questions. Section I is printed in this examination booklet. Section II is printed in a separate booklet.

SECTION I

Time—1 hour

Number of questions—54

Percent of total grade—45

Section I of this examination contains 54 multiple-choice questions. Therefore, please be careful to fill in only the ovals that are preceded by numbers 1 through 54 on your answer sheet.

General Instructions

DO NOT OPEN THIS BOOKLET UNTIL YOU ARE INSTRUCTED TO DO SO.

INDICATE ALL YOUR ANSWERS TO QUESTIONS IN SECTION I ON THE SEPARATE ANSWER SHEET. No credit will be given for anything written in this examination booklet, but you may use the booklet for notes or scratchwork. After you have decided which of the suggested answers is best, COMPLETELY fill in the corresponding oval on the answer sheet.

Example: Sample Answer

Chicago is a

(A) state
(B) city
(C) country
(D) continent
(E) village

Many candidates wonder whether or not to guess the answers to questions about which they are not certain. In this section of the examination, as a correction for haphazard guessing, one-fourth of the number of questions you answer incorrectly will be subtracted from the number of questions you answer correctly. It is improbable, therefore, that mere guessing will improve your score significantly; it may even lower your score, and it does take time. If, however, you are not sure of the best answer but have some knowledge of the question and are able to eliminate one or more of the answer choices as wrong, your chance of getting the right answer is improved, and it may be to your advantage to answer such a question.

Use your time effectively, working as rapidly as you can without losing accuracy. Do not spend too much time on questions that are too difficult. Go on to other questions and come back to the difficult ones later if you have time. It is not expected that everyone will be able to answer all the multiple-choice questions.

The inclusion of the passages in this examination is not intended as an endorsement by The College Board or Educational Testing Service of the content, ideas, values, or styles of the individual authors. The material has been selected from works of various historical periods by a Committee of Examiners who are teachers of language and literature and who have judged that the passages printed here reflect the content of a course of study for which this examination is appropriate.

SECTION I

Time—1 hour

Directions: This part consists of selections from prose works and questions on their content, form, and style. After reading each passage, choose the best answer to each question and completely fill in the corresponding oval on the answer sheet.

Note: Pay particular attention to the requirement of questions that contain the words NOT, LEAST, or EXCEPT.

Questions 1–10. Read the following passage carefully before you choose your answers.

In his 1729 essay "A Modest Proposal," Jonathan Swift wrote the following:

There only remains one hundred and twenty thousand children of poor parents annually born. The question therefore is, how this number shall be reared
Line and provided for, which, as I have already said, under
5 the present situation of affairs, is utterly impossible by all the methods hitherto proposed. For we can neither employ them in handicraft or agriculture; we neither build houses (I mean in the country) nor cultivate land: they can very seldom pick up a livelihood by stealing,
10 till they arrive at six years old, except where they are of towardly parts, although I confess they learn the rudiments much earlier, during which time, they can however be properly looked upon only as probationers, as I have been informed by a principal gentleman in
15 the county of Cavan, who protested to me that he never knew above one or two instances under the age of six, even in a part of the kingdom so renowned for the quickest proficiency in that art.
    I am assured by our merchants, that a boy or a
20 girl before twelve years old is no salable commodity; and even when they come to this age they will not yield above three pounds, or three pounds and half-a-crown at most on the exchange; which cannot turn to account either to the parents or kingdom, the charge of
25 nutriment and rags having been at least four times that value.
    I shall now therefore humbly propose my own thoughts, which I hope will not be liable to the least objection.
30   I have been assured by a very knowing American of my acquaintance in London, that a young healthy child well nursed is at a year old a most delicious, nourishing, and wholesome food, whether stewed, roasted, baked, or boiled; and I make no doubt that it
35 will equally serve in a fricassee or a ragout.
    I do therefore humbly offer it to public consideration that of the hundred and twenty thousand children already computed, twenty thousand may be reserved for breed, whereof only one-fourth part to
40 be males; which is more than we allow to sheep, black cattle or swine; and my reason is, that these children are seldom the fruits of marriage, a circumstance not much regarded by our savages, therefore one male will be sufficient to serve four females. That the remaining
45 hundred thousand may, at a year old, be offered in the sale to the persons of quality and fortune through the kingdom; always advising the mother to let them suck plentifully in the last month, so as to render them plump and fat for a good table. A child will make two
50 dishes at an entertainment for friends; and when the family dines alone, the fore or hind quarter will make a reasonable dish, and seasoned with a little pepper or salt will be very good boiled on the fourth day, especially in winter.
55   I have reckoned upon a medium that a child just born will weigh 12 pounds, and in a solar year, if tolerably nursed, increaseth to 28 pounds.
    I grant this food will be somewhat dear, and therefore very proper for landlords, who, as they have
60 already devoured most of the parents, seem to have the best title to the children.

1. This text can best be described as

    (A) scientific
    (B) satirical
    (C) forthright
    (D) humanitarian
    (E) sadistic

2. In the first, second, and fourth paragraphs the author relies on dubious

    (A) similes
    (B) *ad hominem* arguments
    (C) extended metaphors
    (D) arguments from authority
    (E) appeals to ignorance

GO ON TO THE NEXT PAGE

3. "Probationers" (line 13) are

(A) children learning how to steal
(B) children on probation
(C) adults on probation
(D) apprentices working at a trade
(E) young artists

4. The phrase "the charge of nutriment and rags having been at least four times that value" (lines 24–26) is humorous because

(A) food was relatively cheap at that time
(B) "four times" is a hyperbole
(C) rags could be found free
(D) we don't know who is being charged
(E) "rags" is unexpected diction

5. The word "fricassee" (line 35) is obviously a(n)

(A) animal
(B) child
(C) dish
(D) place
(E) master

6. In lines 36–44 the author adopts the standard rhetorical pattern of

(A) process analysis
(B) example
(C) cause and effect
(D) deductive reasoning
(E) analogy

7. The phrase "always advising the mother to let them suck plentifully in the last month" (lines 47–48) extends the comparison between the children and

(A) properly nourished mammals
(B) poor and ruthless parents
(C) savages
(D) animals raised for slaughter
(E) the poor treatment of animals

8. In line 58, "dear" means

(A) expensive
(B) sweet
(C) cherished
(D) unforgettable
(E) unhealthy

9. In context, "devour" (line 60) is an effective word choice because

(A) it fits both figuratively and literally
(B) it is appropriate only literally
(C) it is indicative of the landlords' plight
(D) it works as a sentimental appeal
(E) it reveals the author's point of view

10. According to the author, the proposal

(A) makes good economic sense and helps the poor
(B) provides food for the needy and the rich, alike
(C) makes good economic sense but does not benefit the poor or rich
(D) benefits the rich in several ways
(E) benefits everyone in many ways

GO ON TO THE NEXT PAGE

Questions 11–14. Read the following passage carefully before you choose your answers.

Of particular interest to me have been the myriad elusive details of earlier times that tend to go unnoticed. In my schooling, I found that teachers
Line and historians, because of their socially prescribed
5 curricular attention toward larger social concepts, often bypassed the smaller and more personal expressions of social custom and conduct, often leaving the novel as the best lens with which to view forgotten elements of everyday life. Take, for instance, the long-defunct
10 activity called *upknocking*, the employment of the *knocker up*, who went house to house in the early morning hours of the nineteenth century to awaken his working-class clients before the advent of affordable alarm clocks. Until encountering this entry, I had never
15 thought about how people of this time managed to awaken with any predictability.

From THE WORD MUSEUM by Jeffrey Kacirk

11. The author of the passage is most likely

   (A) a scientific researcher
   (B) a lexicographer
   (C) a historian
   (D) a sociologist
   (E) a teacher

12. The author has a particular interest in

   (A) old words and alarm clocks
   (B) social and political history
   (C) unusual activities and personal conduct
   (D) historical detail and social conduct
   (E) literature and the nineteenth century

13. In this passage, *"upknocking"* is viewed as

   (A) an interesting anachronism
   (B) a superannuated and silly word
   (C) a working-class word
   (D) a word devoid of historical interest
   (E) the key to understanding the nineteenth century

14. Which word from the passage gives the clearest indication as to where the author encountered the process of *upknocking*?

   (A) entry (line 14)
   (B) novel (line 7)
   (C) schooling (line 3)
   (D) employment (line 10)
   (E) clients (line 13)

Questions 15–22. Read the following passage carefully before you choose your answers.

It can be demonstrated quite satisfactorily that although Romanticism does not erupt into painting until the very end of the eighteenth century it is
Line comparatively untrammeled in literature long before
5 this date. One might remember in this connection not necessarily Jean-Jacques Rousseau, often invoked almost automatically as the patron saint of the movement, but a novelist like the Abbé Prévost, who, in the 1730s and 1740s, writes novels with a
10 full repertory of Gothic effects, such as crêpe-hung mortuary chambers and doomed travelers who insist on telling their life stories to their hapless neighbours in stage-coaches. Even more relevant than the novelists are a number of dramatists who accomplish a
15 revolution in theatrical behaviour which is of singular importance for the morphology of Romanticism. Nivelle de la Chauseée, Diderot, and their numerous and more obscure followers create a type of dramatic genre which calls for the actors to go out of their way to give gratuitous demonstrations of the intensity with
20 which they feel. For a long time these demonstrations were confined to tragic-comedies, or *comédies larmoyantes*, in which the gesticulating characters, often morbid, always extravagant, were united at curtain fall, but when they were transposed to a form of tragedy,
25 dealing with contemporary problems, as they were in the works of the pre-Revolutionary dramatist Louis-Sébastien Mercier, one is already very close to the more rhetorical aspect of Romantic paintings.

From ROMANTICISM AND ITS DISCONTENTS by Anita Brookner

15. It can be inferred from this passage that

   (A) Rousseau's novels predate those of Abbé Prévost
   (B) most critics concur that French Romanticism began with Abbé Prévost's works
   (C) Nivelle de la Chauseée is most famous for his novels
   (D) the eighteenth-century novel is not relevant to the discussion of French Romanticism
   (E) Romantic paintings often depict emotional contemporary issues

GO ON TO THE NEXT PAGE

16. It can be inferred from this passage that Romantic works often include

    (A) scenes in gloomy interiors
    (B) battles with Goths
    (C) scenes from the Wild West
    (D) discussions with neighbors
    (E) vividly decorated chambers

17. The word "morphology" (line 16) most closely means

    (A) structure
    (B) sickness
    (C) psychology
    (D) death
    (E) revolution

18. The "gratuitous demonstrations" (line 19) are

    (A) free of charge
    (B) calm portrayals
    (C) not directly tied to the plot
    (D) tips for the actors
    (E) gratifying plays

19. The "comédies larmoyantes" (lines 21–22) are characterized by

    (A) the overwrought emotionalism of the characters
    (B) the subdued control of the action
    (C) complicated rhetoric
    (D) the death of the main characters at the end of the play
    (E) extravagant sets

20. "Revolutionary" (line 26) is capitalized because it

    (A) refers to a specific revolution
    (B) designates a literary movement
    (C) is a key word in the passage
    (D) is part of the author's title
    (E) refers to a specific dramatist

21. The last sentence (lines 20–28) in the passage is

    (A) a period
    (B) a run-on sentence
    (C) a metaphorical conclusion
    (D) not to be taken literally
    (E) an attack on the dramatist Mercier

22. Most likely, the passage is part of

    (A) a historical study of drama
    (B) a textbook on history
    (C) a study of Romanticism
    (D) an article in a travel magazine
    (E) a political history of France

GO ON TO THE NEXT PAGE

Questions 23–33. Read the following passage carefully before you choose your answers.

In 1792, Mary Wollstonecraft wrote the following in the Introduction to her book *A Vindication of the Rights of Women*:

My own sex, I hope, will excuse me, if I treat
them like rational creatures, instead of flattering their
fascinating graces, and viewing them as if they were in
Line a state of perpetual childhood, unable to stand alone.
5 I earnestly wish to point out in what true dignity
and human happiness consists—I wish to persuade
women to endeavour to acquire strength, both of
mind and body, and to convince them that the soft
phrases, susceptibility of heart, delicacy of sentiment,
10 and refinement of taste, are almost synonymous with
epithets of weakness, and that those beings who are
only the objects of pity and that kind of love, which
has been termed its sister, will soon become objects of
contempt.
15 Dismissing then those pretty feminine phrases,
which the men condescendingly use to soften our
slavish dependence, and despising that weak elegancy
of mind, exquisite sensibility, and sweet docility of
manners, supposed to be the sexual characteristics
20 of the weaker vessel, I wish to show that elegance
is inferior to virtue, that the first object of laudable
ambition is to obtain a character as a human being,
regardless of the distinction of sex; and that secondary
views should be brought to this simple touchstone.
25 This is a rough sketch of my plan; and should I
express my conviction with the energetic emotions
that I feel whenever I think of the subject, the dictates
of experience and reflection will be felt by some of
my readers. Animated by this important object, I
30 shall disdain to cull my phrases or polish my style;—I
aim at being useful, and sincerity will render me
unaffected; for, wishing rather to persuade by the
force of my arguments, than dazzle by the elegance of
my language, I shall not waste my time in rounding
35 periods, nor in fabricating the turgid bombast of
artificial feelings, which, coming from the head, never
reach the heart—I shall be employed about things,
not words!—and, anxious to render my sex more
respectable to members of society, I shall try to avoid
40 that flowery diction which has slided from essays
into novels, and from novels into familiar letters and
conversation.
These pretty nothings—these caricatures of the real
beauty of sensibility, dropping glibly from the tongue,
45 vitiate the taste, and create a kind of sickly delicacy that
turns away from simple unadorned truth; and a deluge
of false sentiments and overstretched feelings, stifling
the natural emotions of the heart, render the domestic
pleasures insipid, that ought to sweeten the exercise

of those severe duties, which educate a rational and
immortal being for a nobler field of action.
50 The education of women has, of late, been more
attended to than formerly; yet they are still reckoned
a frivolous sex, and ridiculed or pitied by the writers
who endeavour by satire or instruction to improve
them. It is acknowledged that they spend many of the
55 first years of their lives in acquiring a smattering of
accomplishments: meanwhile strength of body and
mind are sacrificed to libertine notions of beauty, to
the desire of establishing themselves—the only way
women can rise in the world—by marriage. And this
60 desire making mere animals of them, when they marry
they act as such children may be expected to act—they
dress; they paint, and nickname God's creatures—
Surely these weak beings are only fit for a seraglio!—
Can they govern a family, or take care of the poor babes
65 whom they bring into the world?

23. In the initial paragraph, the author employs both

    (A) apology and classification
    (B) irony and exposition
    (C) analogy and extended metaphor
    (D) flattery and epithets
    (E) induction and persuasion

24. In the initial paragraph, the author decries

    (A) traditional feminine attributes
    (B) traditional male attributes
    (C) modern sexuality
    (D) the importance of love
    (E) the importance of sentiments

25. In the initial paragraph, the author suggests that

    (A) men prefer strong women
    (B) a man will never truly love a strong woman
    (C) men never respect strong women
    (D) women need emotional and physical strength
    (E) women need intellectual and physical strength

26. The author ties the second paragraph to the first by using the words

    (A) "vessel" and "touchstone"
    (B) "soften" and "inferior"
    (C) "laudable" and "sex"
    (D) "slavish" and "virtue"
    (E) "soften" and "weak"

GO ON TO THE NEXT PAGE

27. The word "vessel" (line 20) is a metaphor for

(A) sex
(B) woman
(C) man
(D) phrase
(E) character

28. The author suggests that a woman's worth may be best judged by

(A) comparing her with a praiseworthy man
(B) examining the elegance of her writing
(C) evaluating the strength of her character
(D) evaluating her physical beauty
(E) examining her manners

29. The author proposes to write in a manner that is both

(A) cogent and emotional
(B) polished and intellectual
(C) ornate and rhetorical
(D) elegant and cerebral
(E) convincing and flowery

30. The words "pretty nothings" (line 43) are a reprise of

(A) "letters and conversation" (lines 41–42)
(B) "essays" and "novels" (lines 40–41)
(C) "flowery diction" (line 40)
(D) "rounding periods" (lines 34–35)
(E) "members of society" (line 39)

31. With the phrase "dropping glibly from the tongue" (line 44) the author begins

(A) a caricature of women
(B) a critique of turgid bombast
(C) a panegyric of sugary writing
(D) an analysis of sentimental writing
(E) an extended metaphor

32. One can infer from the passage that to become strong human beings, rather than mere children, young women need

(A) an education different from that of young men
(B) more understanding husbands
(C) obliging husbands
(D) a good marriage
(E) the same education as that of young men

33. The tone of the final paragraph is

(A) sardonic
(B) condescending
(C) ironic
(D) sarcastic
(E) haughty

GO ON TO THE NEXT PAGE

Questions 34–41. Read the following passage carefully before you choose your answers.

In his 1995 book *The End of Education*, Neil Postman wrote the following:

But it is important to keep in mind that the engineering of learning is very often puffed up, assigned an importance it does not deserve. As an old
Line saying goes, *There are one and twenty ways to sing tribal*
5 *lays, and all of them are correct*. So it is with learning. There is no one who can say that this or that is the best way to know things, to feel things, to see things, to remember things, to apply things, to connect things and that no other will do as well. In fact, to make
10 such a claim is to trivialize learning, to reduce it to a mechanical skill.

Of course, there are many learnings that are little else but a mechanical skill, and in such cases, there well may be a best way. But to become a different
15 person because of something you have learned—to appropriate an insight, a concept, a vision, so that your world is altered—that is a different matter. For that to happen, you need a reason. And this is the metaphysical problem I speak of.
20 A reason, as I use the word here, is different from a motivation. Within the context of schooling, motivation refers to a temporary psychic event in which curiosity is aroused and attention is focused. I do not mean to disparage it. But it must not be confused with a reason
25 for being in a classroom, for listening to a teacher, for taking an examination, for doing homework, for putting up with school even if you are not motivated.

This kind of reason is somewhat abstract, not always present in one's consciousness, not at all easy to
30 describe. And yet for all that, without it schooling does not work. For school to make sense, the young, their parents, and their teachers must have a god to serve, or, even better, several gods. If they have none, school is pointless. Nietzsche's famous aphorism is relevant
35 here: "He who has a *why* to live can bear with almost any *how*." This applies as much to learning as to living.

To put it simply, there is no surer way to bring an end to schooling than for it to have no end.

34. The "engineering of learning" (line 2) most nearly means

   (A) development of schools
   (B) building of schools
   (C) educational methodology
   (D) building up of knowledge
   (E) study of engineering

35. The "old saying" (lines 4–5) serves as

   (A) an analogy to the sentences that follow
   (B) a contrast to the sentences that follow
   (C) an illustration of the first sentence
   (D) a historical interlude
   (E) a tribute to tribal lays

36. The series of infinitives in the initial paragraph emphasizes that the learning process is

   (A) long and tedious
   (B) multifaceted and impersonal
   (C) active and varied
   (D) difficult and trivial
   (E) mechanical and complicated

37. According to the author, motivation is

   (A) not important
   (B) synonymous with reason
   (C) abstract and fleeting
   (D) momentary and concrete
   (E) psychological and enduring

38. Both the first and third paragraphs contain

   (A) aphorisms
   (B) ironical statements
   (C) syllogistic reasoning
   (D) *ad hominem* arguments
   (E) notable parallelism

39. In line 32 , "god" most nearly means

   (A) religion
   (B) deity
   (C) reason
   (D) person
   (E) Nietzsche

40. The author employs the argument from authority as

   (A) a contrast to his point of view
   (B) a relevant concrete example
   (C) an apt analogy
   (D) an example of cause and effect
   (E) an illustration of the cruelty in schools

41. The paradox in the final sentence rests on

   (A) different meanings of "end"
   (B) a crass simplification
   (C) the comparison between schooling and learning
   (D) the eternal process of learning
   (E) a new way of bringing schooling to an end

GO ON TO THE NEXT PAGE

Questions 42–47. Read the following passage carefully before you choose your answers.

From *Plessy v. Ferguson*:

It is one thing for railroad carriers to furnish, or to be required by law to furnish, equal accommodations for all whom they are under a legal duty to carry.
Line It is quite another thing for government to forbid
5 citizens of the white and black races from traveling in the same public conveyance, and to punish officers of railroad companies for permitting persons of the two races to occupy the same passenger coach. If a state can prescribe, as a rule of civil conduct, that
10 whites and blacks shall not travel as passengers in the same railroad coach, why may it not so regulate the use of the streets of its cities and towns as to compel white citizens to keep on one side of a street, and black citizens to keep on the other? Why may it not,
15 upon like grounds, punish whites and blacks who ride together in street cars or in open vehicles on a public road or street? Why may it not require sheriffs to assign whites to one side of a court room, and blacks to the other? And why may it not also prohibit
20 the commingling of the two races in the galleries of legislative halls or in public assemblages convened for the consideration of the political questions of the day? Further, if this statute of Louisiana is consistent with the personal liberty of citizens, why may not the state
25 require the separation in railroad coaches of native and naturalized citizens of the United States, or of Protestants and Roman Catholics?

The white race deems itself to be the dominant race in this country. And so it is, in prestige, in
30 achievements, in education, in wealth, and in power. So, I doubt not, it will continue to be for all time, if it remains true to its great heritage, and holds fast to the principles of constitutional liberty. But in view of the constitution, in the eye of the law, there is in this
35 country no superior, dominant, ruling class of citizens. There is no caste here. Our constitution is color-blind, and neither knows nor tolerates classes among citizens. In respect of civil rights, all citizens are equal before the law. The humblest is the peer of the most powerful.
40 The law regards man as man, and takes no account of his surroundings or of his color when his civil rights as guaranteed by the supreme law of the land are involved. It is therefore to be regretted that this high tribunal, the final expositor of the fundamental
45 law of the land, has reached the conclusion that it is competent for a state to regulate the enjoyment by citizens of their civil rights solely upon the basis of race.

In my opinion, the judgment this day rendered will,
50 in time, prove to be quite as pernicious as the decision made by this tribunal in the Dred Scott Case.

It was adjudged in that case that the descendants of Africans who were imported into this country, and sold as slaves, were not included nor intended to be
55 included under the word "citizens" in the constitution, and could not claim any of the rights and privileges which that instrument provided for and secured to citizens of the United States; that, at the time of the adoption of the constitution, they were "considered
60 as a subordinate and inferior class of beings, who had been subjugated by the dominant race, and, whether emancipated or not, yet remained subject to their authority, and had no rights or privileges but such as those who held the power and the government might
65 choose to grant them." The recent amendments of the constitution, it was supposed, had eradicated these principles from our institutions.

I am of opinion that the state of Louisiana is inconsistent with the personal liberty of citizens, white
70 and black, in that state, and hostile to both the spirit and letter of the constitution of the United States. If laws of like character should be enacted in the several states of the Union, the effect would be in the highest degree mischievous. Slavery, as an institution
75 tolerated by law, would, it is true, have disappeared from our country; but there would remain a power in the states, by sinister legislation, to interfere with the full enjoyment of the blessings of freedom, to regulate civil rights, common to all citizens, upon the basis of
80 race, and to place in a condition of legal inferiority a large body of American citizens, now constituting a part of the political community, called the "People of the United States," for whom, and by whom through representatives, our government is administered.
85 Such a system is inconsistent with the guaranty given by the constitution to each state of a republican form of government, and may be stricken down by congressional action, or by the courts in the discharge of their solemn duty to maintain the supreme law of
90 the land, anything in the constitution or laws of any state to the contrary notwithstanding.

For the reason stated, I am constrained to withhold my assent from the opinion and judgment of the majority.

GO ON TO THE NEXT PAGE

42. The speaker in this passage is

    (A) delivering a political speech
    (B) rendering a legal judgment
    (C) reminiscing about the past
    (D) a state governor
    (E) involved with the railroad company

43. In the first paragraph, the series of rhetorical questions serves the speaker's strategy of reasoning by

    (A) appeals to authority
    (B) analogy
    (C) description
    (D) induction
    (E) deduction

44. Based on the passage, the speaker holds that

    (A) racial equality will become a reality in America
    (B) civil equality is guaranteed by the Constitution
    (C) racial equality is guaranteed by the Constitution
    (D) both civil and racial equality are guaranteed by the Constitution
    (E) neither civil nor racial equality is guaranteed by the Constitution

45. In line 50, "pernicious" most nearly means

    (A) just
    (B) unjust
    (C) useful
    (D) propitious
    (E) harmful

46. In the speaker's opinion, the Louisiana law is subject to censure by

    (A) either the United States Congress or the United States Supreme Court
    (B) Louisiana legislation only
    (C) United States legislation only
    (D) the people of Louisiana only
    (E) neither the United States Congress nor the United States Supreme Court

47. The style of the entire passage can be best described as

    (A) ornate and whimsical
    (B) dry and objective
    (C) abstract and legalistic
    (D) terse and opinionated
    (E) probing and subtle

GO ON TO THE NEXT PAGE

Questions 48–54. Read the following passage carefully before you choose your answers.

Sir, believe me, to conduct the Government of this country is a most arduous duty; I may say it without irreverence, that these ancient institutions, like our
Line physical frames, are "fearfully and wonderfully
5 made." It is no easy task to ensure the united action of an ancient monarchy, a proud aristocracy, and a reformed constituency. I have done everything I could do, and have thought it consistent with true Conservative policy to reconcile these three branches
10 of the State. I have thought it consistent with true Conservative policy to promote so much of happiness and contentment among the people that the voice of disaffection should be no longer heard, and that thoughts of the dissolution of our institutions should
15 be forgotten in the midst of physical enjoyment. These were my attempts, and I thought them not inconsistent with true and enlarged Conservative policy. These were my objects in accepting office—it is a burden too great for my physical, and far beyond
20 my intellectual structure; and to be relieved from it with perfect honour would be the greatest favour that could be conferred on me. But as a feeling of honour and strong sense of duty require me to undertake those responsible functions, I declare, Sir, that I am ready to
25 incur these risks, to bear these burdens, and to front all these honourable dangers. But, Sir, I will not take the step with mutilated power and shackled authority. I will not stand at the helm during, such tempestuous nights as I have seen, if the vessel be not allowed fairly
30 to pursue the course which I think she ought to take. I will not, Sir, undertake to direct the course of the vessel by the observations which have been taken in 1842. I will reserve to myself the marking out of that course; and I must, for the public interest, claim for myself the
35 unfettered power of judging of those measures which I conceive will be better for the country to propose.

Sir, I do not wish to be the Minister of England; but while I have the high honour of holding that Office, I am determined to hold it by no servile tenure. I
40 will only hold that office upon the condition of being unshackled by any other obligations than those of consulting the public interests, and of providing for the public safety.

(1846)

48. The opening sentence of the passage contains

(A) an expression of fear
(B) an appeal to authority
(C) a humorous simile
(D) an irreverent attack
(E) equivocation

49. The speaker is addressing

(A) a friend
(B) a group of his peers
(C) a king
(D) a crowd of voters
(E) his political adversaries

50. The most significant transition takes place in

(A) line 10 ("I have thought it consistent…")
(B) line 18 ("These were my objects…")
(C) line 22 ("But as a feeling of honour…")
(D) line 26 ("But, Sir, I will not…")
(E) lines 30–31 ("I will not, Sir, undertake…")

51. All of the following are part of the same extended metaphor EXCEPT

(A) helm (line 28)
(B) vessel (line 29)
(C) fairly (line 29)
(D) course (line 30)
(E) unshackled (line 41)

52. Which term in the first paragraph serves to prepare the dominant point of the final paragraph?

(A) disaffection (line 13)
(B) enjoyment (line 15)
(C) dangers (line 26)
(D) tempestuous (line 28)
(E) unfettered (line 35)

53. Based on the passage, the speaker's motivation to serve as Prime Minister is dictated mostly by

(A) greed
(B) political ambition
(C) sense of honor
(D) political power
(E) youthful exuberance

54. The tone of the entire passage

(A) remains consistently cynical
(B) shifts according to the speaker's mood
(C) shifts from light to serious
(D) becomes more frivolous in the final paragraph
(E) remains consistently lighthearted

END OF SECTION I

ENGLISH

LANGUAGE AND COMPOSITION

SECTION II

Time—2 hours

Number of questions—3

Percent of total grade—55

Each question counts as one-third of the total essay section score.

Question 1 Essay....................................suggested time—40 minutes

Question 2 Essay....................................suggested time—40 minutes

Question 3 Essay....................................suggested time—40 minutes

Section II of this examination requires answers in essay form. To help you use your time well, the coordinator will announce the time at which each question should be completed. If you finish any question before time is announced, you may go on to the following question. If you finish the examination in less than the time allotted, you may go back and work on any essay question you want.

Each essay will be judged on its clarity and effectiveness in dealing with the requirements of the topic assigned and on the quality of the writing. After completing each question, you should check your essay for accuracy of punctuation, spelling, and diction; you are advised, however, not to attempt many longer corrections. Remember that quality is far more important than quantity.

Write your essays with a pen, preferably in black or dark blue ink. Be sure to write CLEARLY and LEGIBLY. Cross out any errors you make.

The questions for Section II are printed in the green insert. You are encouraged to use the green insert to make notes and to plan your essays, but be sure to write your answers in the pink booklet. Number each answer as the question is numbered in the examination. Do not skip lines. Begin each answer on a new page in the pink booklet.

ENGLISH LANGUAGE AND COMPOSITION

SECTION II

Time—1 hour

Question 1

(Suggested time—40 minutes. This question counts as one-third of the total essay section score.)

The passages that follow were published shortly after the appearance of Mary Shelley's *Frankenstein* (1818). At that time, very few people knew the identity of the author. The first passage has been extracted from an anonymous piece from *The Quarterly Review*. The second is part of (Sir) Walter Scott's review in *Blackwood's Edinburgh Magazine*.

Read the passages carefully. Then write a carefully organized essay in which you compare and contrast the manner in which each critic uses language to convey a point of view.

Passage 1

On board this ship poor Frankenstein, after telling his story to Mr. Walton, who has been so kind to write it down for our use, dies of cold, fatigue,
Line and horror; and soon after, the monster, who had
5 borrowed (we presume from the flourishing colony of East Greenland) a kind of raft, comes alongside the ship, and notwithstanding his huge bulk, jumps in at Mr. Walton's cabin window, and is surprised by that gentleman pronouncing a funeral oration over
10 the departed Frankenstein; after which, declaring that he will go back to the Pole, and there burn himself on a funeral pyre (of ice, we conjecture) of his own collecting, he jumps again out the window into his raft, and is out of sight in a moment.
15 Our readers will guess from this summary, what a tissue of horrible and disgusting absurdity this work presents. It is piously dedicated to Mr. Godwin, and is written in the spirit of his school. The dreams of insanity are embodied in the strong
20 and striking language of the insane, and the author, notwithstanding the rationality of his preface, often leaves us in doubt whether he is not as mad as his hero. Mr. Godwin is the patriarch of a literary family, whose chief skill is in delineating the wanderings of
25 the intellect, and which strangely delights in the most affecting and humiliating of human miseries. His disciples are a kind of out pensioners of Bedlam, and like "Mad Bess" or "Mad Tom," are occasionally visited with paroxysms of genius and fits of expression, which
30 makes sober-minded people wonder and shudder.
But when we have thus admitted that Frankenstein has passages which appall the mind and make the flesh creep, we have given it all the praise (if praise it can be called) which we dare to bestow. Our taste and our
35 judgment alike revolt at this kind of writing, and the greater the ability with which it may be executed the worse it is—it inculcates no lesson of conduct, manners, or morality; it cannot mend, and will not even amuse its readers, unless their taste have been deplorably
40 vitiated—it fatigues the feelings without interesting the understanding; it gratuitously harasses the sensations. The author has powers, both of conception and language, which employed in a happier direction might, perhaps (we speak dubiously), give him a name
45 among these whose writings amuse or amend their fellow-creatures; but we take the liberty of assuring him, and hope that he may be in a temper to listen to us, that the style which he has adopted in the present publication merely tends to defeat his own purpose,
50 if he really had any other object in view than that of leaving the wearied reader, after a struggle between laughter and loathing, in doubt whether the head or the heart of the author be the most diseased.

GO ON TO THE NEXT PAGE

Passage 2

Exhausted by his sufferings, but still breathing
vengeance against the being which was at once his
creature and his persecutor, this unhappy victim to
physiological discovery expires just as the clearing
away of the ice permits Captain Walton's vessel to hoist
sail for the return to Britain. At midnight, the daemon,
who had been his destroyer, is discovered in the cabin,
lamenting over the corpse of the person who gave him
being. To Walton he attempts to justify his resentment
towards the human race, while, at the same time, he
acknowledges himself a wretch who had murdered the
lovely and the helpless, and pursued to irremediably
ruin his creator, the select specimen of all that was
worthy of love and admiration.

"Fear not," he continues, addressing the astonished
Walton, "that I shall be the instrument of future
mischief. My work is nearly complete. Neither yours
nor any man's death is needed to consummate the
series of my being, and accomplish that which must
be done; but it requires my own. Do not think that I
shall be slow to perform this sacrifice. I shall quit your
vessel on the ice-raft which brought me hither, and
shall seek the most northern extremity of the globe; I
shall collect my funeral pile and consume to ashes this
miserable frame, that its remains may afford no light to
any curious and unhallowed wretch, who would create
such another as I have been...."

"He sprung from the cabin-window, as he said this,
upon the ice-raft which lay close to the vessel. He was
soon borne away by the waves, and lost in darkness
and distance."

Whether this singular being executed his purpose or
not must necessarily remain an uncertainty, unless the
voyage of discovery to the north pole should throw any
light on the subject.

So concludes this extraordinary tale, in which the
author seems to us to disclose uncommon powers
of poetic imagination. The feeling with which we
perused the unexpected and fearful, yet, allowing the
possibility of the event, very natural conclusion of
Frankenstein's experiment, shook a little even our firm
nerves; although such and so numerous have been
the expedients for exciting terror employed by the
romantic writers of the age, that the reader may adopt
Macbeth's words with a slight alteration:

"We have supp'd full with horrors
Direness, familiar to our "callous" thoughts,
Cannot once startle us."

It is no slight merit in our eyes that the tale, though
wild in incident, is written in plain and forcible
English, without exhibiting that mixture of hyperbolical
Germanisms with which tales of wonder are usually
told, as if it were necessary that the language should
be as extravagant as the fiction. The ideas of the author
are always clearly as well as forcibly expressed; and
his descriptions of landscape have in them the choice
requisites of truth, freshness, precision, and beauty.

GO ON TO THE NEXT PAGE

Question 2

(Suggested time—40 minutes. This question counts as one-third of the total essay section score.)

Read carefully the passage below. Then write an essay in which you support, refute, or qualify the claim that a "neutral" stand on race perpetuates racial imbalance.

I am saying that sometimes colorblindness is racism.
I know that sounds counterintuitive, but let me go on.
Think of society as comprised of lots of different
Line groups of people, identified by their race, gender, etc.
5 Neutrality in our society is supposed to be the great
equalizer because we believe that, if we don't favor
any one group, things will work themselves out and
become more equal. But the thing is this: neutrality has
this effect only if there is no previous social or historical
10 context. But that's not how the real world is. There is, in
fact, a social and historical context for every situation.
So if I were being "neutral" and viewing everyone as
being the same, ignoring personal contexts, I wouldn't
be promoting equality because I would be ignoring the
15 differences that exist and allowing the inequalities to
continue to exist, given that I wouldn't do anything to
help change them. Identifying problems and actively
promoting solutions are necessary to effect useful
change; being neutral is consenting to the status quo.

GO ON TO THE NEXT PAGE

(Suggested time—40 minutes. This question counts as one-third of the total essay section score.)

The passage below is taken from John Stuart Mill's essay "The Utility of Religion" (1874).

Read the passage carefully. Then write an essay in which you analyze the strategies that John Stuart Mill employs to establish his position about the utility of religion.

Anyone who fairly and impartially considers the subject will see reason to believe that those great effects on human conduct, which are commonly
Line ascribed to motives derived directly from religion,
5 have mostly for their proximate cause the influence of human opinion. Religion has been powerful not by its intrinsic force, but because it has wielded that additional and more mighty power. The effect of religion has been immense in giving a direction to
10 public opinion: which has, in many most important respects, been wholly determined by it. But without the sanctions superadded by public opinion, its own proper sanctions have never, save in exceptional characters or in peculiar moods of mind, exercised
15 a very potent influence after the times had gone by in which divine agency was supposed habitually to employ temporal rewards and punishments. When a man firmly believed that if he violated the sacredness of a particular sanctuary he would be struck dead on
20 the spot or smitten suddenly with a mortal disease, he doubtless took care not to incur the penalty: But when any one had the courage to defy the danger and escaped with impunity, the spell was broken. (…) Unquestionably the conviction which experience in
25 time forced on all but the very ignorant, that divine punishments were not to be confidently expected in a temporal form, contributed much to the downfall of the old religions, and the general adoption of one which without absolutely excluding providential interferences
30 in this life for the punishment of guilt or the reward of merit, removed the principal scene of divine retribution to a world after death. But rewards and punishments postponed to that distance of time, and never seen by the eye, are not calculated, even when infinite and
35 eternal, to have, on ordinary minds, a very powerful effect in opposition to strong temptation. Their remoteness alone is a prodigious deduction from their efficacy, on such minds as those which most require the restraint of punishment. A still greater abatement
40 is their uncertainty, which belongs to them from the very nature of the case: for rewards and punishments administered after death, must be awarded not definitely to particular actions, but on a general survey of the person's whole life, and he easily persuades
45 himself that whatever may have been his peccadilloes, there will be a balance in his favour at the last. All positive religions aid this self-delusion. Bad religions teach that divine vengeance may be bought off, by offerings, or personal abasement; the better religious,

50 not to drive sinners to despair, dwell so much on the divine mercy, that hardly any one is compelled to think himself irrevocably condemned. The sole quality in these punishments which might seem calculated to make them efficacious, their overpowering magnitude,
55 is itself a reason why nobody (except a hypochondriac here and there) ever really believes that he is in any very serious danger of incurring them. Even the worst malefactor is hardly able to think that any crime he has had it in his power to commit, any evil he can
60 have inflicted in this short space of existence, can have deserved torture extending through an eternity. Accordingly religious writers and preachers are never tired of complaining how little effect religious motives have on men's lives and conduct, notwithstanding the
65 tremendous penalties denounced.
  Mr. Bentham, whom I have already mentioned as one of the few authors who have written anything to the purpose on the efficacy of the religious sanction, adduces several cases to prove that religious obligation,
70 when not enforced by public opinion, produces scarcely any effect on conduct. His first example is that of oaths. The oaths taken in courts of justice, and any others which from the manifest importance to society of their being kept, public opinion rigidly enforces,
75 are felt as real and binding obligations. But university oaths and custom-house oaths, though in a religious point of view equally obligatory, are in practice utterly disregarded even by men in other respects honourable. The university oath to obey the statutes has been for
80 centuries, with universal acquiescence, set at nought: and utterly false statements are (or used to be) daily and unblushingly sworn to at the Custom-house, by persons as attentive as other people to all the ordinary obligations of life. The explanation being, that veracity
85 in these cases was not enforced by public opinion. The second case which Bentham cites is dueling; a practice now, in this country, obsolete, but in full vigour in several other Christian countries; deemed and admitted to be a sin by almost all who, nevertheless,
90 in obedience to opinion, and to escape from personal humiliation, are guilty of it. The third case is that of illicit sexual intercourse; which in both sexes, stands in the very highest rank of religious sins, yet not being severely censured by opinion in the male sex, they have
95 in general very little scruple in committing it; while in the case of women, though the religious obligation is not stronger, yet being backed in real earnest by public opinion, it is commonly effectual.

GO ON TO THE NEXT PAGE

Question 3B (for May 2007)

(Suggested time—40 minutes. This question counts as one-third of the total essay section score.)

Read or examine carefully the sources that follow; you should keep in mind the validity of the documents, as well as their relevance to the prompt. Then write a well-organized essay in which you include citations from at least four of the sources. You have an extra 15 minutes on this section to study the sources and organize your thoughts.

Relying heavily on the sources that follow, would you have voted for or against women's suffrage, had you been given the opportunity to vote in the late 1880s? Include citations from at least four of the sources in your explanation.

Source 1

In 1872, Susan B. Anthony was arrested and charged with voting illegally. The following passage is the opening of her lecture entitled, "Is It a Crime for a Citizen of the United States to Vote?"

Friends and Fellow-citizens: I stand before you to-night, under indictment for the alleged crime of having voted at the last Presidential election, without having a
Line lawful right to vote. It shall be my work this evening to
5 prove to you that in thus voting, I not only committed no crime, but, instead, simply exercised my citizen's right, guaranteed to me and all United States citizens by the National Constitution, beyond the power of any State to deny.
10 Our democratic-republican government is based on the idea of the natural right of every individual member thereof to a voice and a vote in making and executing the laws. We assert the province of government to be to secure the people in the enjoyment
15 of their unalienable rights. We throw to the winds the old dogma that governments can give rights. Before governments were organized, no one denies that each individual possessed the right to protect his own life, liberty and property. And when 100 or 1,000,000 people
20 enter into a free government, they do not barter away their natural rights; they simply pledge themselves to protect each other in the enjoyment of them, through prescribed judicial and legislative tribunals. They agree to abandon the methods of brute force in the
25 adjustment of their differences, and adopt those of civilization.
Nor can you find a word in any of the grand documents left us by the fathers that assumes for government the power to create or to confer rights.
30 The Declaration of Independence, the United States Constitution, the constitutions of the several states and the organic laws of the territories, all alike propose to protect the people in the exercise of their God-given rights. Not one of them pretends to bestow rights.
35 "All men are created equal, and endowed by their Creator with certain unalienable rights. Among these are life, liberty and the pursuit of happiness. That to secure these, governments are instituted among men,

deriving their just powers from the consent of the
40 governed."
Here is no shadow of government authority over rights, nor exclusion of any from their full and equal enjoyment. Here is pronounced the right of all men, and "consequently," as the Quaker preacher said, "of
45 all women," to a voice in the government. And here, in this very first paragraph of the declaration, is the assertion of the natural right of all to the ballot; for, how can "the consent of the governed" be given, if the right to vote be denied. Again:
50 "That whenever any form of government becomes destructive of these ends, it is the right of the people to alter or abolish it, and to institute a new government, laying its foundations on such principles, and organizing its powers in such forms as to them shall
55 seem most likely to effect their safety and happiness."
Surely, the right of the whole people to vote is here clearly implied. For however destructive in their happiness this government might become, a disfranchised class could neither alter nor abolish it,
60 nor institute a new one, except by the old brute force method of insurrection and rebellion. One-half of the people of this nation to-day are utterly powerless to blot from the statute books an unjust law, or to write there a new and a just one.

GO ON TO THE NEXT PAGE

Source 2

THE DAILY GRAPHIC
AN ILLUSTRATED EVENING NEWSPAPER

VOL. I—NO. 81.   NEW YORK, THURSDAY, JUNE 5, 1873.   FIVE CENTS.

Source 3

An excerpt from Judge Ward Hunt's instructions to the jury in the case of *United States v. Susan B. Anthony*, June 18, 1873.

The right of voting, or the privilege of voting, is a right or privilege arising under the Constitution of the State, and not of the United States. The qualifications are different in the different States. Citizenship, age,
Line
5 sex, residence, are variously required in the different States, or may be so. If the right belongs to any particular person, it is because such person is entitled to it by the laws of the State where he offers to exercise it, and not because of citizenship of the United States.
10 If the State of New York should provide that no person should vote until he had reached the age of 31 years, or after he had reached the age of 50, or that no person having gray hair, or who had not the use of all his limbs, should be entitled to vote, I do not see how it
15 could be held to be a violation of any right derived or held under the Constitution of the United States. We might say that such regulations were unjust, tyrannical, unfit for the regulation of an intelligent State; but if

rights of a citizen are thereby violated, they are of that
20 fundamental class derived from his position as a citizen of the State, and not those limited rights belonging to him as a citizen of the United States. (…)

If she believed she had a right to vote, and voted in reliance upon that belief, does that relieve her from
25 the penalty? It is argued that the knowledge referred to in the act relates to her knowledge of the illegality of the act, and not to the act of voting; for it is said that she must know that she voted. Two principles apply here: First, ignorance of the law excuses no one; second,
30 every person is presumed to understand and to intend the necessary effects of his own acts. Miss Anthony knew that she was a woman, and that the constitution of this State prohibits her from voting. She intended to violate that provision—intended to test it, perhaps,
35 but certainly intended to violate it. The necessary effect of her act was to violate it, and this side is presumed to have intended. There was no ignorance of any fact, but all the facts being known, she undertook to settle a principle in her own person. She takes the risk, and
40 she cannot escape the consequences. It is said, and authorities are cited to sustain the position, that there can be no crime unless there is a culpable intent; to render one criminally responsible a vicious will must be present. A commits a trespass on the land of B, and
45 B, thinking and believing that he has a right to shoot an intruder on his premises, kills A on the spot. Does B's misapprehension of his rights justify his act? Would a Judge be justified in charging the jury that if satisfied that B supposed he had a right to shoot A he was
50 justified, and they should find a verdict of not guilty? No Judge would make such a charge. To constitute a crime, it is true that there must be a criminal intent, but it is equally true that knowledge of the facts of the case is always held to supply this intent. An intentional
55 killing bears with it evidence of malice in law. Whoever, without justifiable cause, intentionally kills his neighbor is guilty of a crime. The principle is the same in the case before us, and in all criminal cases. (…)

Upon this evidence I suppose there is no question
60 for the jury and that the jury should be directed to find a verdict of guilty.

GO ON TO THE NEXT PAGE

Source 4

Sixty-sixth Congress of the United States of America;

At the First Session,

Begun and held at the City of Washington on Monday, the nineteenth day of May, one thousand nine hundred and nineteen.

JOINT RESOLUTION

Proposing an amendment to the Constitution extending the right of suffrage to women.

Resolved by the Senate and House of Representatives of the United States of America in Congress assembled (two-thirds of each House concurring therein), That the following article is proposed as an amendment to the Constitution, which shall be valid to all intents and purposes as part of the Constitution when ratified by the legislatures of three-fourths of the several States.

"ARTICLE ———.

"The right of citizens of the United States to vote shall not be denied or abridged by the United States or by any State on account of sex.

"Congress shall have power to enforce this article by appropriate legislation."

F. H. Gillett

Speaker of the House of Representatives.

Thos. R. Marshall

Vice President of the United States and
President of the Senate.

Source 5

In October, 1874, the Supreme Court voted unanimously that the Constitution of the United States does not confer on women the right to vote in federal elections (*Minor v. Happersett*).

     When the Federal Constitution was adopted, all the States, with the exception of Rhode Island and Connecticut, had constitutions of their own. These two
Line continued to act under their charters from the Crown.
5 Upon an examination of those constitutions we find that in no State were all citizens permitted to vote. Each State determined for itself who should have that power. Thus, in New Hampshire, "every male inhabitant of each town and parish with town privileges, and places
10 unincorporated in the State, of twenty-one years of age and upwards, excepting paupers and persons excused from paying taxes at their own request," were its voters; in Massachusetts "every male inhabitant of twenty-one years of age and upwards, having a
15 freehold estate within the commonwealth of the annual income of three pounds, or any estate of the value of sixty pounds;" in Rhode Island "such as are admitted free of the company and society" of the colony; in

Connecticut such persons as had "maturity in years,
20 quiet and peaceable behavior, a civil conversation, and forty shillings freehold or forty pounds personal estate," if so certified by the selectmen. (…)

     Certainly, if the courts can consider any question settled, this is one. For nearly ninety years the people
25 have acted upon the idea that the Constitution, when it conferred citizenship, did not necessarily confer the right of suffrage. If uniform practice long continued can settle the construction of so important an instrument as the Constitution of the United States confessedly is,
30 most certainly it has been done here. Our province is to decide what the law is, not to declare what it should be.

     We have given this case the careful consideration its importance demands. If the law is wrong, it ought to be changed; but the power for that is not with us. The
35 arguments addressed to us bearing upon such a view of the subject may perhaps be sufficient to induce those having the power, to make the alteration, but they ought not to be permitted to influence our judgment in determining the present rights of the parties now
40 litigating before us. No argument as to woman's need of suffrage can be considered. We can only act upon her rights as they exist. It is not for us to look at the hardship of withholding. Our duty is at an end if we find it is within the power of a State to withhold.
45   Being unanimously of the opinion that the Constitution of the United States does not confer the right of suffrage upon any one, and that the constitutions and laws of the several States which commit that important trust to men alone are not
50 necessarily void, we affirm the judgment.

GO ON TO THE NEXT PAGE

Woman Devotes Her Time to Gossip and Clothes Because She Has Nothing Else to Talk About. Give Her Broader Interests and She Will Cease to Be Vain and Frivolous.

END OF EXAMINATION

13

Practice Test 1: Answers and Explanations

EXPLANATIONS TO THE MULTIPLE-CHOICE SECTION

1. **B** As is often the case on the real exam, this first passage, taken from Jonathan Swift's "A Modest Proposal" is a relatively easy one. This question sets up many of the others that follow it so make sure you get this one correct. If you take the author's proposal seriously, then four of the answers [(A), (C), (D), and (E)] are plausible; of course, the key is to understand that the author is not making a serious proposal, but, rather, he is satirizing other so-called scientific studies that, under the guise of humanitarianism, tend to offer cruel (if not sadistic) "solutions" to poverty. Therefore, (B) is the only acceptable answer.

2. **D** Even if you are not familiar with the term "arguments from authority," you can easily guess the meaning. The authorities cited are "a principal gentleman in the county of Cavan" (paragraph 1), "our merchants" (paragraph 2), and "a very knowing American of my acquaintance in London" (paragraph 4). These are, of course, dubious authorities, indeed, which is one of the sources of humor in the passage.

    The easiest and fastest way to use POE in this case is to examine the shortest of the paragraphs, the fourth. Clearly, there are no similes (A) or extended metaphors (C) in the fourth paragraph, so there is no need to check the first or second paragraphs for these rhetorical devices. The other two answers are more esoteric, but logic leads you to eliminate them, even if you do not fully understand them as rhetorical terms. There is nothing approximating an appeal in paragraph four, so you can eliminate that answer easily; there is also no attempt to argue a point (B).

3. **A** Answers (B) and (C) are shallowly associated with the word "probationers," which appears in the question (and text), and are easily dismissed. Answer (E) tempts you to make a hasty association between the last word in the paragraph ("art") and a practitioner of art. This narrows the choices to (A) and (D); however, it is clear that the children's "livelihood" is not a formal trade, but mere thievery—the only "trade" left open to indigent children during the incipient stages of the Industrial Revolution. So "probationers" refers to "children learning how to steal," or choice A.

4. **E** The humor comes from the clever juxtaposition of the phrase "nutriment and rags." The first term is even more formal than what we may expect (food), and this creates an expectation for the second term: clothing. Instead, the author hits the reader with an unexpected substitute for clothes: rags. The other answers appear to be more or less plausible, but none has anything to do with humor. Hyperbole (B) was thrown in gratuitously; often, students will be tricked into selecting an answer simply because it contains a rhetorical term and appears to be the most sophisticated choice.

5. **C** Even though you are probably not familiar with this word, as long as you read it in context, the answer to this question should be obvious—the entire paragraph is about food, and certainly you understand the other terms (*stewed, roasted, baked, boiled*). Reading the term in context should have at least allowed you to eliminate the other choices; "animal," "child," "place," and "master."

6. **A** The best approach to this question is to use POE. You can eliminate answers (B) and (C) right away. If you remember that "deductive reasoning" means starting with a generality and working logically to a specific conclusion, you can see that answer (D) is way off base too. Answer (E) may be tempting because of the existence of the phrase "which is more than

we allow to sheep, black cattle or swine" in the paragraph, but this paragraph is not dominated by analogy. Although this comparison is extended, it is not really a pattern. "Process analysis" (A) is the best answer; in this paragraph, the author analyzes a problem and proposes a process that will bring about a solution. The proposal describes the process for breeding, fattening, and preparing this very unusual source of protein.

7. **D** This question is related to the previous one. The proposal is to fatten the children for slaughter, just as if they were livestock (sheep, cattle, or pigs).

8. **A** By using POE, you should be able to narrow your choices down to (A) and (C) very quickly. The author is saying that the new meat will be expensive, and only the rich landlords will be able to afford it.

9. **A** By this point, you must have digested (forgive the pun) the satire, so you understand that the landlords have "devoured" the parents by charging unreasonably high rents and that, according to the author, they may as well literally devour (eat) their poor tenants' children. It is understandable that answer (E) may tempt you, but the diction in this sentence is hardly a revelation. We have understood the point of view all along; behind the comical satire is the rage of a man disgusted by the exploitation of the poor by the rich.

10. **D** This farcical proposal does make good economic sense, but it does not help the poor; clearly, this eliminates answers (A), (B), and (E). The "only" in answer (C) allows us to discard that choice too. The proposal benefits the rich by providing a plentiful source of a food that, among other things, will be both chic and appropriate for a wide variety of dishes. Also, by slaughtering the children when they are infants, society will not have to worry about providing for older children, who are too young to work but old enough to need clothing and food. Ostensibly, this responsibility falls on those who have money, the rich; if this cost is eliminated, then again the rich benefit.

11. **B** If you know that lexicon is roughly synonymous with dictionary (and you do if you've studied the Hit Parade), the question is an easy one. If you don't, then it's still a simple matter of POE. Given that the author refers to teachers and historians in a way that appears to set them apart, it is reasonable to assume that the author is not a member of either group. At this point, you could guess and go, or you could note the phrase "until encountering this entry," which is the clue that points to the correct answer—the entry is a dictionary entry.

12. **D** It is wise to use POE again and attempt to eliminate all but one of the answers. Remember that if one of the elements isn't relevant, then the entire answer is invalid. The first answer begins in a promising fashion; the author is interested in old words; however, that interest is only tangentially related to alarm clocks—and the entire topic (upknocking) is only an example used to illustrate a more sweeping interest. Eliminate (A). Answer (B) begins with similar promise, but there is nothing in the passage that addresses political history. All of the remaining answers are at least somewhat plausible, but remember that the example of upknocking is used to illustrate "the smaller and more personal expressions of social custom and conduct" rather than "larger social concepts." That is, the author is interested in the revelatory details of social conduct (or concepts), rather than in the sweeping generalities. The author is, indeed, interested in nineteenth-century literature and unusual activities of that century, but only as they reveal how discrete social groups (in this case, the working class) lived and functioned.

13. **A** If you are not familiar with the word *anachronism*, go back and review the Hit Parade. There are two important meanings of this word. If you were to write a story about one of Ulysses's forgotten adventures, in which the hero uses a machine gun to defeat Schwartza-thon, the King of Califia, then you would have employed an anachronism (the gun); that is, you would have placed a thing (or a person) out of its proper time. But an anachronism can also be something that was once relevant, but no longer is—a definition almost synonymous with "superannuated."

Once again, POE can help you eliminate the incorrect answers. *Upknocking* may sound like a silly word to you, but you should be able to understand the author's sincere, serious inter-est in such a word. Besides, the test writers would never expect you to choose an answer that referred to any aspect of the English language as "silly," so you can always eliminate this type of answer choice when you see it. Answer (C) is off base because, although the word applied to working-class life, there is no reason to suspect that only that class knew of or used the word. If you chose (D), then you need to go back and read the passage very carefully. Choice (E), the final answer, is simply hyperbolic; *upknocking* is a word that gives us a better glimpse into what the nineteenth century was like, but it is not the key to under-standing the entire century.

14. **A** We addressed this in the explanation to question 11; at the very least, you should be able to eliminate answers (C), (D), and (E).

15. **E** In approaching this question, you'll definitely want to use POE. You can infer several things from the first part of the passage.

   a. The passage is about French Romanticism.

   b. Typically, critics agree that French Romanticism begins in the late eighteenth century.

   c. Typically, critics agree that Jean-Jacques Rousseau is the first great French Romantic.

   d. This author emphasizes that French Romanticism is important much earlier in the eigh-teenth century.

   e. This author believes that the novels of Abbé Prévost, who wrote Romantic works in the first half of the century, provide good examples of this earlier phenomenon.

   Thus, answer (A) is clearly false; the reverse is true. The same can be said for (B)—few critics believe this; most critics believe that "the patron saint" is Rousseau. It is easy to eliminate (D). If the novel is not relevant, then why does the critic spend half of the passage discussing it? It is true that the author proposes drama as an even more relevant genre, but that doesn't imply that the consideration of the novel was inappropriate.

   The author discusses Nivelle de la Chaussée along with the group of playwrights; thus, it is reasonable to assume that plays, not novels, are that author's claim to fame. Therefore, you're left with (E); and from how the author has described the books and paintings "often depict emotional contemporary issues."

16. **A** You should be able to eliminate choices (B) and (C) right away. Choice (C) is just ridiculous, and as for (B), the Gothic effects have to do with Gothic art (architecture) and the so-called Gothic Revival. Choice (D) doesn't seem to have much to do with the passage, so get rid of it.

You may get caught up with answer (E); the problem with this answer is the word "vividly." However, between (A) and (E), you should be able to determine that (A) is the better choice, upon reviewing the passage. If you are unfamiliar with Gothic romances, the phrase "such as crêpe-hung mortuary chambers" is the key to arriving at the correct answer.

17. **A** Hopefully, by POE you can use common sense to narrow your choices to (A) and (C). If you are unsure, plug each proposed answer into the sentence and see if the resulting sentence makes sense in the context of what you have read. "Morphology" refers to the form or structure of something. How does (A) sound? "…the revolution in theatrical behaviour which is of singular importance for the <u>structure</u> (or form) of Romanticism." That isn't bad; it's the best of the answer choices!

18. **C** The only overt attempts to trick you are in (D) and (E). When you go to a restaurant, the "gratuity" is the tip; "gratuitous" and "gratifying" contain the same initial letters. Even if you do not know the correct answer, you should never fall for this kind of trick; seldom or never will the question and the correct answer have a relationship such as this one. Words like *intensity* and *gesticulating* should lead you to the correct answer. In this case, the author is saying that the actors "go out of their way to give gratuitous demonstrations of the intensity with which they feel," which implies that their demonstrations are not directly tied to the plot; this shows that (C) is correct. Note that (B) is the exact opposite of the correct answer.

19. **A** This question is related to the previous ones in many respects. Furthermore, answers (C), (D), and (E) are not substantiated in any way by the text, and (B) is the opposite of what is true. A large clue in the passage that should have guided you toward the correct answer is the phrase "the gesticulating characters, often morbid, always extravagant." This implies that the characters were, as (A) states, emotionally overwrought.

20. **A** The word "Revolutionary" is capitalized because it refers to a specific revolution: the French Revolution (of 1789). By the way, there were several other important revolutions in France, most notably in 1830 and 1848; however, the French Revolution is the one that's cited here.

21. **A** Remember that a period (or periodic sentence) is a long, complex, grammatically correct sentence. This is definitely a long sentence, but it flows well and is grammatically correct.

22. **C** Using POE, you can eliminate all the incorrect answers with ease. Clearly, the passage goes beyond a discussion of theater (A), has nothing to do with political history (E), and is far too scholarly to interest tourists (D). Although, conceivably, it could come from a history text (B), the entire passage deals only with Romanticism, and seems to get into a little too much depth, and controversially, to be appropriate for a history text.

23. **B** Again, POE is the best way to approach this question. Answers (A), (C), (D), and (E) are at least half wrong (therefore completely wrong). Take a look at (B). The author is being ironic when she says in the first line "My own sex, I hope, will excuse me, if I treat them like rational creatures…." The second part of choice (B), "exposition," is defined as "a setting forth of meaning or intent," and that is exactly what the author is doing in this first paragraph. Answer choice (B) is correct. For the record, note that, in this context, the author's "apology" has nothing to do with being sorry; it most nearly means "defense of an idea."

24. **A** The author addresses women directly and pretends to excuse herself for addressing them as strong, confident people, instead of the weak, overly sentimental creatures that society wants (and expects) them to be.

25. **E** Your choice should boil down to (D) and (E). When the author says, "I wish to persuade women to endeavour to acquire strength, both of mind and body," she means intellectual and physical strength. Had she wanted to stress emotional strength, she would have replaced mind with heart.

26. **E** *Softer* and *weak* are important adjectives of both paragraphs; the author uses them in the second paragraph to tie this paragraph in with the first one.

27. **A** No doubt you can narrow your choices to (A) and (B). The best way to approach this type of question is to substitute in the answer choices for the original word and see which one makes the most sense. Try (A): "…supposed to be the sexual characteristics of the weaker <u>sex</u>,…". This seems great, but try (B) too, just in case: "…supposed to be the sexual characteristics of the weaker <u>woman</u>,…" Not as good. Naturally, in this case, the weaker sex is woman, but you are asked to find the meaning for "vessel" only. Choice (A) is the best answer.

28. **C** Again, there are only two reasonable answers: (A) and (C). The author states that "the first object of laudable ambition is to obtain a character as a human being, regardless of the distinction of sex;" thus, one must eliminate answer (A) because she is not suggesting that a comparison be made between a man and woman.

29. **A** The author wishes to convince the reader by the force of her cogent arguments and the sincerity of her emotions, so the answer is (A). If you don't have "cogent" on your vocabulary list, put it on now. It means "appealing to the intellect or powers of reasoning; convincing." You can eliminate the other choices: The author states unequivocally that she does not wish to polish her style, to employ the bombast and periodic sentences of a rhetorical style, to write elegantly, or to use flowery diction.

30. **C** The author points out—and rightfully so—that the flowery diction expected of women relegated them to a world outside of that of men. The difference in the social level of men and women was reflected in the way they used language; only men could use the crude words that attempt to express the crude realities of life. Women were not supposed to know those same crude realities, and, therefore, could not use the crude words that fit with those realities.

31. **E** The sugary diction becomes associated with the taste of a cloyingly sweet delicacy; this is an extended metaphor so POE allows you to eliminate (A), (B), and (D). This is not a caricature of women, nor is it a critique of bombast (remember, pompous speech or writing). If you do not know the meaning of "panegyric," then add it to your list of vocabulary. Panegyric means "statement of high praise." It should be clear that the author does not sing the praises of sugary writing.

32. **E** Since, in this passage, the author suggests that women have the capacity to be independent equals of men, she is most likely to agree that if women are educated in the same manner as are men, then they would be more likely to be equals with men in the eyes of the world.

33. **A** Use POE, especially if you don't know what answer choice (A) means. (Sardonic means "harsh, bitter, or caustic.") Although sarcasm is stronger than irony, both answer choices (C) and (D) involve saying one thing and meaning the opposite, so both are incorrect: The author means what she says. It is difficult to imagine a feminist author addressing other women in a condescending or haughty fashion. Only answer (A) remains.

34. **C** What is the entire passage about? It is about learning, and most importantly, the reason for learning. This is simply a big-picture question in disguise. In this passage, the writer claims that teaching methodologies are overrated because there are many ways to teach and learn; what is important is a reason for learning.

35. **A** The phrase "So it is with learning," which follows the example of the ways to learn tribal lays, is a big clue that should tell you that an analogy is being used here. Besides, none of the other answers is plausible; POE can lead you with certainty to the correct answer.

36. **C** Don't be thrown off by the use of the term "infinitives" in this question. Infinitives are simply verb forms that function as substantives, while retaining some verb characteristics. Some examples of infinitives are "We want him to win the lottery," or "To go willingly will prove that you are innocent." So this question specifically refers to the line "There is no one who can say that this or that is the best way to know things, to feel things, to see things, to remember things, to apply things, to connect things and that no other will do as well." From the context—and from your own experience, one hopes—learning is a positive experience, so any answer choice that uses a negative adjective should be eliminated. Learning is (not supposed to be) "tedious" (A), "impersonal" (B), "trivial" (D), or even "mechanical" (E); using POE leaves us with only (C). In fact, learning is an active and a varied process.

37. **D** If you understand the passage, you should be able to quickly narrow your choices to (C) and (D); motivation, in the author's words, is fleeting (or momentary). Although the author does not say outright that a motivation is concrete, he does set up a clear rhetorical contrast between motivation and reason. Given that he describes reason as abstract, it figures that motivation should be roughly the opposite—or at least not the same. The only textual clue that tells us motivation is concrete is the word *event*.

38. **E** We have already drawn attention to the string of infinitives in the first paragraph; in the third paragraph, you may have already noticed the parallel series of prepositional phrases (in which the preposition "to" is repeated). Choice (E), or "notable parallelism" is correct.

Let's go through the other choices. An "aphorism" is a pithy saying or proverb. "Syllogistic reasoning" proceeds along the lines of a syllogism: a major premise, a minor premise, and a conclusion. Here is an example of syllogistic reasoning: All Princeton Review books are useful; this is a Princeton Review book; therefore, this book is useful. *Ad hominem* arguments consist of attacks against a person's character. If you were to say, "This book must be awful because you wrote it," you would be adducing an *ad hominem* argument to prove your point.

39. **C** Answers (A) and (B) are snares for the careless reader who fails to consider the context in which the word is used; "god" in this case has nothing to do with religion. The entire second half of the text is about the reason for education. One big clue that the author isn't using the word "god" literally, is the phrase "…must have a god to serve, or, even better, several gods." If this were a literal use of "god," then the term would not have been pluralized later.

40. **C** In this case, the authority is Nietzsche, and the author gives us a clear rhetorical statement of his use of analogy in the sentence that follows the quote: "This applies as much to learning as to living."

41. **A** Perhaps this is a good time to review two terms that are closely related: *oxymoron* and *paradox*. An oxymoron is an apparent contradiction of terms; a paradox is an apparent contradiction of ideas. The important word here is *apparent*.

In this case, the last sentence is built on an apparent contradiction of terms: Schooling will be brought to an end if it has no end. Nonsense? No. We are supposed to understand that, in context, the second "end" is synonymous with reason (or goal or objective).

42. **B** This is a warm-up question and serves little more than to check that you have a reasonable grasp on the content of the passage.

If you missed the implications of the final statement, then you could eliminate (C) and (E) and guess. Choices (A) and (D) are similar in meaning, and both imply that the speaker is a politician—of which we have no proof. Choice (B) is your best bet. Of course, if you noticed the allusions to law in the body of the text and the judgment of the final statement, then you may have realized that the passage is the dissenting opinion of a judge in a federal case—and you would have been correct to assume that this was a case that went before the Supreme Court.

43. **B** Perhaps the biggest clue that tells us analogy is being employed is the phrase "upon like grounds." Naturally, almost everyone would agree that it would be unthinkable, for example, to segregate passengers by religion (Catholic and Protestant). If we agree that this (and the other examples) are analogous to the case before the court (segregation of passengers by race), then we are forced to agree with this judge.

44. **B** Were you tempted to choose (C)? Did you choose (C)? If so, you fell into a trap. Today, it would be normal to expect this judge to propose both civil and racial equality, but the judge bases his arguments solely on the issue of civil rights. In fact, the judge says that the white race is the dominant one "in prestige, in achievements, in education, in wealth, and in power. So, I doubt not, it will continue to be for all time, if it remains true to its great heritage, and holds fast to the principles of constitutional liberty." Based on the passage, the speaker appears not to believe that racial equality will ever be a reality, although civil equality exists.

45. **E** If you do not know the meaning of the word, begin with POE. Immediately, you will see that (A) and (C) can be eliminated; they mean things that are opposite to the speaker's tone and meaning. If you know that "propitious" is roughly equivalent to (C), "useful," you can eliminate that choice as well. As for choice (B), although "unjust," like "harmful," fits the context, the latter choice is the better synonym for the original term ("pernicious"). Of course, as long as you can narrow the choices down to two or three, you should take a guess even if you are not sure. The definition of pernicious is: "causing great harm."

46. **A** In this passage, the phrases "may be stricken down by congressional action, or by the courts" and "duty to maintain the supreme law of the land" provide the answer; the Louisiana law is subject to censure by either the United States Congress or the United States Supreme Court.

47. **D** POE is the way to go on this one. Remember to look for one inappropriate word in each answer. Neither adjective in answer (A) is really appropriate, so you can eliminate (A). Try (B). Although one may argue that the style is "dry," it is not "objective"—the speaker is arguing only one side of an issue; so (B) is out. How about (C)? Of course, the passage could be thought of as "legalistic," but it is not at all "abstract"—so get rid of (C). As for (E), the passage is "probing," but it is certainly not "subtle." The speaker comes right out and says what he believes; calling this decision as pernicious as the Supreme Court's judgment of the Dred Scott Case. (In the Dred Scott case, the Supreme Court upheld a lower court ruling that the state of Louisiana could fine the railroad company for letting African Americans ride in the same carriages as whites, a situation that was prohibited by Louisiana state law.)

48. **C** The simile in this first sentence compares the great and ancient parliamentary institutions with the august, but somewhat ancient bodies of the members of Parliament. The speaker is warming up his audience with a bit of humor before launching into what amounts to a very serious ultimatum: that the speaker will continue to serve as Prime Minister, but only if they concede to him much greater authority than before (1842).

49. **B** The speaker is addressing a group of his peers, who are the other members of Parliament. The tricky part here is, of course, the repetition of "Sir," a political convention in Great Britain—it is as if the prime minister were addressing each member of Parliament as an individual. We know that he is minister of England because of the final sentences; and these sentences also reveal definitively that he is speaking to peers: "Sir, I do not wish to be the Minister of England; but while I have the high honour of holding that Office, I am determined to hold it by no servile tenure. I will only hold that office upon the condition of being unshackled by any other obligations than those of consulting the public interests, and of providing for the public safety."

50. **D** Everything before this line is an introduction to the minister's real message; until this point, he has joked, given a general review of his former motivations and actions as the leader of the Conservative party, and explained his reasons for accepting to serve again as prime minister ("feeling of honour") in spite of his failing health and aged mind ("a burden too great for my physical, and far beyond my intellectual structure"). The transition comes with "But, Sir, I will not take the step with mutilated power and shackled authority." He will do the country and his peers a favor, but only if he is granted much more authority to rule.

51. **E** It should be easy for you to eliminate (A), (B), and (D), so you're left with (C) and (E), which do not fit neatly into the nautical terminology. Answer (C) is the best choice to eliminate. All the other terms fit neatly into the nautical terminology. However, one could stretch a point and claim that "fairly" is related to fair weather; whereas "unshackled" is clearly unrelated to this metaphor.

52. **E** Naturally, the first step is to determine the "dominant point" of the final paragraph. Thankfully, the second paragraph is short—it is the rhetorical summation of his ultimatum. The key phrases are "servile tenure" and "unshackled by any other obligations." Of course, "unfettered" and "unshackled" are synonyms, so the best answer is (E), "unfettered."

53. **C** The minister states unequivocally that honor is his motivation, in the following passage in particular: "and to be relieved from it [the position] with perfect honour would be the greatest favour that could be conferred on me. But as a feeling of honour and strong sense of duty require me to undertake those responsible functions, I declare, Sir, that I am ready to incur these risks, to bear these burdens, and to front all these honourable dangers." The word *honor* comes up numerous times in this excerpt.

54. **C** You should be able to narrow your options to (B) and (C). But be careful! Do you think that the speaker, the most powerful man in Great Britain, allowed his mood to shift or to affect his tone? The speech was carefully constructed, and the tone was coolly calculated when William Gladstone wrote it. The prime minister began with a light tone because he was looking to set up his audience, not because he started his speech in a good mood. In fact, his real mood never shifts: He manipulates tone for maximum effect.

ANSWERS TO THE FREE-RESPONSE SECTION

QUESTION 1

Analytical/Expository Essay

The sample essay that follows is a strong one; the writer could expect to receive a score of 8 with this work. One important thing to note about this essay is the structure. The writer avoids the common error made in comparison and contrast essays; she does NOT write first about one review in one paragraph and another in a second paragraph. That said, inside each paragraph, the discussion of the articles is clearly segregated; this could have been handled more deftly, but this organization gets the job done. The introduction is a bit on the long side, but it provides a clear outline of the material and engages the reader thoroughly.

Mary Shelley's <u>Frankenstein</u> is, in modern times, heralded as a classic, great work of art. However, when it was first published in 1818, few people regarded it as a worthy work of literary art. As seen in the two passages taken from the critics' reviews of the novel, Frankenstein inspired extreme sentiments and reactions—readers either loved and enjoyed it or abhorred it and were disgusted by it. The two reviews presented convey the two contrasting emotions, as if in response to each other. The first, an anonymous piece from <u>The Quarterly Review</u>, criticizes Mary Shelley's work, using vernacular and plain (yet grotesque) language and popular culture allusions and standards to illustrate the author's condemnation of <u>Frankenstein</u>. Conversely, Sir Walter Scott's review from Blackwood's <u>Edinburgh Magazine</u> is itself written in a worthy literary manner, using heightened terms, literary terms, and quotations from other works to demonstrate his positive point of view. In the 1800s, there were many magazines available for the literate to purchase and indulge in, some were professional journals intended for those who worked in a particular industry (like science or literature), while others were broader publications for the general public. The difference between the two kinds was always (and still is) readily apparent in the type of language used by the authors of the magazine's articles. It can be surmised that Blackwood's <u>Edinburgh Magazine</u> was intended for those immersed in literature, or at least those who were highly educated. Scott's writing is romantic, mentioning "daemons," "the lovely and helpless" and "creature" and "persecutor." All these words and phrases are characteristic of a gothic or a romantic novel, in which the reader is presented with a tortured hero who is persecuted in some form and is faced with something lovely (usually a female). Phrases such as "resentment toward the human race," "expedients for exciting terror," and "uncommon powers of poetic imagination" are meant for a reader with a heightened vocabulary; one capable of understanding Scott's references and intentions. However, juxtaposed with Sir Walter Scott's review, the anonymous review from <u>The Quarterly Review</u> (a seemingly plain publication) is straightforward and simple. Instead of embellishing or elaborating, the author uses language like "strong and striking language," "tissue of horrible and disgusting absurdity," and "fatigues the feelings" to criticize the novel. Overall, the article has a condescending tone; in summarizing the conclusion of the novel, the author adds in his own commentary, sarcastically remarking on the implausibility of the entire situation. All his opinions are presented in a clear, plain manner, which serves to make very clear his utter loathing of Mary Shelley's work.

Both Scott and the anonymous author make use of popular conventions, standards, and allusions of their time period. However, their references again establish a distinct difference between the two articles. Scott, in his piece, quotes <u>Macbeth</u>, by William Shakespeare, to illustrate his point that <u>Frankenstein</u>, while shocking, cannot shock an already jaded audience. Furthermore, he speaks of terror being "employed by the romantic writers of the age" mentioning literary conventions. Another convention is brought up when he states that Shelley does not utilize "hyperbolic Germanisms" with which tales of wonder are usually told. The anonymous author, on the other hand, never quotes another literary work to support his ideas. He alludes to Bedlam, "Mad Bess," and "Mad Tom" as popular cultural figures. Continuing with his appeal to the masses, the anonymous author points out that <u>Frankenstein</u> "inculcates no lessons of conduct, manners or morality." Unlikely popular literature of the time, Shelley's novel disregards the conventions of morals and lessons learned.

Though the two reviews were written in highly different forms of language, both convey their point of view clearly. Scott's review was a positive one, meant for an elite readership. The anonymous author, however, wrote a disgusted condemnation for the pious masses.

QUESTION 2

Argumentative Essay

The following sample essay is very strong. The one noticeable flaw is the discussion of Switzerland; this detour pertains to neutrality, but it is not clear how it relates to racism. It is difficult to gauge just how deleterious the flaw may be. Certainly, the essay would earn a score of at least 7 and may get an 8.

Often, it is believed that if one ignores an issue or a problem, it will merely disappear. Mothers tell their children to ignore bullies, and even the Bible instructs us to turn the other cheek. However, when certain issues are not dealt with, they can fester until they become something far more serious than they were originally; racism is one such issue. As the passage suggests, colorblindness and neutrality are not equalizers; they are merely blinders that allow people to continue as though nothing is out of balance. By adopting a "neutral stand" and by failing to recognize the innate differences between racial groups, one not only perpetuates racism, but also promotes the homogenization of cultures and races, in itself a form of racism.

Sooner or later, the issues one faces must be dealt with. Ignorance, in this case, is not bliss; the longer a problem is put aside, the harder it is to conquer when one finally decides to face it. In the United States, the quintessential example of such a problem is racism. The 1950s and 1960s were a demonstration of just what can happen when an entire nation pretends that nothing is wrong or unequal. Race riots all over the country were the culmination of a race's mounting frustrations. The passage states that "identifying problems and actively promoting solutions are necessary to effect useful change." In fact change, in the form of various civil rights legislatures, only took place when racism was recognized and dealt with by the federal government. Only strong action, like the integration of the Central High School in Little Rock, Arkansas, could ever hope to remedy the situation. By bringing the problem into the spotlight and making everyone consider it and its implications, the government steps toward change, progress, and equality.

The only successful neutral stance ever taken in history was by Switzerland, during all the wars that raged around the country's borders. However, a neutral stance requires more effort to maintain than a stance that is evidently one-sided, because neutrality involves denying the "social and historical context for every situation…[and]…ignoring personal contexts." When this occurs, it would seem that one is assenting that we are all the same equal people, yet that very assertion is flawed, since it eliminates the "differences that exist." If one does not take a side or a stance, one is, in effect, resigning oneself to the current state of affairs, the status quo. As the author of the passage points out, ignoring inequalities and differences allows "the inequalities to continue to exist, given that [one] wouldn't do anything to help change them." Until the public began noticing and sympathizing with the victims of racism, it took no collective action to change the status quo. Finally recognizing the inequality which was the status quo, the public could no longer remain neutral—it split into those who wanted to maintain the status quo and those who wanted to change it and improve the situation.

In essence, neutrality is supposed to be an equalizer because it declares that there are no differences between human beings. However, that denial takes away that which makes us inherently human. Without our cultures and races, we would have nothing to separate one person from another. Thus neutrality states that it is better for a group of people to lack differences than to embrace those differences. Racism is looking down on and rejecting the differences between two people. In much the same way, neutrality turns a blind eye to differences, lending validity to ignorance. Without action and discussion, societies become stale. It is only with a firm stance that one can hope to incite progress and reform; there must be recognition and a definite lack of neutrality if racism is to be prevented. "Being neutral is consenting to the status quo," a status quo which is unequal, unfair, and socially unbalanced.

Question 3A

Analytical/Expository Essay

The following sample should be extremely useful for you because it illustrates the limitations on a good writer who doesn't really know anything about rhetorical strategies. This essay falls in the 8 to 9 category for its writing, but it deserves only a 6 for its handling of the rhetorical strategies; most readers would reward the student for the writing and scoot the score up to a 7. But this is a shame. Were the student to handle the strategies more deftly (appeal to authority, analogy, example, or illustration), the essay would earn a score of 8 or 9. Take our advice seriously: If you are not well versed in the art of rhetoric, study our chapters on rhetorical strategies carefully.

Known as the father of utilitarianism, John Stuart Mill thought that government and societies should work towards securing the greatest happiness for the greatest number of people. In his opinion, the value of a thing was mostly defined by its utility. In his essay "The Utility of Religion," he puts forward the point that religion truly has no value. Without the backing of public opinion, Mill states that religion has nothing—it is a dying institution lacking in any sort of influence. Mill establishes his position using rhetorical strategies like examples and illustration, diction and tone, and counterpoints.

The largest and most important example that Mill utilizes is Jeremy Bentham's discourse on religion's lack of influence and control. In citing Bentham, Mill gives weight to his own argument. Furthermore, Bentham's writing provides specific examples (oaths, dueling and "illicit sexual intercourse") for Mill's position. Of his own accord, Mill brings up general examples, referencing the rewards-and-punishments system imposed by religion. He states that while religion insists that this system is vitally important, it is easily questioned and torn down. His point with discussing this religious system of divine retribution and praise is to point out that the system and the religion itself has no merit if it can be cast aside by anyone with courage and intelligence.

Mill's argument is presented in the most straightforward manner possible in order to reach the greatest amount of people. His diction is clear; instead of using large, important-sounding words, he simplifies his statements so that all who read his essay will understand it (a manifestation of the implementation of his philosophy). Though he naturally utilizes some advanced language, like "peccadilloes" and "malefactor," the meaning of the words can be deduced from the context and implication of the sentences. Furthermore, his common diction underscores his tone—patient, frank, and certain. Mill's simple language emphasizes his belief that he is certain of his position—he needs no fancy vocabulary to lend weight to what he is arguing. Again, his tone suggests openness and his patience implies his desire to broaden the horizons of the greatest number of people.

The counterpoints Mill employs are perhaps the strongest strategy in his essay. In order to make his stance easily understandable, he points out what religions have stipulated and how these stipulations have been challenged over time. Each statement about a quality of religion is followed by a sentence beginning with "but." Furthermore, the counterpoints have a quality of then-and-now. Mill points out that religion once had certain effects and powers over people in the past, however, in Mill's "modern day" period, those effects and powers have been diminished or completely eradicated. Again, he cites the threat of divine punishment and the weight of public opinion as what was but no longer is true and actual.

John Stuart Mill's essay "The Utility of Religion" presents the common people, the middle class, and the upper class with the idea that religion has no purpose or worth. Both his specific and broad examples underline his point. Mill's diction, tone, and counterpoints provide even more emphasis and weight to his argument.

Question 3B

Synthesis Essay

Although it is not perfect, the following sample is about as good as it gets; most likely, it would receive a perfect 9. Writing as a woman and choosing, based on the sources, to vote against women's suffrage is a brilliant strategy; this catches the reader's interest right away. Notice, too, how naturally the student cites the sources; it is easy for the reader to keep track of the citations. Here is a model essay for you.

The late 1880s in the United States were focused on the issue of women's suffrage. As with any debate, there were arguments for and against women's right to vote. The documents provided illustrate both viewpoints and sides of the issues. However, the sources that support the anti-women's-suffrage stance have greater validity and weight. If faced with the choice, I would have voted (though I would not have been allowed to vote, being a woman) against a woman's right to vote.

It is true that Susan B. Anthony's stance is well defended. Citing the documents which created the foundation of the United States, she points out how the founding fathers gave the government no power to award or remove rights. Her appeal to authority, while valid and worthy, simply is not able to compete with the arguments made against women's suffrage. Source 3 presents Judge Ward Hunt's instructions to the jury in the case of the United States v. Susan B. Anthony. The very fact that he is a judge, a person who is typically educated and wise, gives weight to Hunt's position. His references to American law also utilize the strategy of authority; though not an individual, the Constitution of the State dictates the laws of each state. According to Hunt, "The right of voting, or the privilege of voting, is a right or privilege arising under the Constitution of the State, and not of the United States." This statement directly contradicts Anthony's point concerning federal law, in Source 1. By voting, Hunt argues, Anthony deliberately intended to break the existing law and must now face the consequences. Hunt's major point is that voting and its stipulations are at the mercy of the state, and since not all citizens are allowed to vote, it is not a given that women must vote.

Furthering the position against women's suffrage, the Supreme Court's decision, presented in Source 5, was that "the Constitution of the United States does not confer on women the right to vote in federal elections." Again, it is stated that "in no state were all citizens allowed to vote." Each state has its own limits on who is or is not allowed to vote. Unanimously, the judge's decision that the constitution of the United States does "not necessarily confer the right of suffrage" again invalidates Anthony's idea that voting is an unalienable right. Instead, it is a privilege awarded by each state as it sees fit.

Caricatures were a widely popular and an effective, entertaining way of conveying an opinion in print. The caricature of Susan B. Anthony in source 2 is firmly on the side of anti-women's-suffrage. In the foreground is a stern Anthony, wearing a hat usually seen on the heads of lawmakers. Her skirt is far shorter than allowed at the time, and her facial expression resembles that of a military general (her troops are rallying in the background). The idea of the male and female spheres being switched is illustrated behind her—as a consequence of women treading outside of the sphere and being allowed to work, women have taken over the roles typically given to men, like policing, and the men must take up the women's job, motherhood. The implied consequences and chaos that will be caused by allowing women's suffrage overrule any desire to support a woman's right to vote.

Based on the analysis of the presented documents, it would be difficult to vote for women's suffrage. Seeing as it is not an unalienable right, and instead regulated by state constitution, the privilege of voting cannot be seized but awarded. Its threat to the status quo of male-female roles is great and cannot be overlooked.

14

Practice Test 2

ENGLISH LANGUAGE AND COMPOSITION

Three hours are allotted for this examination: 1 hour for Section I, which consists of multiple-choice questions, and 2 hours for Section II, which consists of essay questions. Section I is printed in this examination booklet. Section II is printed in a separate booklet.

SECTION I

Time—1 hour

Number of questions—54

Percent of total grade—45

Section I of this examination contains 54 multiple-choice questions. Therefore, please be careful to fill in only the ovals that are preceded by numbers 1 through 54 on your answer sheet.

General Instructions

DO NOT OPEN THIS BOOKLET UNTIL YOU ARE INSTRUCTED TO DO SO.

INDICATE ALL YOUR ANSWERS TO QUESTIONS IN SECTION I ON THE SEPARATE ANSWER SHEET. No credit will be given for anything written in this examination booklet, but you may use the booklet for notes or scratchwork. After you have decided which of the suggested answers is best, COMPLETELY fill in the corresponding oval on the answer sheet.

Example: Sample Answer

Chicago is a

(A) state
(B) city
(C) country
(D) continent
(E) village

Many candidates wonder whether or not to guess the answers to questions about which they are not certain. In this section of the examination, as a correction for haphazard guessing, one-fourth of the number of questions you answer incorrectly will be subtracted from the number of questions you answer correctly. It is improbable, therefore, that mere guessing will improve your score significantly; it may even lower your score, and it does take time. If, however, you are not sure of the best answer but have some knowledge of the question and are able to eliminate one or more of the answer choices as wrong, your chance of getting the right answer is improved, and it may be to your advantage to answer such a question.

Use your time effectively, working as rapidly as you can without losing accuracy. Do not spend too much time on questions that are too difficult. Go on to other questions and come back to the difficult ones later if you have time. It is not expected that everyone will be able to answer all the multiple-choice questions.

The inclusion of the passages in this examination is not intended as an endorsement by The College Board or Educational Testing Service of the content, ideas, values, or styles of the individual authors. The material has been selected from works of various historical periods by a Committee of Examiners who are teachers of language and literature and who have judged that the passages printed here reflect the content of a course of study for which this examination is appropriate.

ENGLISH LANGUAGE AND COMPOSITION

SECTION I

Time—1 hour

Directions: This part consists of selections from prose works and questions on their content, form, and style. After reading each passage, choose the best answer to each question and completely fill in the corresponding oval on the answer sheet.

Note: Pay particular attention to the requirement of questions that contain the words NOT, LEAST, or EXCEPT.

Questions 1–10. Read the following passage carefully before you choose your answers.

His exuberance of knowledge, and plenitude of ideas, sometimes obstruct the tendency of his reasoning and the clearness of his decisions: on whatever subject
Line he employed his mind, there started up immediately so
5 many images before him, that he lost one by grasping another. His memory supplied him with so many illustrations, parallel or dependent notions, that he was always starting into collateral considerations; but the spirit and vigour of his pursuit always gives
10 delight; and the reader follows him, without reluctance, through his mazes, in themselves flowery and pleasing, and ending at the point originally in view.
"To have great excellencies and great faults, '*magnæ virtutes nec minora vitia*,' is the poesy," says our author,
15 "of the best natures." This poesy may be properly applied to the style of Browne; it is vigorous, but rugged; it is learned, but pedantick; it is deep, but obscure; it strikes, but does not please; it commands, but does not allure; his tropes are harsh, and his
20 combinations uncouth.
He fell into an age in which our language began to lose the stability which it had obtained in the time of Elizabeth; and was considered by every writer as a subject on which he might try his plastick skill, by
25 moulding it according to his own fancy. Milton, in consequence of this encroaching license, began to introduce the Latin idiom: and Browne, though he gave less disturbance to our structures in phraseology, yet poured in a multitude of exotick words; many,
30 indeed, useful and significant, which, if rejected, must be supplied by circumlocution, such as commensality, for the state of many living at the same table; but many superfluous, as a paralogical, for an unreasonable doubt; and some so obscure, that they conceal his
35 meaning rather than explain it, as arthritical analogies, for parts that serve some animals in the place of joints.
His style is, indeed, a tissue of many languages; a mixture of heterogeneous words, brought together from distant regions, with terms originally
40 appropriated to one art, and drawn by violence into the service of another. He must, however, be confessed to have augmented our philosophical diction; and, in defence of his uncommon words and expressions, we must consider, that he had uncommon sentiments, and
45 was not content to express, in many words, that idea for which any language could supply a single term.
But his innovations are sometimes pleasing, and his temerities happy: he has many "verba ardentia" forcible expressions, which he would never have found,
50 but by venturing to the utmost verge of propriety; and flights which would never have been reached, but by one who had very little fear of the shame of falling.

(1756)

1. The reader can infer from the first paragraph that some critics have

(A) chastised Browne for his inability to reason
(B) lauded Browne's frequent linear explanations
(C) complained about Browne's lack of clarity
(D) compared Browne with Shakespeare
(E) compared the author of the passage with Browne

2. In context, "poesy" (line 14) most nearly means

(A) poetry
(B) inspiration for writing
(C) sentimental thoughts
(D) flowery writing
(E) poetic dreaming

3. The meaning of the phrase *magnæ virtutes nec minora vitia* (lines 13–14)

(A) can be ascertained only if one understands Latin
(B) becomes clear at the end of the paragraph
(C) is obvious
(D) has been lost over the centuries
(E) was known only to Browne

GO ON TO THE NEXT PAGE

4. In the second paragraph, the author

(A) is openly critical of Browne's style
(B) hints that Browne's writing is pedantic
(C) justifies the strength of Browne's style
(D) argues in favor of a reexamination of Browne's style
(E) suggests that Browne's writing is too facile

5. The author modifies the strict parallelism of "it is vigorous, but rugged; it is learned, but pedantick; it is deep, but obscure; it strikes, but does not please; it commands, but does not allure; his tropes are harsh, and his combinations uncouth" (lines 16–20) to

(A) better define his point of view
(B) keep the reader off balance
(C) maintain a sense of imbalance
(D) show more respect for Browne's accomplishments
(E) to obfuscate his real opinions

6. According to the author, Browne lived at a time of significant

(A) linguistic experimentation
(B) literary conservatism
(C) linguistic stability
(D) metaphorical license
(E) impoverishment of the English language

7. In lines 27–36 ("Browne, though he gave less disturbance...in the place of joints"), the author classifies Browne's diction in a manner that proceeds from

(A) interesting, to captivating, to intriguing
(B) appropriate, to inappropriate, to superfluous
(C) interesting, to intriguing, to disappointing
(D) useful, to unhelpful, to deleterious
(E) appropriate, to inappropriate, to intriguing

8. The author posits that Browne's unusual diction can be tied to his desire

(A) to mystify his readers
(B) to develop English phraseology
(C) to enrich the English language
(D) to set himself apart from other authors of his time
(E) to express exactly his unusual thoughts

9. According to the author, Browne's style is marked by

(A) heteroclite diction
(B) homogeneous words
(C) mundane vocabulary
(D) humorous phrases
(E) heterogeneous tropes

10. Which of the following best summarizes the passage?

(A) an impartial reconsideration of Browne's style
(B) a scathing critique by a rival
(C) a manifesto by one of Browne's colleagues
(D) a comparative study of Milton and Browne
(E) a virulent polemic

11. The author's tone in this passage is best described as

(A) sarcastic and doctrinaire
(B) analytical and scholarly
(C) expository and harsh
(D) indulgent and condescending
(E) capricious and sentimental

GO ON TO THE NEXT PAGE

But is it upon the heroines that we would cast a final glance. "I have always been finding out my religion since I was a little girl," says Dorothea Casaubon. "I
Line used to pray so much—now I hardly ever pray. I try
5 not to have desires merely for myself..." She is speaking for them all. That is their problem. They cannot live without religion, and they start out on the search for one when they are little girls. Each has the deep feminine passion for goodness, which makes the place
10 where she stands in aspiration and agony the heart of the book—still and cloistered like a place of worship, but that she no longer knows to whom to pray. In learning they seek their goal; in the ordinary tasks of womanhood; in the wider service of their kind. They
15 do not find what they seek, and we cannot wonder. The ancient consciousness of woman, charged with suffering and sensibility, and for so many ages dumb, seems in them to have brimmed and overflowed and uttered a demand for something—they scarcely know
20 what—for something that is perhaps incompatible with the facts of human existence. George Eliot had far too strong an intelligence to tamper with those facts, and too broad a humour to mitigate the truth because it was a stern one. Save for the supreme courage of
25 their endeavour, the struggle ends, for her heroines, in tragedy, or in a compromise that is even more melancholy. But their story is the incomplete version of the story that is George Eliot herself. For her, too, the burden and the complexity of womanhood were
30 not enough; she must reach beyond the sanctuary and pluck for herself the strange bright fruits of art and knowledge. Clasping them as few women have ever clasped them, she would not renounce her own inheritance—the difference of view, the difference
35 of standard—nor accept an inappropriate reward. Thus we behold her, a memorable figure, inordinately praised and shrinking from her fame, despondent, reserved, shuddering back into the arms of love as if there alone were satisfaction and, it might be,
40 justification, at the same time reaching out with "a fastidious yet hungry ambition" for all that life could offer the free and inquiring mind and confronting her feminine aspirations with the real world of men. Triumphant was the issue for her, whatever it may have
45 been for her creations, and as we recollect all that she dared and achieved, how with every obstacle against her—sex and health and convention—she sought more knowledge and more freedom till the body, weighted with its double burden, sank worn out, we must lay
50 upon her grave whatever we have it in our power to bestow of laurel and rose.

(1919)

12. The speaker in the passage above can be described best as

(A) a family member of George Eliot
(B) a member of the clergy
(C) a student
(D) a chauvinist literary critic
(E) a professional writer

13. According to the speaker, George Eliot's heroines are "cloistered" (line 11) because they are

(A) in a church
(B) essentially alone
(C) in a monastery
(D) imprisoned in cloisters
(E) lost in prayer

14. In context, "the facts of human existence" (line 21)

(A) restrict both men and women
(B) restrict women only
(C) are only applicable to Eliot's heroines
(D) pertain to any literary character
(E) pertain to men only

15. "Save for" (line 24) most nearly means

(A) except for
(B) saving
(C) safe for
(D) guarding against
(E) keeping in mind

16. The "differences" mentioned in line 34 pertain to Eliot's

(A) profession
(B) class
(C) upbringing
(D) education
(E) gender

17. According to the speaker, Eliot

(A) enjoyed excellent health
(B) suffered from her independence and knowledge
(C) was prevented from attaining fame by men
(D) was very unlike the heroines of her books
(E) repudiated her feminine nature

GO ON TO THE NEXT PAGE

18. In the sentence beginning "Thus we behold her"
(lines 36–43), the speaker employs all of the following EXCEPT

(A) apposition
(B) hyperbole
(C) personification
(D) relative clauses
(E) parallelism

19. It is reasonable to assume that the phrase "a fastidious yet hungry ambition" (lines 40–41)

(A) is spoken by one of Eliot's heroines
(B) comes from one of the speaker's literary works
(C) is borrowed from one of Eliot's critics
(D) is not to be taken seriously
(E) does not represent the speaker's point of view

20. Generally, the style of the entire passage is best
defined as

(A) effusive and disorganized
(B) pedantic and terse
(C) sympathetic and concrete
(D) abstract and metaphysical
(E) intellectual and cynical

GO ON TO THE NEXT PAGE

Questions 21–25. Read the following passage carefully before you choose your answers.

It will be readily admitted, that a population trained in regular habits of temperance, industry, and sobriety; of genuine charity for the opinions of all
Line mankind, founded on the only knowledge that can
5 implant true charity in the breast of any human being; trained also in a sincere desire to do good to the utmost of their power, and without any exception, to every one of their fellow creatures, cannot, even by their example alone, do otherwise than materially increase
10 the welfare and advantages of the neighbourhood in which such a population may be situated. To feel the due weight of this consideration, only imagine to yourselves 2,000 or 3,000 human beings trained in habits of licentiousness, and allowed to remain in
15 gross ignorance. How much, in such a case, would not the peace, quiet, comfort, and happiness of the neighbourhood be destroyed! But there is not anything I have done, or purpose to do, which is not intended to benefit my fellow-creatures to the greatest extent
20 that my operations can embrace. I wish to benefit all equally; but circumstances limit my present measures for the public good within a narrow circle. I must begin to act at some point; and a combination of singular events has fixed that point at this establishment. The
25 first and greatest advantages will therefore centre here. But, in unison with the principle thus stated, it has ever been my intention that as this Institution, when completed, will accommodate more than the children of parents resident at the village, any persons living
30 at Lanark, or in the neighbourhood anywhere around, who cannot well afford to educate their children, shall be at liberty, on mentioning their wishes, to send them to this place, where they will experience the same care and attention as those who belong to the establishment.
35 Nor will there be any distinction made between the children of those parents who are deemed the worst, and of those who may be esteemed the best, members of society: rather, indeed, would I prefer to receive the offspring of the worst, if they shall be sent at an early
40 age; because they really require more of our care and pity; and by well training these, society will be more essentially benefited, than if the like attention were paid to those whose parents are educating them in comparatively good habits. The system now preparing,
45 and which will ultimately be brought into full practice, is to effect a complete change in all our sentiments and conduct towards those poor miserable creatures whom the errors of past times have denominated the bad, the worthless, and the wicked. A more enlarged and
50 better knowledge of human nature will make it evident that, in strict justice, those who apply these terms to their fellow-men are not only the most ignorant, but are themselves the immediate causes of more misery in the world than those whom they call the outcasts
55 of society. They are, therefore, correctly speaking, the most wicked and worthless; and were they not grossly deceived, and rendered blind from infancy, they would become conscious of the lamentably extensive evils, which, by their well-intended but most mistaken
60 conduct, they have, during so long a period, inflicted on their fellow-men. But the veil of darkness must be removed from their eyes; their erroneous proceedings must be made so palpable that they shall thenceforth reject them with horror. Yes! They will reject with
65 horror even those notions which hitherto they have from infancy been taught to value beyond price.

(1816)

21. In general, the passage reveals a point of view that is

(A) philanthropic and utopian
(B) pessimistic and cynical
(C) altruistic and elitist
(D) quixotic and irrational
(E) positivist and unreasonable

22. The Institution (line 27) is

(A) a hospital
(B) a town
(C) an asylum
(D) a school
(E) a church

23. The sentence that begins "They are, therefore, correctly speaking, the most wicked and worthless…" (lines 55–61) serves to

(A) explain a paradox
(B) prepare an antithesis
(C) present an analogy
(D) resolve an inconsistency
(E) summarize a theme

24. "They" (line 64) refers to

(A) the poor
(B) the wealthy
(C) the inhabitants of Lanark
(D) the inhabitants of neighboring areas
(E) all of the above

GO ON TO THE NEXT PAGE

25. The speaker appears most interested in

    (A) establishing mercantile and financial
         establishments
    (B) creating more employment and cultural
         opportunities
    (C) abolishing socioeconomic and cultural
         differences
    (D) discussing social conduct and poverty
    (E) imparting knowledge and moral values

GO ON TO THE NEXT PAGE

Questions 26–32. Read the following passage carefully before you choose your answers.

And yet, being a problem is a strange experience—peculiar even for one who has never been anything else, save perhaps in babyhood and in Europe. It
Line is in the early days of rollicking boyhood that the
5 revelation first bursts upon one, all in a day, as it were. I remember well when the shadow swept across me. I was a little thing, away up in the hills of New England, where the dark Housatonic winds between Hoosac and Taghkanic to the sea. In a wee wooden schoolhouse,
10 something put it into the boys' and girls' heads to buy gorgeous visiting-cards—ten cents a package—and exchange. The exchange was merry, till one girl, a tall newcomer, refused my card—refused it peremptorily, with a glance. Then it dawned upon me with a certain
15 suddenness that I was different from the others; or like, mayhap, in heart and life and longing, but shut out from their world by a vast veil. I had thereafter no desire to tear down that veil, to creep through; I held all beyond it in common contempt, and lived above it
20 in a region of blue sky and great wandering shadows. That sky was bluest when I could beat my mates at examination-time, or beat them at a foot-race, or even beat their stringy heads. Alas, with the years all this fine contempt began to fade; for the worlds I longed
25 for, and all their dazzling opportunities, were theirs, not mine. But they should not keep these prizes, I said; some, all, I would wrest from them. Just how I would do it I could never decide: by reading law, by healing the sick, by telling the wonderful tales that swam in my
30 head—some way. With other black boys the strife was not so fiercely sunny: their youth shrunk into tasteless sycophancy, or into silent hatred of the pale world about them and mocking distrust of everything white; or wasted itself in a bitter cry, Why did God make me
35 an outcast and a stranger in mine own house? The shades of the prison-house closed round about us all: walls strait and stubborn to the whitest, but relentlessly narrow, tall, and unscalable to sons of night who must plod darkly on in resignation, or beat unavailing palms
40 against the stone, or steadily, half hopelessly, watch the streak of blue above.

From THE SOULS OF BLACK FOLK, W.E.B. Du Bois (1903)

26. The speaker was a problem because

(A) of his ambition
(B) he was involved in schoolyard fights
(C) he was contemptuous of his peers
(D) of his race
(E) of his upbringing

27. In this passage, the anecdote of the visiting-cards serves as

(A) an epiphany for the speaker
(B) a moment of triumph for the speaker
(C) a revelation for the reader
(D) a turning point for the school
(E) a chance for redemption for the speaker

28. After presenting the incident of the visiting-cards, the speaker controls the rest of the passage by employing

(A) repeated appeals to authority
(B) a series of euphemisms
(C) a series of analogies
(D) two extended metaphors
(E) self-deprecating humor

29. The "sons of the night" (line 38) are

(A) evil young men
(B) African American boys
(C) sons of evil parents
(D) lost souls
(E) prisoners

30. One can infer from the passage all of the following EXCEPT that

(A) the speaker considered himself superior to his white peers
(B) the speaker considered himself superior to his African American peers
(C) the other African American boys treated their white peers with deference
(D) the speaker was superior to his white peers in many ways
(E) the speaker felt isolated from both white and African American peers

31. The speaker's contempt wanes and is replaced by

(A) a commitment to become a famous professional
(B) a pledge to beat his peers in athletic contests
(C) a helpless rage against society
(D) a spirit of revenge
(E) actions that eventually lead him to prison

32. The tone of this passage can NOT be described as

(A) self-aware
(B) decisive
(C) fervent
(D) reflective
(E) laudatory

GO ON TO THE NEXT PAGE

Questions 33–39. Read the following passage carefully before you choose your answers.

Now, I hold that Illinois had a right to abolish and prohibit slavery as she did, and I hold that Kentucky has the same right to continue and protect slavery
Line that Illinois had to abolish it. I hold that New York
5 had as much right to abolish slavery as Virginia has to continue it, and that each and every State of this Union is a sovereign power, with the right to do as it pleases upon this question of slavery, and upon all its domestic institutions. Slavery is not the only
10 question which comes up in this controversy. There is a far more important one to you, and that is, what shall be done with the free negro? We have settled the slavery question as far as we are concerned; we have prohibited it in Illinois forever, and in doing so, I think
15 we have done wisely, and there is no man in the State who would be more strenuous in his opposition to the introduction of slavery than I would; but when we settled it for our selves, we exhausted all our power over that subject. We have done our whole duty, and
20 can do no more. We must leave each and every other State to decide for itself the same question. In relation to the policy to be pursued toward the free negroes, we have said that they shall not vote; whilst Maine, on the other hand, has said that they shall vote. Maine is
25 a sovereign State, and has the power to regulate the qualifications of voters within her limits. I would never consent to confer the right of voting and of citizenship upon a negro, but still I am not going to quarrel with Maine for differing from me in opinion. Let Maine take
30 care of her own negroes, and fix the qualifications of her own voters to suit herself, without interfering with Illinois, and Illinois will not interfere with Maine. So with the State of New York. She allows the negro to vote provided he owns two hundred and fifty dollars'
35 worth of property, but not otherwise. While I would not make any distinction whatever between a negro who held property and one who did not, yet if the sovereign State of New York chooses to make that distinction it is her business and not mine, and I will
40 not quarrel with her for it. She can do as she pleases on this question if she minds her own business, and we will do the same thing. Now, my friends, if we will only act conscientiously and rigidly upon this great principle of popular sovereignty, which guarantees to
45 each State and Territory the right to do as it pleases on all things, local and domestic, instead of Congress interfering, we will continue at peace one with another. Why should Illinois be at war with Missouri, or Kentucky with Ohio, or Virginia, with New York,
50 merely because their institutions differ? Our fathers intended that our institutions should differ. They knew that the North and the South, having different climates, productions, and interests, required different

institutions. This doctrine of Mr. Lincoln, of uniformity
55 among the institutions of the different States, is a new doctrine, never dreamed of by Washington, Madison, or the framers of this government. Mr. Lincoln and the Republican party set themselves up as wiser than these men who made this government, which has
60 flourished for seventy years under the principle of popular sovereignty, recognizing the right of each State to do as it pleased. Under that principle, we have grown from a nation of three or four millions to a nation of about thirty millions of people; we have
65 crossed the Allegheny mountains and filled up the whole Northwest, turning the prairie into a garden, and building up churches and schools, thus spreading civilization and Christianity where before there was nothing but savage barbarism. Under that principle we
70 have become, from a feeble nation, the most powerful on the face of the earth, and if we only adhere to that principle, we can go forward increasing in territory, in power, in strength, and in glory until the Republic of America shall be the north star that shall guide the
75 friend of freedom throughout the civilized world. And why can we not adhere to the great principle of self-government upon which our institutions were originally based? I believe that this new doctrine preached by Mr. Lincoln and his party will dissolve
80 the Union if it succeeds. They are trying to array all the Northern States in one body against the South, to excite a sectional war between the free States and the slave States, in order that the one or the other may be driven to the wall.

Stephen Douglas (1858)

33. In this passage the speaker's purpose is to

   (A) analyze the causes of slavery
   (B) argue in favor of states' rights
   (C) criticize individual states
   (D) describe the advantages of a federal
       government
   (E) argue in favor of slavery

34. Which of the following best describes the tone of the passage?

   (A) mock enthusiasm
   (B) righteous indignation
   (C) well-reasoned polemic
   (D) objective rationalization
   (E) ironic detachment

GO ON TO THE NEXT PAGE

35. In the first two sentences (lines 1–9), the speaker grounds his central idea on which of the following rhetorical strategies?

   (A) inductive reasoning
   (B) deductive reasoning
   (C) description
   (D) classification
   (E) appeal to ignorance

36. The most significant rhetorical shift in the passage begins with

   (A) "So with the State of New York." (lines 32–33)
   (B) "Now, my friends…" (line 42)
   (C) "Why should Illinois be at war with Missouri…" (line 48)
   (D) "Under that principle…" (line 69)
   (E) "I believe that this new doctrine…" (line 78)

37. The speaker substantiates his central idea with

   (A) clever anecdotes
   (B) innovative symbols
   (C) unusual paradoxes
   (D) extended metaphors
   (E) appeal to authority

38. From the passage, it appears that the speaker's personal view is that African Americans should be

   (A) slaves and should not be allowed to hold property
   (B) should not be slaves and should be allowed to vote
   (C) should not be free but should be allowed to hold some property
   (D) should be free but not allowed to vote
   (E) should be allowed to hold property and to vote

39. In the final lines of the passage, the speaker attempts to win over his audience by

   (A) inspiring confidence
   (B) shifting blame
   (C) instilling fear
   (D) reconciling differences
   (E) overstating a problem

GO ON TO THE NEXT PAGE

Questions 40–46. Read the following passage carefully before you choose your answers.

Observe, the merchant's function (or manufacturer's, for in the broad sense in which it is here used the word must be understood to include
Line both) is to provide for the nation. It is no more his
5 function to get profit for himself out of that provision than it is a clergyman's function to get his stipend. This stipend is a due and necessary adjunct, but not the object of his life, if he be a true clergyman, any more than his fee (or honorarium) is the object of life
10 to a true physician. Neither is his fee the object of life to a true merchant. All three, if true men, have a work to be done irrespective of fee—to be done even at any cost, or for quite the contrary of fee; the pastor's function being to teach, the physician's to heal, and the
15 merchant's, as I have said, to provide. That is to say, he has to understand to their very root the qualities of the thing he deals in, and the means of obtaining or producing it; and he has to apply all his sagacity and energy to the producing or obtaining it in perfect state,
20 and distributing it at the cheapest possible price where it is most needed.
　　And because the production or obtaining of any commodity involves necessarily the agency of many lives and hands, the merchant becomes in the course
25 of his business the master and governor of large masses of men in a more direct, though less confessed way, than a military officer or pastor; so that on him falls, in great part, the responsibility for the kind of life they lead: and it becomes his duty, not only to be
30 always considering how to produce what he sells, in the purest and cheapest forms, but how to make the various employments involved in the production, or transference of it, most beneficial to the men employed.
　　And as into these two functions, requiring for
35 their right exercise the highest intelligence, as well as patience, kindness, and tact, the merchant is bound to put all his energy, so for their just discharge he is bound, as soldier or physician is bound, to give up, if need be, his life, in such way as it may be demanded of
40 him. Two main points he has in his providing function to maintain: first, his engagements (faithfulness to engagements being the real root of all possibilities, in commerce); and, secondly, the perfectness and purity of the thing provided; so that, rather than fail
45 in any engagement, or consent to any deterioration, adulteration, or unjust and exorbitant price of that which he provides, he is bound to meet fearlessly any form of distress, poverty, or labour, which may, through maintenance of these points, come upon him.

(1860)

40. The author relies principally on which rhetorical strategy?

(A) appeal to authority
(B) classification
(C) description
(D) induction
(E) analogy

41. According to the author, a merchant is

(A) not motivated primarily by the prospect of making a profit
(B) more devoted to material gain than a clergyman
(C) less focused on making money than is a physician
(D) essentially different from a manufacturer
(E) wholly dedicated to material gain

42. In line 7, "adjunct" most nearly means

(A) accompaniment
(B) evil
(C) adjustment
(D) bonus
(E) addition

43. "Agency" (line 23) is directly related semantically to

(A) business (line 25)
(B) merchant (line 24)
(C) master (line 25)
(D) commodity (line 23)
(E) duty (line 29)

44. The author uses "hands" (line 24)

(A) as a synecdoche
(B) to reinforce the manual aspect of most labor of his time
(C) to attenuate the repetition of the word "men"
(D) as a concrete image
(E) all of the above

GO ON TO THE NEXT PAGE

45. The "two functions" in line 34 are

(A) earning high profits and pacifying the workers
(B) manufacturing a good, cheap product and providing for workers
(C) exploiting the workers and maximizing profits
(D) manufacturing good products and making good profits
(E) dealing with unions and keeping profits high

46. Most likely, the author would

(A) support Marxism
(B) neither like nor dislike socialism
(C) support capitalism
(D) support anticlerical groups
(E) dislike the medical profession

GO ON TO THE NEXT PAGE

Questions 47–50. Read the following passage carefully before you choose your answers.

This archipelago consists of ten principal islands, of which five exceed the others in size. They are situated under the Equator, and between five and six hundred miles westward of the coast of America. They are all formed of volcanic rocks; a few fragments of granite curiously glazed and altered by the heat, can hardly be considered as an exception. Some of the craters, surmounting the larger islands, are of immense size, and they rise to a height of between three and four thousand feet. Their flanks are studded by innumerable smaller orifices. I scarcely hesitate to affirm, that there must be in the whole archipelago at least two thousand craters. These consist either of lava or scoriae, or of finely-stratified, sandstone-like tuff. Most of the latter are beautifully symmetrical; they owe their origin to eruptions of volcanic mud without any lava: it is a remarkable circumstance that every one of the twenty-eight tuff-craters which were examined had their southern sides either much lower than the other sides, or quite broken down and removed. As all these craters apparently have been formed when standing in the sea, and as the waves from the trade wind and the swell from the open Pacific here unite their forces on the southern coasts of all the islands, this singular uniformity in the broken state of the craters, composed of the soft and yielding tuff, is easily explained.

(1839)

47. This passage is most notable for its

(A) meticulous classification
(B) unusual point of view
(C) precise description
(D) resourceful analogies
(E) lyrical prose

48. Most likely, the passage is extracted from

(A) an entry in a scientific journal
(B) a nineteenth-century novel
(C) a book on tourism
(D) a letter from a poet
(E) a book on volcanoes

49. In context, one can infer that tuff is

(A) an alternate spelling for tough
(B) a kind of sand
(C) made up principally of grass
(D) volcanic rock
(E) dense and resistant

50. In this passage, the speaker is most notably impressed by

(A) the flora on the islands
(B) the force of the Pacific Ocean
(C) the fragments of granite
(D) the symmetrical craters on the islands
(E) the topography of the smaller islands

GO ON TO THE NEXT PAGE

Questions 51–54. Read the following passage carefully before you choose your answers.

Art begins with abstract decoration, with purely imaginative and pleasurable work dealing with what is unreal and non-existent. This is the first stage. Then
Line Life becomes fascinated with this new wonder, and
5 asks to be admitted into the charmed circle. Art takes life as part of her rough material, re-creates it, and refashions it in fresh forms, is absolutely indifferent to fact, invents, imagines, dreams, and keeps between herself and reality the impenetrable barrier of beautiful
10 style, of decorative or ideal treatment. The third stage is when Life gets the upper hand, and drives Art out into the wilderness. That is the true decadence, and it is from this that we are now suffering.

Take the case of the English drama. At first in
15 the hands of the monks Dramatic Art was abstract, decorative and mythological. Then she enlisted Life in her service, and using some of life's external forms, she created an entirely new race of beings, whose sorrows were more terrible than any sorrow man has
20 ever felt, whose joys were keener than lover's joys, who had the rage of the Titans and the calm of the gods, who had monstrous and marvelous sins, monstrous and marvelous virtues. To them she gave a language different from that of actual use, a language full of
25 resonant music and sweet rhythm, made stately by solemn cadence, or made delicate by fanciful rhyme, jeweled with wonderful words, and enriched with lofty diction. She clothed her children in strange raiment and gave them masks, and at her bidding the antique
30 world rose from its marble tomb. A new Caesar stalked through the streets of risen Rome, and with purple sail and flute-led oars another Cleopatra passed up the river to Antioch. Old myth and legend and dream took shape and substance. History was entirely rewritten,
35 and there was hardly one of the dramatists who did not recognize that the object of Art is not simple truth but complex beauty. In this they were perfectly right. Art itself is really a form of exaggeration; and selection, which is the very spirit of art, is nothing more than an
40 intensified mode of over-emphasis.

But Life soon shattered the perfection of the form. Even in Shakespeare we can see the beginning of the end. It shows itself by the gradual breaking-up of the blank-verse in the later plays, by the predominance
45 given to prose, and by the overimportance assigned to characterization. The passages in Shakespeare—and they are many—where the language is uncouth, vulgar, exaggerated, fantastic, obscene even, are entirely due to Life calling for an echo of her own voice, and rejecting
50 the intervention of beautiful style, through which alone should life be suffered to find expression. Shakespeare is not by any means a flawless artist. He is too fond of going directly to life, and borrowing life's natural utterance. He forgets that when Art surrenders her
55 imaginative medium she surrenders everything.

(1889)

51. The author of this passage is most likely

    (A) a poet
    (B) a novelist
    (C) an art critic
    (D) a journalist
    (E) an actor

52. The author relies principally on which of the following to substantiate his thesis?

    (A) a faulty analogy
    (B) process analysis
    (C) deductive reasoning
    (D) an accumulation of facts
    (E) illustration by example

53. "…when Art surrenders her imaginative medium she surrenders everything" (lines 55–56) is in the form of

    (A) a maxim
    (B) a chiasmus
    (C) an antithesis
    (D) an understatement
    (E) an analogy

54. Above all else, the author reveres

    (A) beauty
    (B) life
    (C) Shakespeare
    (D) Caesar
    (E) English drama

END OF SECTION I

ENGLISH

LANGUAGE AND COMPOSITION

SECTION II

Time—2 hours

Number of questions—3

Percent of total grade—55

Each question counts as one-third of the total essay section score.

Question 1 Essay…………………………………suggested time—40 minutes

Question 2 Essay…………………………………suggested time—40 minutes

Question 3 Essay…………………………………suggested time—40 minutes

Section II of this examination requires answers in essay form. To help you use your time well, the coordinator will announce the time at which each question should be completed. If you finish any question before time is announced, you may go on to the following question. If you finish the examination in less than the time allotted, you may go back and work on any essay question you want.

Each essay will be judged on its clarity and effectiveness in dealing with the requirements of the topic assigned and on the quality of the writing. After completing each question, you should check your essay for accuracy of punctuation, spelling, and diction; you are advised, however, not to attempt many longer corrections. Remember that quality is far more important than quantity.

Write your essays with a pen, preferably in black or dark blue ink. Be sure to write CLEARLY and LEGIBLY. Cross out any errors you make.

The questions for Section II are printed in the green insert. You are encouraged to use the green insert to make notes and to plan your essays, but be sure to write your answers in the pink booklet. Number each answer as the question is numbered in the examination. Do not skip lines. Begin each answer on a new page in the pink booklet.

ENGLISH LANGUAGE AND COMPOSITION

SECTION II

Time—1 hour

Question 1

(Suggested time—40 minutes. This question counts as one-third of the total essay section score.)

The passage below is excerpted from one of Mark Twain's most famous essays, "Fenimore Cooper's Literary Offenses." At the time Twain wrote his essay, Cooper's novels were generally well liked and respected. Read the entire passage carefully. Then write an essay analyzing the rhetorical strategies that Twain uses to convey his attitude.

If Cooper had been an observer his inventive faculty would have worked better; not more interestingly, but more rationally, more plausibly. Cooper's proudest
Line creations in the way of "situations" suffer noticeably
5 from the absence of the observer's protecting gift. Cooper's eye was splendidly inaccurate. Cooper seldom saw anything correctly. He saw nearly all things as through a glass eye, darkly. Of course a man who cannot see the commonest little every-day
10 matters accurately is working at a disadvantage when he is constructing a "situation." In the *Deerslayer* tale Cooper has a stream which is fifty feet wide where it flows out of a lake; it presently narrows to twenty as it meanders along for no given reason, and yet when a
15 stream acts like that it ought to be required to explain itself. Fourteen pages later the width of the brook's outlet from the lake has suddenly shrunk thirty feet, and become "the narrowest part of the stream." This shrinkage is not accounted for. The stream has bends in
20 it, a sure indication that it has alluvial banks and cuts them; yet these bends are only thirty and fifty feet long. If Cooper had been a nice and punctilious observer he would have noticed that the bends were often nine hundred feet long than short of it.
25   Cooper made the exit of that stream fifty feet wide, in the first place, for no particular reason; in the second place, he narrowed it to less than twenty to accommodate some Indians. He bends a "sapling" to form an arch over this narrow passage, and conceals six
30 Indians in its foliage. They are "laying" for a settler's scow or ark which is coming up the stream on its way to the lake; it is being hauled against the stiff current by rope whose stationary end is anchored in the lake; its rate of progress cannot be more than a mile an hour.
35 Cooper describes the ark, but pretty obscurely. In the matter of dimensions "it was little more than a modern canal boat." Let us guess, then, that it was about one hundred and forty feet long. It was of "greater breadth than common." Let us guess then that it was about
40 sixteen feet wide. This leviathan had been prowling

down bends which were but a third as long as itself, and scraping between banks where it only had two feet of space to spare on each side. We cannot too much admire this miracle. A low-roofed dwelling occupies
45 "two-thirds of the ark's length"—a dwelling ninety feet long and sixteen feet wide, let us say—a kind of vestibule train. The dwelling has two rooms—each forty-five feet long and sixteen feet wide, let us guess. One of them is the bedroom of the Hutter girls, Judith
50 and Hetty; the other is the parlor in the daytime, at night it is papa's bedchamber. The ark is arriving at the stream's exit now, whose width has been reduced to less than twenty feet to accommodate the Indians—say to eighteen. There is a foot to spare on each side of the
55 boat. Did the Indians notice that there was going to be a tight squeeze there? Did they notice that they could make money by climbing down out of that arched sapling and just stepping aboard when the ark scraped by? No, other Indians would have noticed these things,
60 but Cooper's Indian's never notice anything. Cooper thinks they are marvelous creatures for noticing, but he was almost always in error about his Indians. There was seldom a sane one among them.
     The ark is one hundred and forty-feet long; the
65 dwelling is ninety feet long. The idea of the Indians is to drop softly and secretly from the arched sapling to the dwelling as the ark creeps along under it at the rate of a mile an hour, and butcher the family. It will take the ark a minute and a half to pass under. It will take
70 the ninety-foot dwelling a minute to pass under. Now, then, what did the six Indians do? It would take you thirty years to guess, and even then you would have to give it up, I believe. Therefore, I will tell you what the Indians did. Their chief, a person of quite extraordinary
75 intellect for a Cooper Indian, warily watched the canal-boat as it squeezed along under him and when he had got his calculations fined down to exactly the right shade, as he judged, he let go and dropped. And missed the boat! That is actually what he did. He
80 missed the house, and landed in the stern of the scow.

GO ON TO THE NEXT PAGE

It was not much of a fall, yet it knocked him silly. He lay there unconscious. If the house had been ninety-seven feet long he would have made the trip. The error lay in the construction of the house. Cooper was no architect.

There still remained in the roost five Indians. The boat has passed under and is now out of their reach. Let me explain what the five did—you would not be able to reason it out for yourself. No. 1 jumped for the boat, but fell in the water astern of it. Then No. 2 jumped for the boat, but fell in the water still further astern of it. Then No. 3 jumped for the boat, and fell a good way astern of it. Then No. 4 jumped for the boat, and fell in the water away astern. Then even No. 5 made a jump for the boat—for he was a Cooper Indian. In that matter of intellect, the difference between a Cooper Indian and the Indian that stands in front of the cigar-shop is not spacious. The scow episode is really a sublime burst of invention; but it does not thrill, because the inaccuracy of details throw a sort of air of fictitiousness and general improbability over it. This comes of Cooper's inadequacy as observer.

GO ON TO THE NEXT PAGE

Question 2

(Suggested time—40 minutes. This question counts as one-third of the total essay section score.)

Read and think carefully about the following quotation. Then write an essay in which you refute, support, or qualify Voltaire's claim. Make sure to use appropriate evidence from literary, historical, or personal sources to develop your argument.

It is dangerous to be right in matters about which the established authorities are wrong.—*Voltaire*

Question 3A (for May 2006)

(Suggested time—40 minutes. This question counts as one-third of the total essay section score.)

On April 23, 1910, President Theodore Roosevelt presented a speech to the mostly privileged students of the Sorbonne [University] in Paris, France. Read carefully the portion of the speech presented below. Then write an essay in which you identify the president's purpose ad analyze how he uses language to achieve his purpose. You may want to consider elements such as syntax, diction, and imagery.

It is well if a large proportion of the leaders in any republic, in any democracy, are, as a matter of course, drawn from the classes represented in this audience
Line to-day; but only provided that those classes possess the
5 gifts of sympathy with plain people and of devotion to great ideals. You and those like you have received special advantages; you have all of you had the opportunity for mental training; many of you have had leisure; most of you have had a chance for enjoyment
10 of life far greater than comes to the majority of your fellows. To you and your kind much has been given, and from you much should be expected. Yet there are certain failings against which it is especially incumbent that both men of trained and cultivated intellect, and
15 men of inherited wealth and position should especially guard themselves, because to these failings they are especially liable; and if yielded to, their—your— chances of useful service are at an end. Let the man of learning, the man of lettered leisure, beware of that
20 queer and cheap temptation to pose to himself and to others as a cynic, as the man who has outgrown emotions and beliefs, the man to whom good and evil are as one. The poorest way to face life is to face it with a sneer. There are many men who feel a kind of
25 twister pride in cynicism; there are many who confine themselves to criticism of the way others do what they themselves dare not even attempt. There is no more unhealthy being, no man less worthy of respect, than he who either really holds, or feigns to hold, an attitude
30 of sneering disbelief toward all that is great and lofty, whether in achievement or in that noble effort which, even if it fails, comes to second achievement. A cynical habit of thought and speech, a readiness to criticize work which the critic himself never tries to perform, an
35 intellectual aloofness which will not accept contact with

life's realities—all these are marks, not as the possessor would fain to think, of superiority but of weakness. They mark the men unfit to bear their part painfully in the stern strife of living, who seek, in the affection of
40 contempt for the achievements of others, to hide from others and from themselves in their own weakness. The rôle is easy; there is none easier, save only the rôle of the man who sneers alike at both criticism and performance.

45 It is not the critic who counts; not the man who points out how the strong man stumbles, or where the doer of deeds could have done them better. The credit belongs to the man who is actually in the arena, whose face is marred by dust and sweat and blood;
50 who strives valiantly; who errs, who comes short again and again, because there is no effort without error and shortcoming; but who does actually strive to do the deeds; who knows great enthusiasms, the great devotions; who spends himself in a worthy cause;
55 who at the best knows in the end the triumph of high achievement, and who at the worst, if he fails, at least fails while daring greatly, so that his place shall never be with those cold and timid souls who neither know victory nor defeat. Shame on the man of cultivated taste
60 who permits refinement to develop into fastidiousness that unfits him for doing the rough work of a workaday world. Among the free peoples who govern themselves there is but a small field of usefulness open for the men of cloistered life who shrink from contact with their
65 fellows. Still less room is there for those who deride

GO ON TO THE NEXT PAGE

of slight what is done by those who actually bear the brunt of the day; nor yet for those others who always profess that they would like to take action, if only the conditions of life were not exactly what they actually
70 are. The man who does nothing cuts the same sordid figure in the pages of history, whether he be a cynic, or fop, or voluptuary. There is little use for the being whose tepid soul knows nothing of great and generous emotion, of the high pride, the stern belief, the lofty
75 enthusiasm, of the men who quell the storm and ride the thunder. Well for these men if they succeed; well also, though not so well, if they fail, given only that they have nobly ventured, and have put forth all their heart and strength.

GO ON TO THE NEXT PAGE

Question 3B (for May 2007)

(Suggested time—55 minutes. This question counts as one-third of the total essay section score.)

Read or examine carefully the sources that follow; you should keep in mind the validity of the documents, as well as their relevance to the prompt. Then write a well-organized essay in which you include citations from at least four of the sources. You have an extra 15 minutes on this section to study the sources and organize your thoughts.

Basing your answer on the information below, support, refute, or qualify the assertion that the Swiss architect Le Corbusier made in 1923: "Space and light and order. Those are the things that men need just as much as they need bread or a place to sleep."

Source 1

Charles Fourier (*Theory of Universal Unity*, 1822)

The center of the palace or Phalanstery should be a place for quiet activity; it should include the dining rooms, the exchange, meeting rooms, library,
Line studies, etc. This central section includes the temple,
5 the tower, the telegraph, the coops for carrier pigeons, the ceremonial chimes, the observatory, and a winter courtyard adorned with vines. The parade grounds are located just behind the central section.

One of the wings of the Phalanstery should include
10 all the noisy workshops, like the carpenter shop, the forge, and the other workshops where hammering is done. It should also be the place for all the industrial gatherings involving children, who are generally very noisy at work and even at music. The grouping
15 of these activities will avoid an annoying drawback of our civilized cities where every street has its own hammerer, or blacksmith, or beginning clarinet player to shatter the ear drums of fifty families in the vicinity.

All the children, both rich and poor, are lodged
20 together on the mezzanine of the Phalanstery, for they should be kept separate from the adolescents, and in general from all those who are capable of making love, at most times and particularly during the late evening and the early morning hours. The reasons for this will
25 be explained later. For the time being let us assume that those who are capable of forming amorous relations will be concentrated on the second floor, while the very young and the very old should have meeting-halls on the ground floor and the mezzanine.

30 The other wing should contain the ballrooms and halls for meetings with outsiders, who should not be allowed to encumber the center of the palace or to disturb the domestic relations of the Phalanstery. This precaution of isolating outsiders and concentrating
35 their meetings in one of the wings will be most important in the trial Phalanstery, for it will attract thousands of curiosity seekers whose entry fees will provide a profit that I estimate at not less than twenty million.

Source 2

The United States Housing Act of 1949 provided federal funds for urban redevelopment and slum removal; this prompted the city of Saint Louis to hire
Line architect Minoru Yamasaki to design a monumental
5 public housing project baptized Pruitt-Igoe by the architect. The housing project, located on a 57-acre site, consisted of 33 identical eleven-story, flat-topped apartment blocks designed to engineer better people through better architecture; by making Pruitt-Igoe
10 clean, safe, and democratic, Yamasaki hoped to ameliorate the housing project's residents.

Pruitt-Igoe was supposed to be surrounded by a green space and trees winding through the open spaces, which was to help make the area its
15 own Garden of Eden. The greenery never really materialized. The stark, Spartan surfaces lacked any ornamentation, which was an intentional attempt to strip away the implication of socioeconomic inequality. The repetition of perfectly similar apartments opening
20 to streets that were situated inside the buildings, where tenants and their children would be safe from traffic, was allegedly based on the metaphor of the hospital. Pruitt-Igoe, in theory, would offer a safe, hygienic, and healthy environment. Somehow, even in the highest
25 density public housing ever built in the United States, neighborhoods would establish an identify centered around the corridor-streets. Children could play in the street, and mothers could gather there and talk or do their laundry. At its height, nearly twelve thousand
30 residents inhabited Pruitt-Igoe, thus creating a small city within the larger city.

Originally, the city had planned two projects: Pruitt for blacks and Igoe for whites—a plan that was not exactly in line with the democratic glory of
35 the architectural plan. The buildings were integrated when they opened in 1954, but during the following decade, only African-Americans lived in the high-rises that, as it turned out, did nothing to improve the tenants. Crime and drugs were as common as roaches
40 and mice, and no one took care of the common areas, which slowly deteriorated. The elevators worked, but they stopped at only three of the eleven floors. Soon, the utopian project was worse than the slums it had replaced.

April 22, 1972: the Demolition of Pruitt-Igoe

GO ON TO THE NEXT PAGE

Source 4

Sir Thomas More (*Utopia*, 1516)

The town of Amaurot is compassed with a high and thick wall, in which there are many towers and forts; there is also a broad and deep dry ditch, set thick with thorns, cast round three sides of the town, and the river is instead of a ditch on the fourth side. The streets are very convenient for all carriage, and are well sheltered from the winds. Their buildings are good, and are so uniform that a whole side of a street looks like one house. The streets are twenty feet broad; there lie gardens behind all their houses; these are large but enclosed with buildings that on all hands face the streets; so that every house has both a door to the street, and a back door to the garden. Their doors have all two leaves, which, as they are easily opened, so they shut of their own accord; and there being no property among them, every man may freely enter into any house whatsoever. At every ten years' end they shift their houses by lots.

They cultivate their gardens with great care, so that they have vines, fruits, herbs, and flowers in them; and all is so well ordered, and so finely kept, that I never saw gardens anywhere that were both so fruitful and so beautiful as theirs. Their records, that contain the history of their town and State, are preserved with an exact care and run backward 1,760 years. From these it appears that their houses were at first low and mean, like cottages, made of any sort of timber, and were built with mud walls and thatched with straw. But now their houses are three stories high: the fronts of them are faced with stone, plastering, or brick; and between the facings of their walls they throw in their rubbish. Their roofs are flat, and on them they lay a sort of plaster, which costs very little, and yet is so tempered that it is not apt to take fire, and yet resists the weather more than lead. They have great quantities of glass among them, with which they glaze their windows. They use also in their windows a thin linen cloth, that is so oiled or gummed that it both keeps out the wind and gives free admission to the light.

Source 5

Ebenezer Howard (*Garden Cities of Tomorrow*, 1902)

Six magnificent boulevards—each 120 feet wide—traverse the city from centre to circumference, dividing it into six equal parts or wards. In the centre is a circular space containing about five and a half acres, laid out as a beautiful and well-watered garden; and, surrounding this garden, each standing in its own ample grounds, are the larger public buildings—town hall, principal concert and lecture hall, theatre, library, museum, picture-gallery, and hospital.

The rest of the large space encircled by the Crystal Palace is a public park, containing 145 acres, which includes ample recreation grounds within very easy access of all the people.

Running all round the Central Park (except where it is intersected by the boulevards) is a wide glass arcade called the 'Crystal Palace', opening on to the park. This building is in wet weather one of the favourite resorts of the people, whilst the knowledge that its bright shelter is ever close at hand tempts people into Central Park, even in the most doubtful of weathers. Here manufactured goods are exposed for sale, and here most of that class of shopping which requires the joy of deliberation and selection is done. The space enclosed by the Crystal Palace is, however, a good deal larger than is required for these purposes, and a considerable part of it is used as a Winter Garden—the whole forming a permanent exhibition of a most attractive character, whilst its circular form brings it near to every dweller in the town—the furthest removed inhabitant being within 600 yards.

Passing out of the Crystal Palace on our way to the outer ring of the town, we cross Fifth Avenue—lined, as are all the roads of the town, with trees—fronting which, and looking on to the Crystal Palace, we find a ring of very excellently built houses, each standing in its own ample grounds; and, as we continue our walk, we observe that the houses are for the most part built either in concentric rings, facing the various avenues (as the circular roads are termed), or fronting the boulevards and roads which all converge to the centre of the town. Asking the friend who accompanies us on our journey what the population of this little city may be, we are told about 30,000 in the city itself, and about 2,000 in the agricultural estate, and that there are in the town 5,500 building lots of an average size of 20 feet × 130 feet—the minimum space allotted for the purpose being 20 × 100. Noticing the very varied architecture and design which the houses and groups of houses display—some having common gardens and co-operative kitchens—we learn that general observance of street line or harmonious departure from it are the chief points as to

GO ON TO THE NEXT PAGE

house building, over which the municipal authorities exercise control, for, though proper sanitary arrangements are strictly enforced, the fullest measure of individual taste and preference is encouraged.

Walking still toward the outskirts of the town, we come upon "Grand Avenue." This avenue is fully entitled to the name it bears, for it is 420 feet wide, and, forming a belt of green upwards of three miles long, divides that part of the town which lies outside Central Park into two belts. It really constitutes an additional park of 115 acres—a park which is within 240 yards of the furthest removed inhabitant. In this splendid avenue six sites, each of four acres, are occupied by public schools and their surrounding playgrounds and gardens, while other sites are reserved for churches, of such denominations as the religious beliefs of the people may determine, to be erected and maintained out of the funds of the worshippers and their friends. We observe that the houses fronting on Grand Avenue have departed (at least in one of the wards—that of which Diagram 3 is a representation)—from the general plan of concentric rings, and, in order to ensure a longer line of frontage on Grand Avenue, are arranged in crescents—thus also to the eye yet further enlarging the already splendid width of Grand Avenue.

On the outer ring of the town are factories, warehouses, dairies, markets, coal yards, timber yards, etc., all fronting on the circle railway, which encompasses the whole town, and which has sidings connecting it with a main line of railway which passes through the estate. This arrangement enables goods to be loaded direct into trucks from the warehouses and workshops, and so sent by railway to distant markets, or to be taken direct from the trucks into the warehouses or factories; thus not only effecting a very great saving in regard to packing and cartage, and reducing to a minimum loss from breakage, but also, by reducing the traffic on the roads of the town, lessening to a very marked extent the cost of their maintenance. The smoke fiend is kept well within bounds in Garden City; for all machinery is driven by electric energy, with the result that the cost of electricity for lighting and other purposes is greatly reduced.

The refuse of the town is utilized on the agricultural portions of the estate, which are held by various individuals in large farms, small holdings, allotments, cow pastures, etc.; the natural competition of these various methods of agriculture, tested by the willingness of occupiers to offer the highest rent to the municipality, tending to bring about the best system of husbandry, or, what is more probable, the best systems adapted for various purposes.

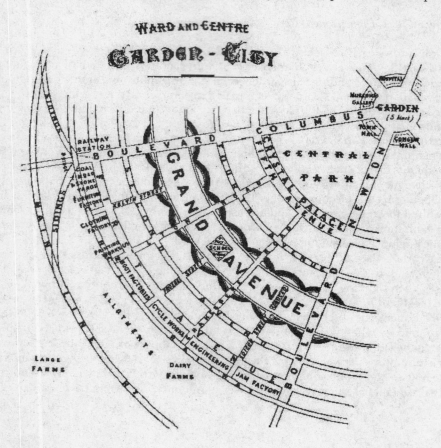

GO ON TO THE NEXT PAGE

La Candelaria, the old town of Bogotá, Colombia

END OF EXAMINATION

15

Practice Test 2:
Answers and
Explanations

EXPLANATIONS TO THE MULTIPLE-CHOICE SECTION

1. **C** Remember that oftentimes AP questions will ask you to infer—to draw a conclusion based on what is said in the text.

   The best course of action to take when approaching this question is POE. Answer (B) is the only one that posits a positive answer (to "laud" means to praise), and it can be eliminated easily because of the word "linear." The final sentence of the first paragraph does laud Browne's writing, but the author suggests that the reading process is like going through a series of mazes. This is anything but straightforward—or linear. Later in the text, there is an oblique allusion to William Shakespeare ("the time of Elizabeth"), but there is nothing resembling a comparison between Browne and Shakespeare; eliminate (D). There is even less reason to suspect that there is any suggestion of a comparison between the author of the passage (Samuel Johnson, by the way) and Browne; so you can eliminate answer (E). Now you're down to two choices. The author criticizes the exuberance and lack of clarity that makes it difficult to understand his reasoning; he does not suggest that Browne reasons poorly (or not at all); thus, answer (A) is not correct. You're left with (C), which fits: The author complains about Browne's lack of clarity.

2. **B** This question also requires you to use POE. The first answer should be suspect—it would be far too easy if they just expected you to equate "poesy" and "poetry." Remember that the author applies the poesy to Browne's style, which the author qualifies with a combination of positive and negative attributes. In essence, you must match the positive qualities ("excellencies") and negative ones ("faults") with one of the answers. None of the last three answers, which all are tied to "poetry" to keep you leaning toward a simplistic answer, is appropriate. Browne says that greatness is connected to certain extremes (both good and bad) in an individual's character; the author of the passage suggests that the extremes of Browne's character help explain the eccentricities of his style.

   As is common on this test, there is no answer that is a perfect match. More often than not the correct answer will be similar, but not identical, to the answer that you come up with from reading the passage. Your goal is to identify the best answer, and (B) is the only plausible one.

3. **C** The meaning is obvious because the author translates the expression for us, putting the translation just before the Latin phrase: "To have great excellencies and great faults." By the way, more often than not, authors who insert foreign words or phrases will tip their hands and either suggest the meaning or simply state it.

4. **A** Here's another example where POE comes in handy. At first glance, answer (B) seems plausible, but the problem lies in the word "hints." The author does not hint; rather, he says outright that the style is pedantic. The author describes, but does not justify or argue, so (C) and (D) are out. Choice (E) can't be correct; Browne's style is many things (including complex), but it is definitely not facile (easy). True, there are some positive elements in the author's evaluation, but these are outweighed by the negative epithets: rugged, pedantic (overly bookish), obscure, harsh, and uncouth. This appears to be open criticism, so (A) is the best answer.

5. **A** The key to answering this question correctly is to recognize that the author establishes a clear parallel pattern: a sequence of positive qualifiers contrasted with related negative ones (this, but that). At the end of the sentence, however, the author combines two pejorative statements (this and that). This modificant of the parallelism tips the balance toward the

negative. Remember that the passage begins with Browne's own comment that suggests that greatness originates in a sort of balance between the great qualities and great faults. By adding on only faults at the end of the sentence describing Browne's style, the author of the passage shows that he sees more faults than "excellencies." Some of the answers are deliberately misleading. Both (B) and (C) pertain to "balance," although each has nothing to do with our answer. Choice (D) appears to function only as "filler." If you chose this answer, you should review the meaning of parallelism before going any further. Choice (E) is the exact opposite of the correct answer; "obfuscate" means to intentionally mislead.

6. **A** The first sentence of the third paragraph allows you to use POE to begin eliminating incorrect answer choices. "He fell into an age in which our language began to lose the stability...." Right away, you can eliminate answers (B), (C), and (E). You should be suspicious of (D) because of the word "metaphorical." Where does "metaphorical" come in? It doesn't, which is why (D) is not the best answer. Browne lived in a time of linguistic experimentation, and the author of the passage takes the time to discuss this to put some of Browne's excesses in context.

7. **D** The author at first classifies Browne's use of vocabulary as "useful" then goes on to describe some of it as "superfluous" and then "obscure." You can use POE to eliminate all but the correct answer. The last word in the correct answer, "deleterious," may have given you problems; this word means "harmful." The idea that some of his vocabulary is, in fact, harmful to his writing is given in the lines that say that some words "conceal his meaning rather than explain it."

8. **E** For this question, all of the answers probably seemed plausible. Your first step should have been to find the appropriate part of the text. In the last paragraph, the author writes: "in defence of his uncommon words and expressions, we must consider that he had uncommon sentiments, and was not content to express, in many words, that idea for which any language could supply a single term." Thus, the author attributes Browne's unusual diction (word choice) to his desire to find the exact word that expresses his uncommon thoughts or feelings, instead of circuitously expressing them through the use of many words.

9. **A** This question does not ask anything new; in essence, it addresses the same content as the preceding question, but in a slightly different way and while also indirectly testing your knowledge of a couple of words. If you understand that "heteroclite diction" signifies the use of words that are unusual or unusually varied, you can probably pick out the correct answer immediately. If not, use POE. You can eliminate (D) right away. Hopefully, you are familiar with the word "homogeneous" and can eliminate choice (B) too. Even if you aren't sure about the meaning of "mundane" (ordinary, usual, worldly) or "trope" (similar in meaning to rhetorical figure, for example, metaphor), you will have narrowed your choices to three, and should guess and move on.

10. **A** This question is relatively straightforward; using POE would enable you to eliminate answers (B) and (D). You may have been tempted by (C), but you should have noticed that the author of the passage discusses Browne as though he were writing in the past; for example, the third paragraph begins, "He fell into an age in which our language began to lose the stability which it had obtained in the time of Elizabeth." Finally, if you know that polemic means "debate" and that "virulent polemic" means something like a "heated debate," then you can dismiss answer (E). If not, then you should have guessed and moved on.

11. **B** Remember that with this type of question, if you can determine that half of the answer is untrue, then you can eliminate the entire answer. Thus, the fact that "sarcastic" seems way off-base allows you to eliminate (A), the inappropriateness of "harsh" allows you to discard (C), and the use of "sentimental" (or "capricious") disqualifies (E). It may not seem unreasonable to claim that the author of the passage is somewhat condescending, but it would be inaccurate to say that he is indulgent; the author appears to genuinely appreciate and admire certain aspects of Browne's style. In fact, he analyzes the style in a scholarly manner, which is why (B) is the best answer.

12. **E** One of the most important questions that you can ask while reading is: Who is speaking? With more modern literary texts, the question is often difficult to answer. Clearly, in this case, the speaker is a talented writer who knows the works of George Eliot (a nineteenth-century female writer). We have no reason to suspect that the speaker is a family member, so choice (A) is incorrect. Answer (B) is a trap for those casual readers who note that in the initial part of the text there is a discussion of religion, but fail to see how this fits into a discussion of the heroines in a feminist construct. Answer (D) would be a legitimate answer were it not for the qualifier, "chauvinist." If you had to attach a label to the speaker, it would probably be feminist, not chauvinist. After using POE, the only answer choice left is (E), and it seems appropriate enough.

13. **B** This question digs deeper into the relevance of the discussion of religion as it applies to the speaker's view of Eliot as a feminist writer (or as a writer about the feminine condition). Don't let the simile ("like a place of worship") mislead you. The speaker claims that at the heart of Eliot's novels the reader finds a young woman's struggle "in aspiration and agony" for "something that is perhaps incompatible with the facts of human existence." There is no statement about where the heroine might be physically, so answers (A), (C), and (D) should be eliminated right away. Answer (E) may have seemed plausible, but in fact, the heroine, as a woman in a world dominated by men, is shut off from "the real world" and forced into herself, not necessarily "lost in prayer." She is more precisely "essentially alone."

14. **B** If you understood the last explanation, there is little to add here. The great fact of human existence in the context of this passage is that it's a man's world (remember that Eliot wrote in nineteenth-century England). The entire passage is about women and their place in "the human condition." Answer (C) may have tempted you, but "the facts of human existence" cannot be limited to these women protagonists. You may have felt that answer (A) was correct because human existence restricts both men and women in some way; however, the aspirations of the heroines are incompatible only with "the facts of human existence." In this context, the incompatibility pertains only to women.

15. **A** Every once in a while, the exam will surprise you with a question as easy as this one. "Save for," which you may have seen written before, is sometimes substituted for the phrase "except for."

16. **E** "The difference of [point of] view" and "the difference of standard" are Eliot's "inheritance." Like men, Eliot sought and achieved a significant grasp of art and culture, but, according to the speaker, she did not renounce the feminine qualities—the results of her gender—that made her different.

17. **B** At the end of the passage, the speaker calls Eliot's knowledge and freedom a "double burden" and suggests that the burden led directly to Eliot's death, in the phrase "sank worn out." Clearly, Eliot was not in good health, since she has died, and answer (A) can be elimi-

nated. The other answer choices are very obviously incorrect; choice (C) is incorrect since Eliot was in fact famous. Choice (D) is also untrue according to the passage, and (E) is the opposite of what is stated in the passage. Choice (B) is the best answer.

18. **D** The best way to approach this type of question is to use POE. The apposition ("her, a memorable figure") appears almost at the beginning of the sentence, so (A) is not the correct answer. The claim that Eliot reached out "for all that life could offer" may be intended literally, but the statement is hyperbolic (it is an overstatement). As for choice (C), there is a clear example of personification when Eliot shrinks "back into the arms of love." One could also argue that there are multiple examples of not very noteworthy parallelism, but perhaps the most obvious one is the construction "reaching out with … confronting her feminine aspirations with." You may expect to find a relative clause in such a long periodic sentence, however, there is none, and the correct answer is (D).

19. **A** The question boils down to this: Who is speaking? Let's use POE. The speaker put the phrase in quotation marks to show that it is not hers; therefore, (B) is incorrect. If the speaker borrowed it from one of Eliot's critics, she would need to identify the citation somehow; (C), therefore, does not seem plausible. From context, it is clear that the reader should, indeed, take the phrase seriously, and the phrase *does* represent the speaker's point of view, which is why the phrase is there in the first place. So answers (D) and (E) can be eliminated. The entire text centers on Eliot's relationship to her feminine protagonists, and so it seems very probable (in this case, certain) that the speaker would integrate a phrase from one of Eliot's heroines. Choice (A) is the best answer.

20. **C** This type of question is very common on actual AP exams; fortunately, these types of questions usually contain two terms—as this one does.
It would be difficult to accept either qualifier in (A), but "disorganized" is far too pejorative and couldn't possibly be appropriate for this passage. Answer (B) is far off the mark too, especially if you can discern between "scholarship" and "pedantry." Pedantic means "characterized by a narrow, often ostentatious concern for book learning and formal rules." You could probably dismiss both terms in answer (D), also; this passage cannot accurately be described as "metaphysical." Answer (E) is half right; the style could be called "intellectual," but there is no cynicism here. POE leaves us with "sympathetic and concrete." This answer may not be ideal, but it's the best choice available.

21. **A** Choice (A) is the only answer that lists two appropriate adjectives, but go through the other choices to make sure none of them is equally good: Both parts of (B) are untrue. Answer (C) starts out well; the point of view could be considered "altruistic." The second term ("elitist"), however, does not seem appropriate at all. Remember that you need to eliminate only one element of the answer to discount the entire answer. "Quixotic" (overly idealistic) might fit, but the plan is presented in a rational manner, so you can eliminate (D). The point of view is "positivist" (having to do with faith in progress), but "unreasonable" is too strong. Although (E) is a possibility, (A) is a better answer.

22. **D** The key in this question is to recognize that the "Institution" the author of this passage describes is meant to serve only children. The other answer choices are institutions that serve both children and adults. The author, who did, in fact, establish a utopian community (Lanark, in Southern Scotland) never uses the word *school*, but it is clear what kind of institution he is proposing because of this sentence: "It has ever been my intention that as this Institution, when completed, will accommodate more than the children of parents resident

at the village, any persons living at Lanark, or in the neighbourhood anywhere around, who cannot well afford to educate their children, shall be at liberty, on mentioning their wishes, to send them to this place, where they will experience the same care and attention as those who belong to the establishment."

23. **A** The pronoun at the beginning of the sentence refers to "those who apply these terms to their fellow-men," and we can infer that the "those" referred to are the wealthy and privileged middle class. Essentially, the sentence states that the "men of worth" (the wealthy) are the worthless. That is a paradox or apparent contradiction. The wealthy who believe that the poor are worthless creatures help perpetuate their poverty; this, states the author, is far worse than the condition of being poor. The entire sentence both states, and partly explains, the paradox.

24. **B** This question is merely a continuation of the previous one. The pronoun that they're asking about in this question is the same one they asked about in question 23—"they." Again, "they" refers to "those who apply these terms to their fellow-men." We can infer that the author most nearly means "the wealthy."

25. **E** At first glance, all of the answers seem to be correct. But what is the speaker most interested in? The passage is centered on the establishment of the (educational) "Institution" and its goals. Note that the author blames poor upbringing (education) for the "wicked" attitude of the privileged classes. Thus, the real focus of the passage is on education—"imparting knowledge and moral values."

26. **D** This is a warm-up question. The incorrect answers are all related to the text, but only (D) explains the opening sentence of the passage ("And yet, being a problem is a strange experience"). The passage is written by an African American author (W. E. B. Du Bois) and deals with racism.

27. **A** An epiphany is a sudden realization; in this passage, there is a rhetorical statement that announces the moment of epiphany: "Then it dawned upon me with a certain suddenness...." Even if you didn't know the meaning of epiphany, you could use POE to arrive at the correct answer. The author is definitely not describing the incident as a moment of triumph (B). Answer (C) is partly true because the moment is a revelation, but the epiphany is for the boy, not for the reader. The remaining answers have no grounding in the passage.

28. **D** The more obvious of the metaphors is the sky, which is extended by "dazzling," "sunny," and "streak of blue." The blue, dazzling, and sunny sky represents the world of opportunity that shines above the white children and, for a while, the author. As the child matures, he realizes the narrowness of his opportunities (the blue is reduced to a streak). The other metaphor is the house/prison with its straight, narrow, tall, and unscalable walls of stone; of course, this edifice is not a real prison, but the limiting restrictions of racism. You may have noticed that the walls of the prison are white.
You can eliminate the other answers with ease, unless you are not familiar with "euphemism," which means "a word or words that replace a crass, crude, or simply inappropriate word or phrase."

29. **B** This is a common AP exam phenomenon: Two questions so closely linked that you are more likely to get both right or both wrong. In light of the previous explanation, the "night" is used metonymically to suggest the color of the boys' skin. (In metonymy, one term is substituted for another term with which it is closely associated.)

30. **A** Using POE is the best way to attack this question. You can eliminate (C), (D), and (E) with certainty. The author states that his comrades shrank into "sycophancy" (obsequiousness, or, in the vernacular, "brown-nosing"); he implies that he had moments of intellectual and physical triumph over his white peers; he also sets himself somewhat apart from his African American comrades ("other black boys"). Choosing between (A) and (B) is the tricky part. On the one hand, even though the author does finally include himself ("the shades of the prison-house closed around us all"), the author places himself above them by accusing the other black boys of being sycophants, and saying that only he wrested his share of opportunity. On the other hand, he suggests that he is superior to his white peers by saying that he could win his share of prizes and contests at school, he suggests that he could at least hold his own in professional life (law, medicine, literature), if given the opportunity.

31. **A** The previous explanation hints at the answer to this question. The author's first reaction was to remain aloof and "above" the racism at school; however, he realizes that this attitude would do nothing to change one stark reality: that he would not be able to remain apart if he were to somehow "wrest from them" the opportunities open to white boys. He vows to succeed in a field restricted almost exclusively to white men: law, medicine, or literature.

32. **E** Laudatory means "praiseworthy or congratulatory," and if you know this, the question is not too difficult. If you didn't know this, then POE will enable you to eliminate all of the answers except (E). Watch out for questions that say "EXCEPT" or "NOT"—in these questions, you're looking for the opposite of what you'd usually look for.

33. **B** This passage is from one of the famous Lincoln-Douglas debates; here, Douglas argues in favor of states' rights.
    You should note that it is possible to eliminate several of the choices based on the verb used. The speaker presents an argument; he does not analyze (A), criticize (C), or describe (D). Douglas says directly that he is vehemently opposed to the idea of slavery in his home state of Illinois; he argues in favor of letting each state decide the issue for itself and goes on to claim that the greatness of the country rests on the sovereignty of the states to do so.

34. **C** You might not agree with what Douglas is saying in this passage, but he controls his tone carefully; remember, he is engaged in a debate at a time when people turned out in droves, expecting not colossal home runs, spectacular slam-dunks, hockey fights, or touchdown passes, but brilliantly conceived, expertly delivered rhetoric.
    If you use POE, you can narrow it down to three choices by eliminating (A) and (E). Answer (D) may be alluring, but be careful not to apply twenty-first-century point of view to nineteenth-century reality. It may be tempting to see Douglas's defense of states' rights as a mask for his true feelings on slavery or, at least, as a poor veil for a racist bias. However, none of that is appropriate to the task at hand. The tone is best described as the tone of a debate; in other words, the speaker attempts to step back and let the force of his words (the voice of reason, if you will) carry the day. Also, remember that polemic means "controversial argument."

35. **A** The speaker uses inductive reasoning (which is defined as reasoning derived from detailed facts, to form general principles) that goes something like this: You all agree that it was right for Illinois to vote as it chose and abolish slavery; thus, every state should be able to make its own choice on this issue. Moreover, every state should be able to make its own choices on just about everything.

36. **B** The shift that begins with "Now, my friends…" is important because at this point in the passage, Douglas shifts from the issue of states' rights and slavery to what the consequences will be if voters do not support his platform—the consequences are civil war. This is a scare tactic. Douglas is saying that voters should support states' rights because that is the only way to maintain peace between North and South.

37. **E** The correct answer may not have been readily apparent, but using POE allows you to eliminate (A) through (D). Douglas uses no anecdotes, much less clever ones; likewise, there are no symbols, paradoxes, or metaphors. The authorities in this case are not only the other states (meaning the voters in the other states), but also the founding fathers: "Washington, Madison, or the framers of this government."

38. **D** Douglas states his own opinion on slavery (his official opinion, at least) at the beginning of the passage ("there is no man in the State who would be more strenuous in his opposition to the introduction of slavery than I would"). Douglas also presents a clear position on voting: "I would never consent to confer the right of voting and of citizenship upon a negro…." Finally, there is a clear position on property: "I would not make any distinction whatever between a negro who held property and one who did not…." Of course, this implies that he would allow African Americans to have property, but he states that, propertied or not, they should not be able to vote. With this information, it is possible to answer the question with certainty; the correct answer is (D).

39. **C** In a way, this is simply a reprise of Question 36, but here Douglas pushes his scare tactic even further by saying that Lincoln and his party are deliberately infringing on states' rights to incite a civil war. Hopefully, you were not fooled by (B). While it is true that Douglas is blaming the war (that hadn't yet begun) on Lincoln and his political party, he is not shifting any blame; nowhere does he imply that anyone was blaming or accusing Douglas and his party of trying to provoke a war, and to shift blame, Douglas would have had to have *had* blame at some point.

40. **E** In this passage, the author builds his case by claiming that the role of the merchant is analogous to that of a physician or clergyman; this is a clear analogy. Note that the author is not referring to physicians and clergymen as authorities; so answer choice (A), "appeal to authorities," is not correct.

41. **A** If you understood the previous question, you could probably have eliminated (B) and (C) immediately. At the beginning of the passage, the author tells us that he includes manufacturer in the category of merchant, so (D) is not correct, and you have already narrowed down the answer choices significantly. You may have expected (E) to be true, but in the context of this particular passage, the merchant is said to be motivated by the same altruistic motives that guide a doctor or clergyman.

42. **A** The author claims that "the stipend" (salary or profit) is a necessary adjunct to the work of a merchant, physician, or clergyman, but not the true motivational force. Only answer choice (A) comes close to being correct. Remember that in questions like this one, you should take the original sentence and insert each answer choice to see which one sounds the best. How does (A) sound? "This stipend is a due and necessary <u>acccompaniment</u>, but not the object of his life, if he be a true clergyman, any more than his fee (or honorarium) is the object of life to a true physician." The best answer is (A).

43. **C** In this context, agency means "direction" or "governance," and the term is, therefore, tied to "master and governor of large masses of men." The question asks you to tie together words by semantics; that is, to tie them together by *meaning*. The merchant must oversee or govern all his workers, and this leads logically to the role of governor. It is the semantic connection that allows the reader to understand the writer's logic in this sentence. By using POE, you can narrow the answers to (C) and (E). If you're not sure, guess and move on.

44. **E** This is a tricky question. If you understand the term "synecdoche," you increase your odds of getting the question right. This rhetorical figure is a limited form of metonymy (which is defined as any time a characteristic represents something, or something stands for its characteristic). Synecdoche is when a part stands for the whole. In this case, the merchant doesn't govern hands, he governs workers, but the workers are mostly manual laborers, so the hands represent the workers (by synecdoche) and reinforce the idea of manual labor. The author employs the word *men* twice in the paragraph, and the synecdoche also helps with diction. Answer (D) is less important, but surely "hands" is a concrete, rather than an abstract, image. Thus, all four answers are appropriate.

45. **B** The answer to this question is embedded in the final part of the paragraph discussed above. If you read and understood the passage, you should have been fine; the question should cause problems only for those who guess by using the context of the twenty-first century. He says that the merchant's two obligations are to produce quality, affordable goods and take care of his workers. From the initial paragraph, we saw that according to this author, profits are only secondary to the merchants' real functions, so you can eliminate every answer but (B) right off the bat.

46. **C** This passage is a kind of an ode to the merchant, and this is tantamount to an ode to capitalism.
If you decide to use POE, then you can eliminate (D) and (E) right away: The author posits merchants, clerics, and physicians in a decidedly positive light. By extolling the virtues of the merchant (and manufacturer), he cannot possibly be a supporter of socialism, so even (B) is an unreasonable choice.

47. **C** This is a scientifically precise description of the Galapagos Islands. Choice (A) is incorrect since nothing is being classified in this passage. Choice (B) is also wrong—no point of view is presented here—just facts. The passage is not dominated by analogies, so (D) can't be right. Finally, you know that (E) is incorrect, since "lyrical" pertains to personal sentiment, and there are practically no personal feelings expressed at all; the closest we get to personal sentiment is the statement that some of the craters are "beautifully symmetrical."

48. **A** Unless you recognized the passage (by Charles Darwin), you should have used POE to answer this question. Answer (D) is the easiest to eliminate; the passage is neither lyrical nor poetic—it was not written by a poet. The passage is about the islands themselves, not about volcanoes as (E) suggests. Answers (B) and (C) are somewhat plausible; however if this passage were emblematic of an entire novel, what boring reading that would be. Finally, a book for tourists about the Galapagos Islands would make the islands far more alluring than this passage does.

49. **D** In this case, the answer is made clear from the passage; the craters have a border of soft stone (tuff) that has worn away on the southern side. The specific line from the passage that allows you to answer this question is: "These consist either of lava or scoriae, or of finely-

stratified, sandstone-like tuff." Sandstone is a type of rock. The definition of "tuff" is actually "a rock composed of compacted volcanic ash varying in size from fine sand to coarse gravel."

50. **D** The author doesn't address (A) or (E), so you can eliminate those and look more closely at the middle three choices. While it is true that the speaker mentions the Pacific Ocean and the fragments of granite, he incorporates these elements in his overarching discussion of the symmetrical craters.

51. **A** In reality, the author is both a poet and a novelist, but you are asked to make a judgment based on the passage. To answer this question correctly, you would need to use POE and your best judgment to eliminate all of the least likely answer choices. The passage is an attack against the intrusion of prosaic life into the realm of art. The panegyric (high praise) of classical language is a key to understanding the author's point of view: "a language different from that of actual use, a language full of resonant music and sweet rhythm, made stately by solemn cadence, or made delicate by fanciful rhyme, jeweled with wonderful words, and enriched with lofty diction." In a word, this is poetry.
The writing is far too lyrical for the author of the passage to be a journalist (D) or an actor (E); the latter choice is thrown in for those superficial readers who assume that a passage that purports to deal with English drama should be somehow related to a theatrical term. The same may be said for (C). The author capitalizes "art" because he is not discussing painting specifically, but the general realm of artistic creation that encompasses all the arts.

52. **E** The example is stated rhetorically: "Take the case of the English drama," and lasts for most of the passage. "Illustration by example" is definitely the defining rhetorical device of this passage.

53. **A** A maxim is a truism or pithy saying, a gnomic statement similar to a proverb, so (A) is the best answer.
POE can help you narrow down your choices. Clearly, the statement does not compare Art something else, so you can eliminate (E). If anything, the statement is overstatement (hyperbole), and for that reason (D) can be discarded. For the statement to be an antithesis, the author would have needed to put two things or concepts in opposition, but we have only one element (Art); thus, you can eliminate answer (C). At this point, your chances are fifty-fifty, so you could guess and move on.
But let's look at (B). A "chiasmus" is a syntactic figure wherein the elements in one clause are reversed in another. The most famous example is President Kennedy's statement: "Ask not what your country can do for you, but what you can do for your country."

54. **A** The author does not revere life above everything else—for example, he clearly states that he doesn't like life as an intrusion in Art, at the very least or as it appears in certain parts of William Shakespeare's work. He includes these examples of Caesar and English drama for rhetorical reasons, and while he admires English drama, he does not appear to revere it. (By the way, to "revere" something is "to regard it with awe, deference, and devotion.") Beauty is held up as an ideal, and this is clear when the author says, "the object of Art is not simple truth but complex beauty."

EXPLANATIONS TO THE FREE-RESPONSE SECTION

QUESTION 1

Analytical/Expository Essay

The following sample is a slightly better than adequate response; the strong writing would probably carry it to a 7 or 8, despite the tenuous grasp of rhetorical strategies. It would be possible to question the student's assertion that Mark Twain's comment that "the scow episode is really a sublime burst of invention" proves that "he is a reasonable critic and not bent on purely insulting the popular author." Most likely, this represents more of Twain's sarcasm.

Mark Twain's well-known essay "Fenimore Cooper's Literary Offenses" seeks to mock both the work itself and its devoted readers. Though Twain's piece has a decidedly ironic tone and is not meant to be serious literary criticism, he employs a variety of rhetorical tactics to argue his point and persuade the audience that not only is Cooper's work flawed and ridiculous, but also that they are mislead in having enjoyed Cooper's writing. Twain uses rhetorical devices rooted in both language and content to convince the reader of the validity of his scathing conclusion about Cooper.

By subtle choices of persuasive writing, Twain conveys his meaning through his language. He uses the first person plural as his point of view to connect with the reader and to give an impression of a sympathetic guide alerting the reader to literary inadequacy. Instead of always presenting his evidence outright, Twain uses rhetorical questions to intensify his essay and to catch the reader's attention. By demanding "Did the Indians notice [...]?" he highlights the unrealistic nature of Cooper's work. In the final paragraph, he employs an anaphora, beginning several successive sentences with "Then No...." This repetitive wording emphasizes his message of Cooper's inadequacy. His phrasing plays a key role in convincing the reader of his point.

In addition, Twain's choice of evidence is clearly intended to strengthen his argument. He uses a simile, "He saw nearly all things as through a glass eye, darkly" to help the audience visualize and better comprehend his meaning. To dramatize his critique, Twain writes "It would take you thirty years to guess," an obvious hyperbole that vividly depicts the ridiculousness of Cooper's work. Throughout the essay, Twain relies on mathematical computations and logic to undermine Cooper's credibility, hoping that objective reasoning will sway his readers. Finally, in a concession to Cooper's competency, Twain admits that "the scow episode is really a sublime burst of invention" to illustrate that he is a reasonable critic and not bent on purely insulting the popular author.

Twain's wide range of rhetorical techniques serve to convince his audience in as many different ways as possible that he is a logical, credible critic and that his argument is valid.

QUESTION 2

Argumentative Essay

The sample essay below serves as a great model, for it exudes an ease that can come only with great practice with the art of writing. There is a clear thesis and organizational structure. Quality replaces quantity, and the clarity is pristine. Remember that above all else, the AP reader craves clarity. The work might not earn a 9, but it would definitely receive an 8.

> For as long as authority has existed, there have been those who have challenged it, rebelled against it, and even refused to acknowledge it. Institutions that hold great power—the government, the church, public opinion—have dictated what is right and wrong to those under their control. However, when an individual's personal convictions come into conflict with authority's established morality, persecution, isolation, and other such punishments often follow. Voltaire was correct in his assertion that "it is dangerous to be right" in opposition to the status quo, as demonstrated in history and literature.
>
> As science developed during the Renaissance and humans began to have a more objective understanding of the world, the church held vehemently to its tenets and persecuted those who contradicted its teachings. Italian astronomer Galileo Galilei, whose observations played a pivotal role in our model for the solar system, was one such man who suffered greatly for his non-Christian hypotheses. Though Galileo's theories were indeed correct, the Church nonetheless suppressed his work and placed him under house arrest. Similarly, during the 1950s, McCarthyism swept America, as the government tried to root out "Communists." For the few who condemned the inherent immorality of McCarthy's campaign and tactics, the result was that they too would be blacklisted and effectively ruined. In contradicting the Church and the government, independent thinkers have suffered greatly for "being right" throughout history.
>
> The dangers of questioning authority have not been neglected in world literature. In Milan Kundera's The Joke, the protagonist Ludvik is expelled from the university and the Communist Party for making comments derogatory to the Party. Though his criticisms would certainly be deemed valid by later generations, his correct thinking is rewarded with isolation and prison-like punishment in the military. Fighting against both the establishment and the majority, Arthur Miller's character John Proctor is indeed "right" that the Salem witch trials depicted in The Crucible are madness, and ruining the lives of innocent people. However, his unpopular beliefs only cause him danger as he, too, is soon labeled as a witch. These two protagonists, whose lone voices of reason decry the authorities' "wrong" stance, suffer great dangers as a result of their challenges to the establishment. Voltaire's claim has been continually confirmed by history and literature.

QUESTION 3A

Analytical/Expository Essay

The following is another strong sample that it would earn an 8 or a 9. If it falls short, it would be the abrupt ending. It is difficult to find much fault elsewhere.

In his speech to students at the Sorbonne, President Theodore Roosevelt seeks to inspire these educated young people to make good use of their blessings by attempting to change the world. The outcome of their efforts, he argues, is not as important as venturing out itself. He especially warns against the cynicism to which the learned are highly vulnerable. Through his syntactical choices, diction, and use of imagery, Roosevelt conveys his message of empowerment and social responsibility.

With unique sentence structure, the President is able to highlight certain points to the audience that make clear his meaning. Periodic sentences occur throughout the speech, heighten the tension, and underscore the importance of each phrase in the series. These lengthy sentences are often combined with inverted syntax, as when Roosevelt proclaims, "There are certain failings against which it is especially incumbent that...[men]...should especially guard themselves." By placing these "certain failings" in an unexpected place in the sentence, he imbues a greater significance to them. The audience understands the gravity of these shortcomings from the syntax Roosevelt employs.

The President uses strong, emphatic diction in his speech to enhance the power and impact of his message. He uses superlative terms to decry those "cynics" who he considers weak: their lifestyle is "the poorest," there are "none more unhealthy" than them. By painting the consequences of inaction in such ultimate terms, he encourages the audience to take to heart his message. Similarly, he often pairs antithetical words like "good and evil" and "superiority and weakness" to emphasize the contrast between the route he prefers the audience to take and the path of the weak. His highly polarized choice of words adds to the persuasiveness of his argument.

Finally, Roosevelt uses imagery to provide a visual representation of his message to convince the audience. He extols "the man who is actually in the arena, whose face is marred by dust and sweat and blood," evoking a clear image of bravery, struggle, and nobility that would sway those unmoved by the President's more conceptual reasoning. Later he describes these men of action as those "who quell the storm and ride the thunder," giving the audience a sense of the grandeur and scope of the task Roosevelt sets for them. These images, like his syntax and diction, make clear his purpose.

Question 3B

Synthesis Essay

This sample essay is only slightly above average, thanks to the excellent writing. Although the student takes a clear stand and writes a strong introduction, the essay doesn't seem to go anywhere after that. The reader can sense the writer's lack of interest in the subject, and that lack of interest is immediately transferred to the reader. There is no conclusion, and one can only assume that time management was not good. The best that this essay can hope for is a 6.

The types of needs considered to be common to all humans varies considerably depending on the source of the information. While some necessities, like food and water, are undeniably required for survival, other more abstract concepts provoke much more controversy over what is truly essential. In 1923, Swiss architect Le Corbusier declared that "space and light and order" were as necessary as nourishment and shelter. While it is true that humanity has long prized these aesthetic values, it would be incorrect to attribute to them an equal importance as more basic human needs. The beautiful surroundings described by Le Corbusier can be enjoyed only when the fundamental drives to obtain food and shelter have been fulfilled.

History clearly demonstrates the relative importance of aesthetic and biological needs. The Pruitt-Igoe housing project was an extremely ordered development, composed of "33 identical…[]…apartment blocks." Were "space and light and order" as essential as "bread or a place to sleep," the impoverished condition of the project's tenants would be offset by the richness of their environment. This was clearly not the case, for the Pruitt-Igoe was soon "worse than the slums it replaced." Poverty prevented the occupants from adequately addressing their basic needs, and thus they could not make successful use of their well-ordered project. With rampant "crime and drugs," the failed development eventually had to be demolished. Evidently, superior architecture could not elevate the status of those living in desperate circumstances.

In descriptions of Utopian communities, authors often include Le Corbusier's three tenets of aesthetic needs, but unlike the creator of Pruitt-Igoe, they take fundamental necessities into consideration and provide for physiological comforts as well. While Fourier considers the sounds of industry to be "an annoying drawback," that ostensibly threatens the order and harmony of the city, he still provides for a wing of the palace where "noisy workshops" will ensure the economy needed to keep residents fed and sheltered. Howard, too, includes an area for "factories, warehouses, dairies, markets, coal yards, timber yards, etc.," in his plans for Garden City to support the city center that personifies space, light, and order. In this way, aesthetic needs are able to be fulfilled because more primary necessities have been provided.

ABOUT THE AUTHOR

During his 31-year career, Richard Hartzell has served as a teacher, a coach, and an administrator at a variety of prestigious institutions, including Brown University, Phillips Exeter Academy, Horace Mann School, St. Mark's School of Texas, The American School in Switzerland, Fundación Nuevo Marymount (Colombia), The Webb Schools, and The Harker School. He has taught Advanced Placement courses in seven subjects (English Language, English Literature, European History, Art History, French Literature, French Language, and Spanish Literature), as well as multitudinous "standard" and elective classes. Dr. Hartzell has been head varsity coach of football, soccer, ice hockey, basketball, track, and baseball teams, but his most cherished afternoons were spent as assistant varsity golf coach.

Once a reasonably prolific writer of both literary criticism and fiction, Richard Hartzell has said good-bye to all that and now devotes his "free time" to his wife, reading, cooking, and hiking. His students are not always pleased with his propensity for literary allusion, and the preceding tip of the hat to Robert Graves would make most of them absolutely furious.

Richard Hartzell holds A. B. Honors and Ph.D. degrees from Brown University. Currently, he serves as head of Upper School and teacher of AP English at The Harker School in San Jose, California.

Completely darken bubbles with a No. 2 pencil. If you make a mistake, be sure to erase mark completely. Erase all stray marks.

1. YOUR NAME: _____
(Print)   Last   First   M.I.

SIGNATURE: _____   **DATE:** ____ / ____ / ____

HOME ADDRESS: _____
(Print)   Number and Street

_____
City   State   Zip Code

PHONE NO. : _____
(Print)

IMPORTANT: Please fill in these boxes exactly as shown on the back cover of your test book.

2. TEST FORM

3. TEST CODE

4. REGISTRATION NUMBER

5. YOUR NAME

First 4 letters of last name				FIRST INIT	MID INIT

6. DATE OF BIRTH

Month	Day	Year
JAN		
FEB		
MAR	0 0	0 0
APR	1 1	1 1
MAY	2 2	2 2
JUN	3 3	3 3
JUL		4 4
AUG		5 5
SEP		7 7
OCT		8 8
NOV		9 9
DEC		

7. SEX
MALE
FEMALE

The Princeton Review
© The Princeton Review, Inc.
FORM NO. 00001-PR

Section 1 Start with number 1 for each new section.
If a section has fewer questions than answer spaces, leave the extra answer spaces blank.

1. A B C D   31. A B C D   61. A B C D   91. A B C D
2. A B C D   32. A B C D   62. A B C D   92. A B C D
3. A B C D   33. A B C D   63. A B C D   93. A B C D
4. A B C D   34. A B C D   64. A B C D   94. A B C D
5. A B C D   35. A B C D   65. A B C D   95. A B C D
6. A B C D   36. A B C D   66. A B C D   96. A B C D
7. A B C D   37. A B C D   67. A B C D   97. A B C D
8. A B C D   38. A B C D   68. A B C D   98. A B C D
9. A B C D   39. A B C D   69. A B C D   99. A B C D
10. A B C D   40. A B C D   70. A B C D   100. A B C D
11. A B C D   41. A B C D   71. A B C D   101. A B C D
12. A B C D   42. A B C D   72. A B C D   102. A B C D
13. A B C D   43. A B C D   73. A B C D   103. A B C D
14. A B C D   44. A B C D   74. A B C D   104. A B C D
15. A B C D   45. A B C D   75. A B C D   105. A B C D
16. A B C D   46. A B C D   76. A B C D   106. A B C D
17. A B C D   47. A B C D   77. A B C D   107. A B C D
18. A B C D   48. A B C D   78. A B C D   108. A B C D
19. A B C D   49. A B C D   79. A B C D   109. A B C D
20. A B C D   50. A B C D   80. A B C D   110. A B C D
21. A B C D   51. A B C D   81. A B C D   111. A B C D
22. A B C D   52. A B C D   82. A B C D   112. A B C D
23. A B C D   53. A B C D   83. A B C D   113. A B C D
24. A B C D   54. A B C D   84. A B C D   114. A B C D
25. A B C D   55. A B C D   85. A B C D   115. A B C D
26. A B C D   56. A B C D   86. A B C D   116. A B C D
27. A B C D   57. A B C D   87. A B C D   117. A B C D
28. A B C D   58. A B C D   88. A B C D   118. A B C D
29. A B C D   59. A B C D   89. A B C D   119. A B C D
30. A B C D   60. A B C D   90. A B C D   120. A B C D

Completely darken bubbles with a No. 2 pencil. If you make a mistake, be sure to erase mark completely. Erase all stray marks.

1. YOUR NAME:
(Print) Last First M.I.
SIGNATURE: _____ DATE: ___ / ___ / ___

HOME ADDRESS: _____
(Print) Number and Street

_____
City State Zip Code

PHONE NO. : _____
(Print)

5. YOUR NAME

First 4 letters of last name				FIRST INIT	MID INIT
A	A	A	A	A	A
B	B	B	B	B	B
C	C	C	C	C	C
D	D	D	D	D	D
E	E	E	E	E	E
F	F	F	F	F	F
G	G	G	G	G	G
H	H	H	H	H	H
I	I	I	I	I	I
J	J	J	J	J	J
K	K	K	K	K	K
L	L	L	L	L	L
M	M	M	M	M	M
N	N	N	N	N	N
O	O	O	O	O	O
P	P	P	P	P	P
Q	Q	Q	Q	Q	Q
R	R	R	R	R	R
S	S	S	S	S	S
T	T	T	T	T	T
U	U	U	U	U	U
V	V	V	V	V	V
W	W	W	W	W	W
X	X	X	X	X	X
Y	Y	Y	Y	Y	Y
Z	Z	Z	Z	Z	Z

IMPORTANT: Please fill in these boxes exactly as shown on the back cover of your test book.

2. TEST FORM

3. TEST CODE

4. REGISTRATION NUMBER

0 A 0 0 0 0 0 0 0 0 0
1 B 1 1 1 1 1 1 1 1 1
2 C 2 2 2 2 2 2 2 2 2
3 D 3 3 3 3 3 3 3 3 3
4 E 4 4 4 4 4 4 4 4 4
5 F 5 5 5 5 5 5 5 5 5
7 G 7 7 7 7 7 7 7 7 7
8 8 8 8 8 8 8 8 8 8
9 9 9 9 9 9 9 9 9 9

6. DATE OF BIRTH

Month	Day		Year	
JAN				
FEB				
MAR	0	0	0	0
APR	1	1	1	1
MAY	2	2	2	2
JUN	3	3	3	3
JUL		4	4	4
AUG		5	5	5
SEP		7	7	7
OCT		8	8	8
NOV		9	9	9
DEC				

7. SEX
MALE
FEMALE

The Princeton Review
© The Princeton Review, Inc.
FORM NO. 00001-PR

Section 1

Start with number 1 for each new section.
If a section has fewer questions than answer spaces, leave the extra answer spaces blank.

1. A B C D
2. A B C D
3. A B C D
4. A B C D
5. A B C D
6. A B C D
7. A B C D
8. A B C D
9. A B C D
10. A B C D
11. A B C D
12. A B C D
13. A B C D
14. A B C D
15. A B C D
16. A B C D
17. A B C D
18. A B C D
19. A B C D
20. A B C D
21. A B C D
22. A B C D
23. A B C D
24. A B C D
25. A B C D
26. A B C D
27. A B C D
28. A B C D
29. A B C D
30. A B C D

31. A B C D
32. A B C D
33. A B C D
34. A B C D
35. A B C D
36. A B C D
37. A B C D
38. A B C D
39. A B C D
40. A B C D
41. A B C D
42. A B C D
43. A B C D
44. A B C D
45. A B C D
46. A B C D
47. A B C D
48. A B C D
49. A B C D
50. A B C D
51. A B C D
52. A B C D
53. A B C D
54. A B C D
55. A B C D
56. A B C D
57. A B C D
58. A B C D
59. A B C D
60. A B C D

61. A B C D
62. A B C D
63. A B C D
64. A B C D
65. A B C D
66. A B C D
67. A B C D
68. A B C D
69. A B C D
70. A B C D
71. A B C D
72. A B C D
73. A B C D
74. A B C D
75. A B C D
76. A B C D
77. A B C D
78. A B C D
79. A B C D
80. A B C D
81. A B C D
82. A B C D
83. A B C D
84. A B C D
85. A B C D
86. A B C D
87. A B C D
88. A B C D
89. A B C D
90. A B C D

91. A B C D
92. A B C D
93. A B C D
94. A B C D
95. A B C D
96. A B C D
97. A B C D
98. A B C D
99. A B C D
100. A B C D
101. A B C D
102. A B C D
103. A B C D
104. A B C D
105. A B C D
106. A B C D
107. A B C D
108. A B C D
109. A B C D
110. A B C D
111. A B C D
112. A B C D
113. A B C D
114. A B C D
115. A B C D
116. A B C D
117. A B C D
118. A B C D
119. A B C D
120. A B C D

Need More?

If you're looking to learn more about how to excel on the AP Exams, you're in the right place. The Princeton Review has three great options.

Princeton Review for the AP Exams

Our online review programs for 14 different AP Exams include:
- Content that is fully aligned with the actual exam topics
- Tailored study plan
- Full-length diagnostic exam
- Drills that build skills and develop conceptual understanding
- Loads of practice questions, written in the AP Exam format

Private Tutoring

If you need maximum flexibility and test prep tailored to your particular learning style, then this is your preferred option. Tutoring is best if you:
- Learn better with personal instruction
- Need flexibility with dates and locations
- Only need to focus on specific areas of the test or specific academic areas

Cracking the AP Exams Book Series

If you like our *Cracking the AP English Language Exam*, check out:
- *Cracking the AP Physics Exam*
- *Cracking the AP European History Exam*
- *Cracking the AP Chemistry Exam*
- *Cracking the AP English Literature Exam*

To learn more, visit *PrincetonReview.com/AP* or call 800-2Review.